EUROPE

ASIA

Seychelles

Guam

Vanuatu

AUSTRALIA

ISLAS

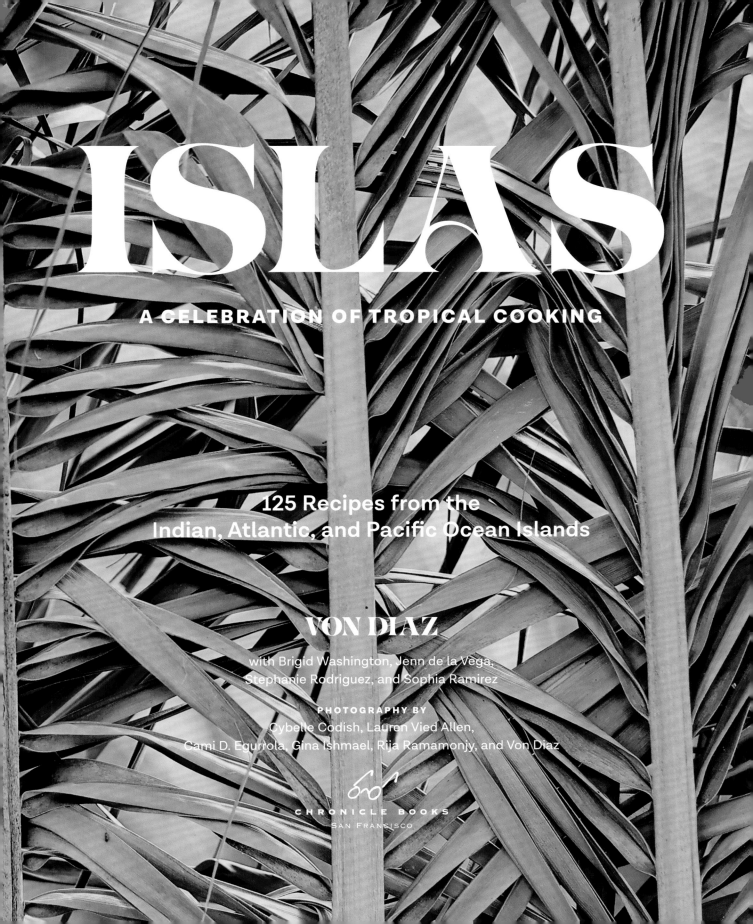

ISLAS

A CELEBRATION OF TROPICAL COOKING

125 Recipes from the
Indian, Atlantic, and Pacific Ocean Islands

VON DIAZ

with Brigid Washington, Jenn de la Vega,
Stephanie Rodriguez, and Sophia Ramirez

PHOTOGRAPHY BY
Cybelle Codish, Lauren Vied Allen,
Cami D. Eguriola, Gina Ishmael, Rija Ramamonjy, and Von Diaz

CHRONICLE BOOKS
SAN FRANCISCO

Library of Congress Cataloging-in-Publication Data available.

ISBN 978-1-7972-1524-2

Manufactured in China.

FSC
www.fsc.org
MIX
Paper from
responsible sources
FSC™ C169962

Design by **LIZZIE VAUGHAN**.
Additional photo curation, editing, and location scouting by **CYBELLE CODISH**.
Typesetting by **TAYLOR ROY**.
Typeset in Alma, Lota Grotesque, Ramo, and Sisteron.

7-Up is a registered trademark of Dr Pepper/Seven Up Inc. Badia is a registered trademark of Badia Spices, Inc. Chief is a registered trademark of Chief Brand Products,
Limited. Diamond Crystal is a registered trademark of Cargill, Inc. Libby's is a registered
trademark of Libby's Brand Holding. Loisa is a registered trademark of Loisa, Inc. Old
Bay is a registered trademark of McCormick & Company, Inc. Sazon is a registered
trademark of Sancho Sazon Seasonings LLC. Sprite is a registered trademark of The
Coca-Cola Company. Tabasco is a registered trademark of McIlhenny Company.

10 9 8 7 6 5 4 3 2 1

Chronicle books and gifts are available at special quantity discounts to
corporations, professional associations, literacy programs, and other
organizations. For details and discount information, please contact
our premiums department at corporatesales@chroniclebooks.com
or at 1-800-759-0190.

Chronicle Books LLC
680 Second Street
San Francisco, California 94107
www.chroniclebooks.com

Para toda mi gente isleña

For all of my island people

CONTENTS

NEVER TAKE THE FIRST.
NEVER TAKE THE LAST.
TAKE ONLY WHAT YOU NEED.
TAKE ONLY THAT WHICH IS GIVEN.
NEVER TAKE MORE THAN HALF.
LEAVE SOME FOR OTHERS.
HARVEST IN A WAY THAT MINIMIZES HARM.
USE IT RESPECTFULLY.
NEVER WASTE WHAT YOU HAVE TAKEN. SHARE.
GIVE THANKS FOR WHAT YOU HAVE BEEN GIVEN.
GIVE A GIFT, IN RECIPROCITY FOR WHAT YOU HAVE TAKEN.
SUSTAIN THE ONES WHO SUSTAIN YOU
AND THE EARTH WILL LAST FOREVER.

—Robin Wall Kimmerer, *Braiding Sweetgrass*

INTRODUCTION

Rain starts beating on my windshield as I drive through the winding mountain roads between Rincón and San Juan, Puerto Rico. The day before, meteorologists announced that a tropical depression was forming in the Caribbean just east of the island, which was predicted to bring heavy wind and rain. That morning, the skies were relatively clear as I set out to visit family on the west side of the island, but the radio announcers kept me on edge. The specter of Hurricane Maria hung heavy in their voices, vacillating between disbelief, disinterest, and real fear. People from different parts of the island called in throughout the day, saying the wind had kicked up, there were heavy rains, or they'd already lost power. I, too, became afraid.

I was born in Puerto Rico but raised in the American South, and I had never been on the island during a storm. My family avoided travel there during hurricane season, which used to start in late July and last through early October. Now, meteorologists have extended the season from May through early November. The unpredictability is worsened by lessons learned from Maria, and more recently from Fiona—that the storms are getting stronger and more destructive.

On this day, traffic got thick once I arrived in Mayagüez. I soon realized there was a snaking line for the gas station, so I got in it. There, I filled my tank and bought a couple gallons of water and a large bottle of white rum (just in case). I continued my journey, but as a foreigner in my own homeland, I was panicking. I didn't have any wisdom to draw from; I couldn't read the color of the sky, the disconcerting hollowness of the breeze. I called my mother, who was also panicking back home in Tennessee. We both, perhaps, felt retraumatized, remembering frightened phone calls from family members when previous storms had threatened the island.

Finally, back at my rental apartment, I did things I remembered my mother and grandmother describing. I found every available vessel and filled it with water. I pulled out all the nonperishable food I could find, plus the can opener, candles, lighters, and matches. I secured everything that looked as if it might fly away. I pulled everything I might need into the more secure bedroom—a concrete block with metal shutters over the windows—and away from the sliding-glass-doored living room. I went to bed that night and prayed, holding my grandmother's rosary, which I often travel with.

I woke up the next morning to sunshine and seabirds, and not a drop of rain on the ground. I felt disoriented, my plans for the day completely disrupted. So I drove to the beach, bought some Alcapurrias de Jueyes (page 220) and a cold beer, and looked out at the ocean. I was fortunate, but millions of people are not so lucky, as storm systems are shifting and worsening not just in the Caribbean, but across the tropics.

I wondered how folks make do when their whole lives are based in an environment under constant threat. What can we learn from the elders of those communities, who have spent their lives testing strategies for overcoming adversity?

The people who live on tropical islands are among the toughest, scrappiest, most resilient people on this planet. Storms have always been unpredictable, and generations of islanders have cultivated ancestral knowledge around how to survive and, importantly, how to feed themselves despite it all. With limited ingredients, they cook in ways that are soul-nourishing and emphasize flavor. Making magic out of what's available—the leaves that sprout from root vegetables such as taro; the otherwise inedible parts of animals such as hoofs and tails—is the way they've always cooked. It's an expression of ancestry, adaptability, and fortitude. Because what we eat is about much more than what tastes good or what is available—our cuisines tell rich stories, preserve our histories, and provide a road map for survival.

Take Puerto Rican Mofongo (page 207): Plantains are deep-fried—a technique with African roots—and then combined with Spanish ingredients such as garlic and pork cracklings, and mashed in a large wooden pilón, a mortar and pestle with indigenous Taíno roots. Or Filipino Sinigang (page 116): bright soup with a signature tangy sourness—a cornerstone of the cuisine, in this case derived from green mango—that's brimming with fresh seafood, herbs, and lime. And Mas Riha from the Maldives (page 148): A coconut-based, aromatic curry that reflects the nation's history as a port of call for merchants traveling west, it blends nearby South Indian ingredients and techniques with riches of the Spice Islands—cardamom, fennel, turmeric, cumin, black pepper, and cinnamon—and is served with fresh tuna (abundant in local waters) and basmati rice.

Islas is a book about these remarkable places and the people there who have so much to teach us. It celebrates island cuisines spanning the Indian, Atlantic, and Pacific Oceans. These islands share dozens of ingredients and cooking techniques, including marinating, fermenting, deep-frying, smoking, and in-ground roasting. Bold flavors—tastes that represent their cultures of origin—burst from each dish.

These flavors, despite distance and cultural differences, pair remarkably well together: The bright citruses and vinegars, grassy herbs, slow-cooked and smoky grilled meats, fresh seafood, aromatic rice, and earthy root vegetables that typify these island cuisines have a harmonious, synchronous spirit, rife with potential for exploration and fusion. This book explores these flavors side by side, noting the simplicity of ancestral cooking that continues to yield delicious results.

What most people think of as island cuisine is documented by tourists, and often focuses on seafood and tropical fruit. Those are indeed signature flavors of island cooking, but so too are earthiness, richness, intensity, saltiness, sourness, brininess. You are more likely to be served hearty stewed meat than a citrusy ceviche on most islands, alongside foods that call up the fleeting crisp of a glazed donut, the loud crunch of fried pork skins, the fiery heat of chili sauces and pickles. And even when dishes are tender and slow-cooked, they are likely quite beautiful: the golden hues of turmeric and saffron, the almost electric red of annatto, the royal purple of ube, the verdant green of fresh okra.

These islands also share more than just fruits, vegetables, spices, meat, and seafood. Island nations also struggle with isolation and environmental vulnerability, which force the inhabitants to get creative with layering flavors using local produce and shelf-stable ingredients. Many also grapple with colonial legacies, impacted by policies that limit what foods are available. In fact, the little that has been disseminated about these remote places has come from the outside—from anthropologists, who for generations were white scholars, arriving in paradise with an imperialist gaze. As such, those from the region were framed as savages: scantily clad pagans living in villages with palm-thatched roofs, their faces decorated with tribal markings. And, of course, with incredibly foreign food customs: eating on the floor with hands (often family style from communal vessels), dishes layered with coconut and spices, abundant seafood and tropical fruit, pungent side dishes produced through fermentation.

But the tropics is a vast region, with as many differences as similarities. This is not a comprehensive book of island cuisines, and it's not organized by place, because many nations in the region are archipelagos comprising dozens—sometimes thousands—of islands. Instead, this book is organized by the ancestral cooking techniques that define island cooking. These techniques, among the oldest known to humanity, enable people to make delicious food with limited ingredients, often without modern tools or energy sources.

The recipes in this book celebrate the ingenuity of traditional techniques and dishes, while also keeping the cuisines alive through adaptations that make it possible to prepare them in a modern kitchen. Many of these dishes are prepared for celebrations or holidays, but there are just as many simple dishes—such as grilled Chuletas al Carbón (page 263) and the coconut ceviche Oka I'a (page 68)—that take minutes to prepare. The dishes range widely in difficulty, some decidedly project meals with overnight marinades or elaborate banana leaf wrappers. Others are quite simple: Cucumber Chow (page 107), fried green plantain Tostones (page 213), and Arroz Caldo, chicken rice porridge (page 155).

The people profiled in this book represent the richness of their cultures and are the beating hearts of these islands. Some are food business owners and farmers, but others are average citizens who have lived on islands their entire lives. Their ingenuity, time-tested family recipes, and age-old cooking techniques provide a window into island life and the ways in which their cuisines and, importantly, *how* they cook reflect a profound connection to tradition and ancestry.

And so, *Islas* comes from the perspective of the islanders themselves. *Islas* is about preserving the wisdom and values of the people who live in some of the most volatile, vulnerable places on this planet. It tells stories of continuous adaptation and captures the spirit of places that are uniquely preserved, that remain connected to older ways of living. This book is, in many ways, an archive of strategies for persistence, creativity, ingenuity, and resilience. And it honors the keepers of these cultures, who are so often women. Above all, these stories and recipes acknowledge that cooking delicious food for others is a selfless act. Cooks are givers, always.

Our world is changing. Political unrest, environmental chaos, and—most recently—global pandemics are transforming how we eat. The impact of our changing world on global food systems feels immeasurable at times, and the COVID-19 crisis thrust many of us into unprecedented food insecurity. And yet, while much of the developing world—particularly those living in island nations—grapple with new realities, they've long been accustomed to cooking in crisis. Exploring these disparate island nations' foodways will both preserve the ancestral legacy, adaptability, and fortitude of their cultures and provide a road map for cooking delicious food under the most challenging conditions.

WELCOME

Bon-Bini

THE TECHNIQUES OF THE ISLANDS

Islas will introduce you to cooking methods that range from the simplest marinade to the most complex banana leaf–wrapped parcels. Many of these techniques aren't intuitive to those of us who don't live on islands. Folks living in big, urban cities likely don't have a safe place to dig a hole for an in-ground whole-hog roast. Most other places don't cook like this because they have other ingredients, other tools, other options. These techniques are primal and utilitarian in a way that is increasingly rare, and it's remarkable that such delicious cuisine stems from such simple origins.

MARINATING can turn tough cuts of meat and flavorless vegetables into dynamic, sumptuous dishes. But there's an art to marinating, and choosing your base—vinegar, citrus, or yogurt—is key. The balance of aromatics, such as garlic, onion, and fresh or dried herbs, adds dimension. And timing is crucial. An overnight marinade can truly transform a tough ingredient into something spectacular, while a quick marinade gives you bright, punchy flavors ideal for seafood and vegetables.

FERMENTATION AND PICKLING use natural chemical processes that balance sugars and acids to preserve and give life to sauces, beverages, mixed vegetables, and bread dough.

BRAISING AND STEWING, techniques often associated with cold climates, are among the most prominently featured throughout the tropics.

These techniques are foolproof ways to make use of available ingredients and can render the inedible (such as cow hoof) edible. The layering of this "kitchen-sink" approach creates unforgettable flavors and truly treasured dishes.

DEEP-FRYING, a technique attributed to enslaved African workers in the Caribbean and beyond, can make just about anything delicious. Frying both cooks and preserves, often leaving surplus cooking oil that can be used again and again.

GRILLING imbues foods with magic smoke flavor. Cooking over open fires is among the earliest forms of cooking known to humanity, and the term *barbacoa*, the origin of the word *barbecue*, is rooted in indigenous Taíno traditions.

STEAMING, whether of singular ingredients, of rice dishes in large casseroles, or of carefully composed tamales wrapped in aromatic banana leaves, is a technique used on every island in the tropics.

And finally, IN-GROUND COOKING, practiced throughout the tropical band, leads to dishes that tell powerful stories about history and ancestry. Jamaican jerk, for example, is believed to have been invented by Maroons fleeing enslavement, using in-ground pits to cook without exposing their location.

TASTE
米味
RUONG
ENRICHED
SUPER SPECIAL QUALITY

HAN KUK MI
WN RICE

New Crop
Long Grain Red Rice

RESEALABLE -For Freshness and Convenience

ornia's Original
SHI RICE

東北黑米

ily Elephan

RANCIA

Enriched Medium Grain Rice

ARROZ
RICO

"EL MEJOR DE PUERTO RICO"
Does not contain more than 4% broken rice.
NET WT. 32 OUNCES (2 POUNDS) 0.906 kg.

最高級
PREMIUM
CALIFOR
5 LBS. NET

THE RESILIENT PANTRY

Despite seemingly infinite distances, separate oceans, and differing climates, island cultures share a remarkable number of core ingredients. Intensely flavored fruits, herbs, chiles, and spices thrive in tropical climates. Paired with rice (these regions' most important grain) and coconut (abundant and generous in its uses), these ingredients form the foundation for the dynamic dishes in this book.

RICE

By Jenn de la Vega

Rice is such an important ingredient for island cooking that it requires a dedicated section. Across all the cultures represented in this book, most meals will have rice at the table to accompany everything from braised dishes to pickles. Rice is a glorious, gluten-free, vegan substrate for stewed dishes. It tempers intense spice, cuts through tartness, and soaks up fat. The main types of rice you'll encounter in these cuisines are white, jasmine, basmati, brown, black, and sticky. You'll find there are subtle differences in texture, aroma, and flavor between the different types, and in turn, there are a few nuances to cooking them.

Washing the Rice

Regardless of what type of rice you're using, washing your uncooked rice is essential for most of the recipes in this book. It lifts out extra starches that can make your grains gummy or mushy. Swish the rice in cold water and drain through a fine-mesh sieve three or four times until the cloudy water runs clear. (You can save this conditioned rice water for starting broths, stocks, or cooking other heartier grains.) You'll see a few exceptions in this book, such as with the Arroz con Tocino

(page 292), because when in doubt, I have followed the guidance of aunties, which is ripe for adaptations.

Cooking Best Practices

For the purposes of this book, we'll be focused on varieties of steamed rice. If cooking rice on the stovetop, make sure to use a large pot so there is plenty of room for the cooked rice. When it comes to salt, it depends largely on what you will be eating with the rice. If the dish is on the lighter side of salinity, add ¼ tsp per cup of rice before you cook it. You can always add a finishing salt if you think it needs more. On the stovetop, bring the rinsed rice and cold water to a boil over medium-high heat, uncovered. Once boiling, lower the heat to medium-low and cover for 12 minutes. Resist the urge to stir! Rice needs to be left alone while steaming or you will end up with risotto or something closer to congee. Turn off the heat and let stand for 10 minutes.

For those of you skeptical about rice cookers, hear us out. Most have one button or a latch for turning it on and keeping cooked rice warm. Fancier appliances have multiple options for different types of rice. The brown rice or sushi

settings have longer cooking times to make it possible to skip soaking. Just be careful not to overfill the basin—rice expands greatly no matter how you cook it. Note: Most rice cookers come with their own cups and settings for different kinds of rice, so make sure to follow the manufacturer's instructions for your rice cooker.

Always let your rice sit, covered, for 10 to 15 minutes once it is done cooking. This is because condensation has gathered on the underside of the lid and this extra time allows the droplets to redistribute and avoid mushy spots. If you're not serving immediately, fluff the rice with two forks, a slicing motion with a rice paddle, or a spatula and put the lid back on until ready to serve.

Types of Rice

Plain white rice, distinct from jasmine and basmati, is ubiquitous across the tropics and beyond, and is typically found in short/medium- or long-grain varieties. Compared to other rice it has a particularly mild flavor, which makes it ideal for composed rice dishes such as Hawaiian Chicken Jook (page 152) and Malagasy Vary Amin'Anana (page 183).

RICE RATIOS

TYPE	DRY AMOUNT *	WATER AMOUNT	ADDITIONAL INGREDIENTS
White (long or short grain)	1 cup [200 g]	2 cups [480 ml]	Salt, oil, butter, chicken bouillon or broth
Jasmine	1 cup [167 g]	1¼ cups [300 ml]	Salt, coconut oil, butter
Basmati	1 cup [179 g]	1¾ cups [420 ml]	Salt, ghee, butter, bay leaves
Brown	1 cup [190 g]	2 cups [480 ml]	Salt, oil
Black Rice	1 cup [201 g]	2¼ cups [540 ml]	Salt, oil
Sticky Rice	1 cup [185 g]	3 cups [720 ml]	Salt, oil

each makes approximately 4 servings

To cook on the stovetop, bring the rinsed rice and cold water to a boil over medium-high heat, uncovered. Once boiling, turn the heat to medium-low and cover for 12 minutes. Turn off the heat and let stand for 10 minutes.

JASMINE is a long-grain white rice originating from Southeast Asia—specifically Thailand, Cambodia, Laos, and Vietnam. It is a naturally soft grain that plumps easily and tastes faintly of buttery popcorn and a tinge of floral pandan. It appears slightly sticky but is not considered "sticky rice" (see page 25).

To cook on the stovetop, bring the rinsed rice and cold water to a boil over medium-high heat, uncovered. Once boiling, turn the heat to medium-low and cover for 12 minutes. Turn off the heat and let stand for 10 minutes.

BASMATI is a long-grain rice grown in India, Pakistan, and Nepal. Compared side by side, basmati is a bit longer and thinner than jasmine. Named for the Hindi word for "fragrant," basmati is light, tender, and fluffy, with a more defined separation between the grains. Basmati has a medium

glycemic index, so it is safer than jasmine and white rices for diabetics to consume.

To cook on the stovetop, combine the rinsed rice with water and ghee or oil and bring to a boil over medium-high heat, stirring once to make sure the grains are coated in fat. Lower the heat to medium-low and cook, covered, for 15 minutes. Turn off the heat and let stand for 10 minutes.

BROWN RICE, available as both long- and short-grain, is considered a whole-grain rice with the inedible outer hull removed. Compared to white jasmine and basmati rice, brown rice has a chewier texture, nutty flavor, and more nutrients. The bran and germ are intact, which provides its signature brown color (without it, it would be white rice). As a result, it takes a little longer to cook compared to white rice. To cut down the time, soak the rice in the cooking water for 30 minutes after washing.

To cook on the stovetop, bring the rinsed, soaked brown rice and cold water to a boil over medium-high heat. Lower the heat to medium-low and cook, covered, for 25 minutes. (If using unsoaked brown rice, let cook, covered, for

45 minutes.) Turn off the heat and let stand for 10 minutes.

BLACK RICE is a healthful whole grain with the bran, germ, and endosperm still attached—as with brown rice. Black rice is also known as "forbidden rice" in China because it was originally prohibitively expensive—available only to emperors and aristocrats—but it is now widely available. It derives its signature dark color from an antioxidant with anti-inflammatory properties called anthocyanin. It's the same nutrient that you'll find in other purple flora like eggplant and blueberries. Black rice is a little more forgiving and not sticky like jasmine, basmati, or brown rice. You can boil it in a lot of water and drain, much like pasta. There's no need to soak black rice, but if you have a sensitive digestive tract, soaking will break down the outer hull a bit more. You can cook black rice alone or mix a tablespoon of it with other rice to give the dish an inky burst of purple.

To cook on the stovetop, bring the rinsed black rice and cold water to a boil over medium-high heat. Lower the heat to medium-low and cook, covered, for 45 minutes. Turn off the heat and let stand for

10 minutes. If after that time there is excess liquid, simply drain it off.

STICKY RICE is a short-grain variety from Southeast Asia, East Asia, Bhutan, and North India. It is also called glutinous rice because it is sticky, not because it contains gluten. This is due to high amounts of amylopectin, one of the two molecules that make up starch. Sticky rice works in both sweet and savory applications. It can also be ground and used for various dumplings, thickening agents, and baked goods. It's so versatile that it makes up a whole class of rice-based desserts called kakanin in the Philippines.

The stovetop preparation for sticky rice is a bit different from what you might do with other grains: throwing it in a pot and calling it a day. First, rinse sticky rice and soak for at least 30 minutes or up to 4 hours. In a pot large enough to put a bamboo steamer basket on top, bring the water to a boil. Drain the soaked rice, then transfer it to a cheesecloth, thin kitchen towel, or banana leaf. Place it in the steamer basket and set over boiling water, then steam for 30 to 45 minutes, until tender. Turn off the heat and let stand for 10 minutes.

Pro tip: Wet your serving tools and hands before handling sticky rice. Be aware that it can dry out and harden quite quickly at room temperature, so make sure that the rice stays warm and covered until you are ready to use it.

Troubleshooting Tips

Sometimes you'll need to trouble-shoot rice in different kitchens and altitudes, but these basic principles will help you get the hang of cooking all kinds of rice.

When cooking large batches, account for an additional 2 to 3 minutes of steaming per cup, checking the doneness every 10 minutes after the suggested cook time.

If the rice scorches at the bottom of the pot, the heat was too high during cooking. You need only bring the rice to a boil and lower the heat immediately.

As far as texture goes, you can adjust up or down with ¼ cup [60 ml] of water for softer grains or harder if you like more chew. It's better to have drier rice than rice that is too wet. In the former case, add ¼ cup [60 ml] of water to the still-hot vessel and put the lid back on the warm burner or "keep warm" cooker setting. The rice should fluff up and absorb the additional water within 10 minutes. Overly wet rice cannot be completely saved, but try letting it steam with the lid off—and resist stirring.

If you've stirred or overcooked the rice, the grains will not retain their shape and will break. Don't worry, it's still edible despite the broken grains! But if you want to use it another way, you're already halfway to Chicken Jook (page 152).

Once you've mastered steamed rice, you can play with incorporating other ingredients while it steams to add more flavor dimension. Try adding a bay leaf, pandan leaf, cardamom pods, a pinch of saffron threads, or a cinnamon stick as the rice comes to a boil. When it's all steamed through, remove the harder aromatics before serving.

If you're using a rice cooker, it can pull double duty with steamer inserts, and can withstand you throwing in peeled, diced tubers like sweet potato or taro with the rice to stretch it out with more carbs.

You can save any rice by letting it cool completely for up to 1 hour before storing in the refrigerator for up to 5 days.

COCONUT

By Brigid Washington

Coconuts and their many derivatives hold an outsize importance to the culture, diets, and revenue streams of many tropical and some subtropical nations. Truly, the coconut must be nature's highest form of enterprise. From the bark to the leaves, the husk to the fruit, most every part of this palm has both fibrous and fluid utility, making it a global nutritional sensation as well as a socioeconomic staple for countries that lie within the warm equatorial band.

While the evolutionary origin of coconuts remains shrouded in mystery, what is known about their proliferation through the East and West Indies has much to do with the plant's pattern of dispersal. Botanists and researchers have long established that the seed nuts in coconuts can germinate after having floated in seawater for upward of 3 months. This uncanny ability to sprout in less-than-favorable situations reaffirms coconuts' wonder. With a heavy assist from trade winds and ocean currents—and a habit of shallow rooting in sandy, saline-rich soil—coconuts thrive along sun-drenched, lowland tropical coasts, making them an indispensable mainstay of island life the world over.

For centuries, islanders from all geographies have been self-taught master engineers when it comes to extracting the inherent bounty of this powerhouse palm. Manual harvesting—mostly by climbing—remains a common method of retrieval, although other approaches exist (like employing lengthy bamboo poles with an attached sickle-like blade). Recently, researchers in countries such as India and Sri Lanka have made headway in developing automated tree-climbing robots that can scale the trees and remove the coconuts. These soon-to-be-patented machines significantly reduce the risk of human injury that is common in coconut harvesting. Harvesting takes on greater significance in storm-prone island regions, as fresh coconuts are shelf-stable for roughly four months. This makes the coconut an ideal food source during times of duress.

This versatility is compounded by the fact that utilization of its many derivative products is low cost and high reward, both in and out of the culinary arena. And when it comes to food-related uses, coconuts are an ingredient with vast and vibrant contributions, including but not limited to fats, dairy substitutes, sweeteners, and starches.

Coconut Oil

Coconut oil is a saturated fat mixture that is processed by one of two methods: wet or dry. In the wet process, an emulsion of oil and water is created from coconut milk, then broken up by an extensive boiling period to separate out the oil. In the Philippines, coconut curds called latik, produced during the wet oil extraction process, are a popular garnish for desserts. Unrefined coconut oil, which is produced from the wet process, is minimally treated, and as such has a distinct nutty flavor and clean coconut aroma as well as a lower smoke point. Unrefined coconut oil is a good candidate for baked goods.

The dry process for creating coconut oil involves removing the coconut meat from the shell, then drying the meat either by sunlight, fire, or an oven. The dried meat is then dissolved with various solvents to produce the oil. Refined coconut oil produced by the dry process has a higher smoke point because it undergoes more treatment and processing. That additional processing also tends to make it more neutral and subtle tasting, with less of an aroma, which makes it well suited for stir-frying and sautéing.

Coconut Water

Coconut water is the naturally occurring clear liquid present in young green coconuts. Today it's a popular beverage that's mass produced and widely available in stores. Its purest form is extracted by slicing the top hard outer layers of the green coconut with a machete or cutlass and then puncturing a hole through the coconut to release the liquid as well as a thin layer of pulp. Coconut water is deeply refreshing, crisp, and luscious, with the added health benefits of vitamins, minerals, and electrolytes.

Coconut Vinegar

Coconut vinegar is produced by fermenting either coconut water or the sap of coconut tree blossoms. It has a white coloring with a cutting, astringent, acidic taste and delicate yeasty undertones. Coconut vinegar is a staple in Southeast Asian cuisines.

Coconut Milk + Coconut Cream

Coconut milk is made from the hard white inner pulp of mature coconut meat that is grated or shredded—either manually or mechanically—that is then mixed, strained, and squeezed in warm or hot water. The resulting thick, bright white, viscous milk is a clean, wholly vegan, and hefty nondairy milk that boasts varying degrees of fat. Freshly grated and strained coconut milk has a very short shelf life (rancidity occurs when it is exposed at room temperature for an hour), so it should always be refrigerated with a tightly fitting lid, which can extend its life for up to 3 days.

The biggest difference between coconut milk and cream is the fat content. Coconut cream has the highest amount of fat. It is the first press of the grated coconut, extracted using very little to no added water. Conversely, coconut milk is made by subsequent presses following the already-squeezed pulp.

Canned coconut milk and cream are distinct from the coconut milk you might find in the refrigerated section of your local grocery store. Carton coconut milk has more fillers and is significantly watered down, making it lower in fat but also less flavorful than canned coconut milk, which makes it great for your coffee or cereal but not ideal for cooking. Canned coconut milk and coconut cream are the purest form you can find without pressing the milk yourself.

It is important to note that coconut cream is not the same as cream of coconut. The latter is a commercially processed, highly artificially sweetened and syrupy product that is used as the basis of many desserts and cocktails such as piña coladas and coconut cream pie.

Shredded Coconut + Coconut Flakes

Both shredded coconut and coconut flakes are made from the flesh of young coconuts, and the biggest difference between the two is that shredded comprises smaller pieces.

Shredded coconut and coconut flakes are easy to make at home with only a few simple tools. A hard hit through the middle of a young coconut (with outer green husk removed) with a hammer will crack the shell, allowing you to pull the coconut open with your hands. This should be done over a bowl so that the encased coconut water can be saved and enjoyed. To remove the white meat from the shell, use a paring knife to pry the meat from the hard outer layer. (A vegetable peeler works to remove any residual brown skin on the flesh.)

To make shredded coconut, grate the coconut meat on either the larger or smaller holes of a box grater. This now-shredded coconut can be dried at room temperature, which is typically the norm in most humid island nations, or in the oven on a very low temperature (135 to 145°F [57 to 63°C]) for an hour.

To make coconut flakes, use a vegetable peeler to achieve long, thick strips, which can then be dried. Sweetened coconut flakes, commonly sold in most American grocery stores, can be made by incorporating a simple syrup (¼ cup [60 ml] of water plus ¼ cup [50 g] sugar) per every 1½ cups [120 g] freshly grated and dried coconut, which is then simmered until the syrup has been fully absorbed into the coconut.

Coconut Sugar

Coconut sugar, also known as coconut palm sugar, is a natural sugar derived from the circulating fluid (or sap) from coconuts. Coconut sugar is made by collecting liquid sap from an incision on the flower of the coconut palm, and then heating that sap until the water has evaporated. The resulting product is a mahogany-brown granulated sugar that is highly caloric but not as sweet as cane sugar. Coconut sugar is very minimally processed and, as a result of its origin, it contains small amounts of minerals, antioxidants, and fiber.

Coconut Flour

Coconut flour is a natural and versatile byproduct of coconut milk production. It is made from dried, ground coconut meat. It has a dense grain that retains more water than wheat flour. Gluten-free; high in fat, fiber, and protein; and with a low glycemic index (which aids in stabilizing blood sugar), coconut flour has long been used as an ingredient to aid against malnutrition.

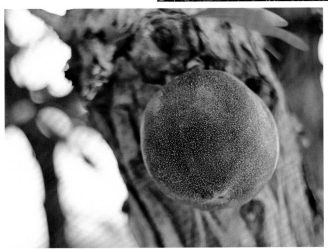

ESSENTIALS

When I began my research for this book, I expected this list of island-cuisine staples to be full of things I hadn't heard of. And while some of these ingredients may be tougher to find away from the islands—breadfruit (a bright green starchy fruit ubiquitous across the tropics, but rarely found elsewhere) and galangal (a root similar to ginger but with notes of citrus and pine)—most of these items are relatively common and easy to source. Some ingredients, however, will require going to a specialty Asian, Indian, Caribbean, or Latin American grocery store, or can increasingly be sourced online. Wherever possible, substitutions are suggested in individual recipes.

AROMATICS + HERBS

Banana leaves

Bay leaves

Capers

Chiles

    Bird's eye

    Habanero

    Jalapeño

    Scotch bonnet

Cilantro

Citrus zest

Culantro/chadon beni/recao

Curry leaves

Galangal

Garlic

Ginger

Green onions

Lemongrass

Makrut lime leaves

Mint

Olives

Onions

    Red

    White

    Yellow

Oregano

Parsley

Peppers

Shallots

Thyme

DRESSINGS, SAUCES + PASTES

Coconut milk

Fish sauce

Honey

Kecap manis (Indonesian sweet soy sauce)

Ketchup

Liquid smoke

Maggi

Mayonnaise

Miso

Molasses

Shrimp paste

Soy sauce

Sriracha

Sweet chili sauce

Tamarind purée and paste

Tomato paste

Worcestershire sauce

FRUITS + VEGETABLES

Avocados

Bananas

Bok choy

Breadfruit

Cabbage

Carrots

Celery

Cucumbers

Eggplant

Green beans

Greens
- Arugula
- Cassava
- Collards
- Moringa
- Spinach

Mango

Okra

Papaya

Peas

Pineapple

Plantains

Potatoes

Radishes

Taro

Tomatoes

SPICES

Adobo

Allspice

Annatto (achiote)

Bouillon (cubes or powder)

Cardamom

Cinnamon

Cloves

Coriander

Cumin

Curry powder

Garam masala

Mustard seeds

Nutmeg

Paprika

Pepper
- Black pepper
- White pepper
- Whole black peppercorns

Saffron

Salt
- Hawaiian
- Kosher (Diamond Crystal brand)
- Sea

Sazón seasoning

Sesame seeds

Star anise

Turmeric

SWEETENERS

Brown sugar

Demerara sugar

Honey

Jaggery

White cane sugar

ACIDS

Calamansi

Lemons

Limes

Oranges

Sour oranges

Vinegars
- Coconut
- Palm
- Rice
- Sugarcane
- White

Yogurt

FATS

Butter

Coconut oil

Ghee

Grapeseed oil

Nuts
- Almonds
- Macadamia nuts
- Peanuts

Olive oil

Sesame oil

Vegetable oil

ISLAS

ESSENTIAL TOOLS

I grew up on the US mainland at a time when it was difficult to find tools from my homeland. We would eventually buy a pilón (wooden mortar and pestle) and a tostonera (a press used for smashing fried green plantains) when we visited family in Puerto Rico, but before that we had to improvise. For example, when making Tostones (page 213), you can use a small plate and the bottom of a large coffee cup for similar results. Over the course of my research and cooking, I identified a handful of tools that are now essential to my kitchen and will make cooking island dishes a breeze.

Pots + Pans
Heavy-duty cast-iron pots and skillets are ideal for many island dishes because they can withstand extreme heat and can be transferred easily between your stovetop, grill, and oven.

DUTCH OVEN
This heavy-bottomed cooking pot has a tight-fitting lid and is typically made of enameled cast iron. I also recommend a camping pot: a completely cast-iron pot, typically with feet on the bottom and a heatproof handle, that can be placed directly on hot coals or hung over an open fire.

CAST-IRON SKILLET
A properly seasoned cast-iron skillet is like a well-honed knife, and may become your favorite pan. It can be used to sear, sauté, and fry, and like a Dutch oven, it's versatile and can be put in the oven at any temperature or directly atop an open fire.

WOK
I use my wok for everything from scrambling eggs to frying fish. The shape makes it particularly versatile, as the large surface area is ideal for sautéing vegetables, simmering sauces, or fitting a bamboo steamer basket.

STOCKPOT
Across the islands, huge metal pots are used to prepare vats of soups, stews, and rices to feed a group. In your average kitchen, you may not get as much use out of it, but you will be happy to have one on hand for making stocks and other dishes with a lot of ingredients or large bones.

CALDERO
A thin metal pot with a lid that's perfect for making rice on the stovetop.

Appliances
COFFEE GRINDER
Many recipes in this book call for homemade spice and curry blends. A mortar and pestle is the traditional method for grinding spices, but a standard, inexpensive coffee grinder is infinitely more effective and efficient.

COOKERS
I use my pressure, slow, and rice cookers often, as do many islanders. Pressure cookers can speed up long braises and stews, and rice cookers can also be used to make composed rice dishes, such as Jamaican Rice and Peas (page 160).

FOOD PROCESSOR/BLENDER
My food processor is one of the most indispensable tools in my kitchen. It's heavy and takes up a lot of space, but it's crucial for blending up root vegetable masa for Puerto Rican Pasteles de Masa (page 284), or grinding up dozens of chiles for Sambal Oelek (page 49).

Utensils + Grilling Supplies
GLOVES
Heatproof gloves are an excellent safety precaution for building fires and working over a hot grill, particularly when you need to flip skewered meats or grill baskets. Similarly, disposable plastic gloves are a must when handling fiery chiles.

GRILL TOOLS
- Grill basket
- Long tongs
- Bamboo skewers
- Grill brush
- Charcoal grill
- Tripod
- Kitchen twine
- Meat thermometer
- Pilón (large wooden mortar and pestle)
- Wooden spoons

CHOPSTICKS
Both long and short to use for stirring and as utensils.

SAUCES, CONDIMENTS + SPICE BLENDS

The vital sauces and spice blends from these island nations are dynamic and versatile. Throughout the tropics, it's common to be served well-seasoned seafood or meat alongside rice or root vegetables, with a flavorful, sometimes spicy sauce on the side to give it a kick. The intensity of foundational dry spices and pastes transform basic ingredients such as lamb stew meat for Lamb Colombo (page 182) or red kidney beans in Habichuelas Guisadas con Calabaza (page 145). The sauces add acidity and dynamism to both balance and turn up the flavors of otherwise simple dishes, such as Mojo (page 46) on Tostones (page 213). They can also add a whole other dimension to a dish, as when you pair fruity, spicy, citrusy Lasos Pimam (page 48) with Seychellois Cari de Poisson et Potiron (Pumpkin Fish Curry) (page 151). These condiments also reflect similarities across islands, as they share many ingredients—particularly garlic, chiles, cilantro, citrus juice or vinegar, and soy sauce. You can easily serve a Caribbean dish with a Mint-Cilantro Chutney (page 44), or a CHamoru dish with a Caribbean Wasakaka (page 47). Above all, these sauces are incredibly adaptable and can be adjusted to match your personal tastes.

RECIPES

Island	Yield	Total Time
Puerto Rico	2¼ cups [540 ml]	5 minutes

SOFRITO

Sofrito—a blend of garlic, onions, peppers, and recao (culantro)—is the backbone of flavor for Puerto Rican dishes. Also referred to as recaito, it's typically sautéed in oil as the foundation for sauces, braises, beans, stews, and rice dishes. It's also adaptable: Sauté for 2 to 3 minutes for a lighter, more verdant flavor or sauté for 7 to 10 minutes and combine with tomato sauce for a richer flavor. This recipe yields a little more than 2 cups [540 ml]—probably more than you'll use for any recipe—but it keeps well. If kept in the refrigerator, it's best if used within a week, but it can be frozen for up to 6 months and thawed before using. You can also put it into a pan with hot oil straight from the freezer, though it may sputter a smidge. My grandmother often kept sofrito in the freezer stored in a repurposed plastic margarine container or frozen into cubes and saved in resealable bags.

1 medium red bell pepper, seeded and quartered

3 ají dulce, amarillo, or mild banana chile peppers, seeded and coarsely chopped (see Tips)

6 large garlic cloves

1 large yellow onion, coarsely chopped

6 fresh culantro sprigs, both leaves and tender stems, coarsely chopped (see Tips)

6 fresh cilantro sprigs, both leaves and tender stems, coarsely chopped

In a food processor or blender, blend the bell pepper, chile peppers, and garlic until smooth. Add the onion and blend until smooth, then add the culantro and cilantro and blend until smooth.

The sofrito will keep, covered, in the refrigerator for up to 1 week or in the freezer for up to 6 months.

TIPS If you can't find ají dulce or amarillo peppers, use another half of a bell pepper—yellow or orange—to add color!

Culantro, also called sawtooth herb or wild coriander, has long leaves with jagged edges and a stronger, earthier flavor than cilantro. You can find it in the produce section of most Latin American markets, as well as many Asian grocery stores.

Island	Yield	Total Time
Puerto Rico	About ½ cup [64 g]	5 minutes

Island	Yield	Total Time
Puerto Rico	About 4½ tsp [13 g]	5 minutes

SAZÓN SEASONING

Cumin-heavy sazón, along with Adobo (right), is among the most commonly used spice blends in Puerto Rican cooking. It's also popular throughout Latin America, and commercial brands are widely available. This is my take on sazón, which includes turmeric along with the standard annatto to imbue dishes with a golden hue. Adaptation is encouraged based on preference, and if you can't find ground annatto, then sweet paprika is a perfect substitute. It will keep in an airtight container for years.

2 Tbsp fine sea salt

2 Tbsp ground annatto (achiote) or sweet paprika

1 Tbsp garlic powder

1 Tbsp onion powder

1 Tbsp ground cumin

1 Tbsp ground turmeric

½ tsp freshly ground black pepper

In an airtight container, combine all ingredients. Cover and shake well to incorporate.

ADOBO SEASONING

Adobo is an all-purpose seasoned salt commonly used in Puerto Rico and across Latin America. It's a great addition to just about any savory Puerto Rican dish. Unlike Sazón (left) it doesn't include annatto, so it doesn't add the same vibrant orange color. It's an incredible cheat, and is particularly good in marinades for grilled meats.

2 tsp garlic powder

1½ tsp kosher salt, plus more as needed

¼ tsp dried oregano

¼ tsp ground turmeric

¼ tsp freshly ground black pepper

In a small bowl, combine all ingredients and mix well with a fork. Taste and add more salt if desired.

Island	Yield	Total Time
Seychelles	½ cup [64 g]	5 minutes

Island	Yield	Total Time
Martinique	8 tsp [25 g]	5 minutes

SEYCHELLOIS MASSALÉ

Curries abound in Seychelles, and massalé is among the most common. Like most spice blends, there are numerous variations and approaches. The signature flavor comes from the combination of clove, cinnamon, cardamom, nutmeg, and pepper—all of which grow abundantly on the island.

3 Tbsp coriander seeds

1 Tbsp cumin seeds

1 Tbsp black peppercorns

9 green cardamom pods

1 tsp whole cloves

1 small cinnamon stick, snapped into small pieces

2 tsp chili powder

1 tsp freshly grated nutmeg

In a medium skillet over high heat, combine the coriander, cumin seeds, peppercorns, cardamom, cloves, and cinnamon and toast for 1 minute or less, swirling continuously to ensure even toasting and so that the spices do not burn. Do not overcook, or you'll get a bitter, burnt taste. If you burn the first batch (it happens!), start over with fresh spices. Let cool, then grind to a powder using a mortar and pestle or a clean coffee grinder. Stir in the chili powder and nutmeg.

COLOMBO SEASONING

This simple spice blend combines turmeric and spicy black pepper from Asia with Caribbean allspice, representing the flow of ingredients through the spice trade from East to West.

2 tsp ground allspice

2 tsp ground coriander

2 tsp ground cumin

1 tsp ground turmeric

1 tsp freshly ground black pepper

In a small bowl, combine all ingredients and mix well with a fork.

Island	Yield	Total Time
Fiji	½ cup [64 g]	5 minutes

FIJIAN CURRY PASTE

The foundation of Fijian Lamb Barbecue (page 257), this flavorful, heavily spiced paste pairs particularly well with gamey meats.

1 Tbsp brown sugar

1 Tbsp ground ginger

1 Tbsp paprika

1 Tbsp ground turmeric

2 tsp ground cumin

2 tsp ground coriander

1 tsp garlic powder

1 tsp kosher salt

½ tsp cayenne pepper

¼ tsp freshly ground black pepper

2 Tbsp dark soy sauce

1 Tbsp vegetable or coconut oil

In a medium bowl, combine the brown sugar, ginger, paprika, turmeric, cumin, coriander, garlic powder, salt, cayenne, and pepper, and mix well with a fork. Add the soy sauce and oil and whisk into a thick paste.

Island	Yield	Total Time
Madagascar	3 Tbsp [26 g]	5 minutes

MALAGASY CURRY

Similar to Madras, this mild curry blend is incredibly adaptable. It works particularly well with braises and stews.

2 tsp ground coriander

1 tsp ground cumin

1 tsp sweet paprika

1 tsp ground turmeric

¼ tsp chili powder

¼ tsp ground cardamom

¼ tsp ground cinnamon

⅛ tsp ground allspice

In a small bowl, combine all ingredients and mix well with a fork.

Island	Yield	Total Time
St. Lucia	2 cups [480 ml]	40 minutes

BANANA KETCHUP

This fun, fruity condiment is flavorful, tangy, and mildly sweet. While this version is from the Caribbean, variations are also popular in the Philippines and across Southeast Asia. Use as you would standard tomato ketchup on french fries or alongside any of the doughy fried snacks in this book.

2 Tbsp peanut or vegetable oil

½ cup [70 g] finely chopped white onion

2 medium garlic cloves, minced

1 small jalapeño, seeded if desired to mitigate spiciness, finely chopped

2 tsp finely grated peeled fresh ginger

½ tsp ground turmeric

¼ tsp ground allspice

1¼ cups [236 g] mashed ripe banana (about 2 bananas)

½ cup [120 ml] rice vinegar

2 Tbsp honey

2 Tbsp rum (optional)

1 Tbsp tomato paste

1 Tbsp soy sauce, plus more as needed

½ tsp kosher salt, plus more as needed

In a medium saucepan over medium-high, heat the peanut oil until shimmering, 1 to 2 minutes.

Add the onion and sauté, stirring occasionally, until softened, about 5 minutes. Add the garlic, jalapeño, ginger, turmeric, and allspice and cook until fragrant, about 30 seconds.

Stir in the banana, vinegar, honey, rum (if using), tomato paste, soy sauce, and salt, then bring back to a simmer.

Lower the heat, cover, and simmer for 15 minutes, stirring often. Remove from the heat, uncover, and let cool for at least 10 minutes.

Transfer the mixture to a heat-tolerant food processor or blender or use an immersion blender to process until smooth, about 1 minute. Thin with water as needed to reach a ketchup-like consistency.

Season with additional soy sauce or salt as needed. Transfer to an airtight container and store in the refrigerator for up to 2 weeks.

Island	Yield	Total Time
Indonesia	1 cup [240 ml]	10 minutes

Island	Yield	Total Time
Guam	1½ cups [360 ml]	5 minutes

COCONUT PEANUT SAUCE

A variation on classic Indonesian peanut sauce, this recipe combines coconut milk, garlic, and fresh cilantro with peanut butter for a rich, flavorful dipping sauce. Serve alongside Sate Ayam (page 253).

1 garlic clove, minced

2 tsp jaggery or demerara sugar

2 tsp sriracha or chile oil, plus more as needed

2 Tbsp fresh lime juice

½ cup [120 ml] canned full-fat coconut milk, well shaken and stirred

¼ cup [226 g] creamy peanut butter

2 tsp minced fresh cilantro leaves

2 tsp soy sauce, plus more as needed

In a blender or small food processor, combine the garlic, sugar, sriracha, and lime juice and pulse four or five times until the garlic is ground to a paste. Scrape the sides of the blender, then add the coconut milk, peanut butter, cilantro, and soy sauce and purée to a thick sauce. Taste and add more soy sauce or sriracha, for added umami or spiciness respectively, if desired.

TIP To make a thinner sauce, add more coconut milk or warm water 1 Tbsp at a time until you reach your desired consistency.

FINA'DENNE'
CHAMORU SOY DIPPING SAUCE

A staple of CHamoru cuisine, this soy-based dipping sauce is flavored with lemon, green onions, and fiery chiles. You can replace the vinegar with additional lemon juice if desired. This recipe was inspired by Juanita Blaz, profiled on page 57.

¾ cup [180 ml] soy sauce, plus more as needed

½ cup [24 g] thinly sliced green onions or shallots

3 to 6 red bird's eye chiles

½ cup [80 g] halved cherry tomatoes

¼ cup [60 ml] coconut vinegar or apple cider vinegar

¼ cup [60 ml] fresh lemon juice

In a medium bowl, combine all ingredients and mix well. Taste and adjust soy sauce and chiles as desired.

Island	Yield	Total Time
Puerto Rico	1 cup [240 ml]	5 minutes

Island	Yield	Total Time
Mauritius	1 cup [240 ml]	5 minutes

MAYO-KETCHUP

A favorite Puerto Rican condiment, mayonnaise and ketchup are blended with garlic, lime juice, and a bit of hot sauce to make a delightful pink sauce. It comes together in minutes and pairs well with Tostones (page 213) and most other fried snacks.

½ cup [120 g] mayonnaise

⅓ cup [85 g] ketchup

1 medium garlic clove, minced

½ tsp fresh lime juice, plus more as needed

¼ tsp kosher salt, plus more as needed

Dash of hot sauce, such as Frank's RedHot, plus more as needed

In a small bowl, combine all ingredients and mix well with a fork. Taste and adjust the lime juice, salt, and hot sauce as needed. Store in an airtight container and chill before serving.

MINT-CILANTRO CHUTNEY

Fresh, bright, and herbaceous, this chutney pairs well with any of the curries in this book, particularly Mauritian Kalia de Poulet (page 80), or as a dipping sauce for fried snacks such as Pates from St. Croix (page 198) and Seychellois Gato Pima (page 197).

3 to 6 serrano or jalapeño chiles, stemmed, seeded if desired to mitigate spiciness, chopped

2 tsp sugar

½ tsp kosher salt, plus more as needed

1 cup [12 g] packed fresh mint leaves, chopped

½ cup [6 g] packed fresh cilantro leaves, chopped

½ cup [120 ml] fresh lime juice

In a food processor, combine the chiles, sugar, and salt and pulse several times to chop into a loose paste. Add the mint, cilantro, and lime juice and process to a smooth paste. For a looser chutney, add water 1 Tbsp at a time until you reach your desired consistency. This sauce is best served fresh, though you can store any remaining sauce in the refrigerator for up to 2 days.

TIP If desired, you can also make this chutney using a large mortar and pestle.

Island	Yield	Total Time
Trinidad	1 cup [240 ml]	30 minutes

TAMARIND SAUCE

Islas contributor Brigid Washington's signature tangy Trinidadian condiment is spiced with amchar masala, a traditional local blend that's similar to garam masala. The sauce pairs beautifully with fritters such as Pates (page 198) or Festival (page 196) and is also a great accompaniment to saucy curry dishes such as Cari de Poisson et Potiron (page 151).

1 cup [200 g] brown sugar

¼ cup [60 g] tamarind paste

¼ cup [24 g] amchar masala

4 garlic cloves, minced

1 tsp kosher salt

2 Tbsp finely chopped fresh culantro leaves, or 3 Tbsp finely chopped fresh cilantro leaves

In a small saucepan, bring 1½ cups [360 ml] of water to a boil. Add the brown sugar, tamarind paste, amchar masala, garlic, and salt, and whisk to combine.

Lower the heat and simmer, uncovered, for 15 minutes. The consistency should be viscous and the sauce will stick to the back of a spoon. Add the culantro and simmer uncovered for another 5 minutes. This sauce keeps well for several weeks in a sealed container in the refrigerator.

Island	Yield	Total Time
Philippines	1 cup [240 ml]	5 minutes

TOYOMANSI

This Filipino dipping sauce is a staple of the cuisine, and it is meant to be adapted to your personal taste. Add fish sauce or thinly sliced green onions as desired for a subtle variation. Serve it with grilled chicken and seafood.

½ cup [120 ml] calamansi juice

½ cup [120 ml] soy sauce

3 large garlic cloves, minced

3 or 4 red bird's eye chiles, stemmed and chopped

In a medium bowl, combine all ingredients and stir well. This sauce keeps for 1 week in a non-reactive, sealed container in the refrigerator.

TIP Calamansi juice is available frozen or bottled, typically in Asian grocery stores. If you can't find it, substitute half tangerine juice and half fresh lime juice.

Island	Yield	Total Time
Cuba	1 cup [240 ml]	10 minutes

Island	Yield	Total Time
Mauritius	½ cup [120 ml]	5 minutes

MOJO

This classic garlic, citrus, and herb Cuban dipping sauce is great with Tostones (page 213) and Pescado Frito (page 219).

1 head garlic, 10 to 12 cloves, minced

½ cup [120 ml] sour orange juice (see Tips)

⅓ cup [80 ml] olive oil

1½ tsp kosher salt, plus more as needed

1 tsp finely chopped fresh oregano (see Tips)

¼ tsp ground cumin

In a medium bowl, combine all ingredients and blend with a fork. Alternatively, for a thicker mojo, purée the ingredients in a blender or small food processor. Mojo will keep, refrigerated in an airtight container, for 3 to 5 days.

TIPS If you can't find sour orange juice, combine ¼ cup [60 ml] tangerine juice with ¼ cup [60 ml] fresh lime juice.

You can substitute ½ tsp dried oregano for fresh.

SPICED YOGURT SAUCE

This simple spiced yogurt sauce is a great accompaniment to curries and fritters. Add diced cucumber for a cooling variation, which is similar to Indian raita.

½ cup [120 g] plain yogurt

1 Tbsp chopped fresh cilantro or mint leaves

1 tsp fresh lime juice

½ tsp garam masala

Pinch of cayenne pepper

½ cup diced cucumber (optional)

In a small bowl, combine the yogurt, cilantro, lime juice, and garam masala and whisk with a fork. Dust with cayenne, add the cucumber (if using), and serve immediately or chill until ready to use. Stored in an airtight container, the sauce will keep for at least 1 week in the refrigerator.

Island	Yield	Total Time
Dominican Republic	1 cup [240 ml]	5 minutes

WASAKAKA

This herbaceous Dominican take on Latin American chimichurri uses lime juice instead of the more traditional red wine vinegar.

⅓ cup [80 ml] fresh lime juice

½ cup [20 g] finely chopped fresh flat-leaf parsley

¼ cup [10 g] finely chopped fresh cilantro leaves

¼ cup [7 g] finely chopped fresh oregano

¼ cup [60 ml] olive oil

2 garlic cloves, minced

1 tsp kosher salt

¼ tsp freshly ground black pepper

In a small bowl, combine all ingredients and whisk to incorporate. If you'd like a creamier sauce, blend the ingredients in a small food processor or blender. This sauce keeps for about 1 week in a sealed container in the refrigerator, though it should come to room temperature before using, as the oil will congeal when cooled.

SPICY SAUCES

Island	Yield	Total Time
Philippines	1½ cups [360 ml]	3 days

Island	Yield	Total Time
Seychelles	2 cups [480 ml]	1 day

SINAMAK
ILCOS-STYLE SPICED VINEGAR

This sinamak is a type of sawsawan—Tagalog for dipping sauces that are typically made with vinegar, garlic, onion, chiles, herbs, and spices. It's a Filipino staple with numerous regional variations.

2 cups [475 ml] palm vinegar or rice vinegar (see Tip)

15 whole red bird's eye chiles, stemmed

10 whole long green chiles, stemmed

2 Tbsp julienned peeled galangal

1 Tbsp julienned peeled fresh ginger

8 garlic cloves, thinly sliced

1 tsp black peppercorns

In a sterilized, airtight jar or other nonreactive container with a lid, combine the vinegar, chiles, galangal, ginger, garlic, and peppercorns. Let rest at room temperature for at least 3 days before using. Transfer to a long-neck bottle with a speed pourer for easier use. Sinamak will keep for several months on the countertop or in your pantry and will deepen in flavor over time.

TIP   Datu Puti brand has a native sugarcane vinegar that's a good substitute for palm vinegar.

LASOS PIMAN

Lasos piman, a condiment known simply as "chili" in Seychelles, is fundamental to Seychellois cuisine. This fruity version balances intense heat with a bit of sweetness. Bilimbi is a small cucumber that's indigenous to the island but can be difficult to source. A tart, firm carambol or star fruit is a good substitute.

¼ lb [115 g] spicy red chiles, such as bird's eye, stemmed and chopped

½ cup [70 g] minced white onion

1 or 2 large garlic cloves, minced

½ tsp kosher salt, plus more as needed

⅛ tsp freshly ground black pepper

½ cup [80 g] chopped tomato

1 small bilimbi, or ¼ cup [35 g] star fruit, seeded and chopped (see Tip)

¼ cup [60 ml] fresh lemon juice

1 Tbsp olive oil

In a large mortar or food processor, combine the chiles, onion, garlic, salt, and pepper and grind or pulse into a paste. Add the tomato and bilimbi, and grind or pulse to fully incorporate.

Add the lemon juice and olive oil and stir well to fully blend. The sauce can be served immediately, but it's best left at room temperature for at least 1 day, or preferably 3 to 5 days. Stored in an airtight container in the refrigerator, it will keep for several months.

TIP   If you don't have access to bilimbi or star fruit, substitute ¼ cup [60 ml] more lemon juice or ¼ cup [60 ml] soursop juice.

PIQUE
PUERTO RICAN–STYLE HOT SAUCE

Chiles are rarely used in Puerto Rican cooking. Even the commonly used ají dulce is typically quite mild. But Puerto Ricans do like a kick to their food, which is often added with this simple vinegar-based hot sauce. While *pique* is a catchall term for hot sauces across the island, each cook has their own take. This recipe comes from Serena and Toriano Fredericks, owners of Boricua Soul, a Puerto Rican/Southern restaurant in Durham, North Carolina.

SAMBAL OELEK

This traditional Indonesian chili paste is lightly fermented and fiery hot. Use gloves when handling the chiles, being careful not to touch your face. Use the sauce sparingly at first. The heat will mellow out and the flavors will deepen the longer it ferments.

6 medium jalapeños (about 10 oz [285 g]), stemmed, seeded, and roughly chopped (about 2½ cups)

6 medium habanero chiles (about 2¼ oz [65 g]), stemmed, seeded, and roughly chopped (about ¾ cup)

3 medium garlic cloves, smashed

10 black peppercorns

2 cups [475 ml] white vinegar

½ tsp kosher salt

In a 1 qt [945 ml] wide-mouth jar with a lid, combine the jalapeños, habaneros, garlic, peppercorns, vinegar, and salt. Stir until the salt is dissolved. Cover and let stand at room temperature for 3 days. Transfer to narrow-necked sealable bottles for easier pouring, if desired. Pique will keep for up to 2 weeks in a sealed container in the refrigerator.

1 lb [455 g] bird's eye or long green chiles or Fresno, red jalapeño, or red serrano peppers

1 or 2 large garlic cloves (optional)

1 Tbsp kosher salt, plus more as needed

2 Tbsp rice vinegar or white vinegar

1 tsp fresh lime juice (optional)

In a food processor, combine the chiles, garlic (if using), and salt and pulse several times to chop. Add the vinegar and lime juice (if using) and purée into a thick paste. Transfer to an airtight glass container and let sit at room temperature for at least 4 days. Taste (with care) and refrigerate when it tastes right. Sambal oelek keeps for several months in the refrigerator.

Buni
Snuk
Mula
Dradu
Masbango
Lion Fish
Piska'i Fondo
Karko

CHAPTER ONE

MARINATING

Guam

Ginger, garlic, green onions, soy, lemon. These are the ingredients for CHamoru marinade. It's from Guam, an island of fewer than 200,000 people, set deep in the Pacific Ocean—about halfway between Japan and Australia. This classic marinade tells many stories: that of geography, and the ways in which ingredients flow across southeast Asia; that of the CHamoru, the indigenous people of the Mariana Islands; that of US colonization.

Guam is lush and fertile, and crops grow readily due to its humid, tropical climate. Honeydew, cantaloupe, watermelon, and a small melon known as the pipinu; citrus such as lemonchina, calamansi, tangerines, and pomelos; trees bearing coconuts, papayas, bananas, guavas, star fruits, gooseberries, mangoes, avocados, breadfruit, soursops, and jackfruit— all growing on an island perfumed by ginger blossoms, plumeria, and jasmine. Yet despite the lushness and abundance of the landscape, the food people eat in Guam is perhaps not what you'd expect, and in many ways mirrors the cuisines of Caribbean islands halfway across the planet.

The volcanic island, which is part of the Mariana Islands archipelago, has existed for at least 33 million years. It is among the first islands to be settled by humans in the region: The indigenous CHamoru have been there since about 2000 BCE. The earliest invaders of Guam described the people living there as having long hair past their waists (regardless of gender) and having stained their teeth black or red with varnish as a symbol of beauty. Although CHamorus have remained the dominant ethnic group on the island, they have suffered because of colonization. They were labeled "Chamorros" (with that spelling) by Spanish colonizers who took the island in 1565 and immediately began a civilizing mission—much in the way they had everywhere else they conquered. Catholicism was strictly enforced, cultural expression was controlled, and the native language slowly became infused with Spanish. Today, more than half of the CHamoru vocabulary includes words derived from Spanish, although efforts to define an indigenous orthography have shifted the spelling to *CHamoru*, because the indigenous alphabet does not contain *rr* or *c*.

The United States acquired Guam in 1898 in the Treaty of Paris, which ended the Spanish–American War and also led to the absorption of Puerto Rico, the Philippines, and Cuba into the United States. Much like their predecessors, Americans sought to "civilize" Guam, even banning the CHamoru language—a restriction that was upheld through the mid-1970s. American interest in the Mariana Islands stemmed from its strategic location relatively close to powerful Asian countries including China, Japan, and Korea. Despite being incredibly remote—its closest neighbor, Papua New Guinea, is 1,100 miles [1,800 km] away—it is a gateway between East Asia and the Americas, a tiny sentry ensuring American eyes on the region.

The relationship between the modern CHamorus and the US military is complex. During World War II, Japan occupied Guam following the bombing of Pearl Harbor. It was a brutal period, after which the American government recaptured the island. This military intervention was initially welcomed, even celebrated, until the US government began claiming ancestral farmlands for military compounds (officially this land was "purchased," though sometimes for just one dollar an acre). Today, Guam is—like Puerto Rico—an unincorporated territory of the United States, which maintains a significant military presence there and remains one of the most substantial employers for the island.

Despite its tropical abundance, much of the modern CHamoru diet is imported. Starting in the 1940s, the United States introduced canned foods such as Spam, corned beef, and other processed meats that remain fixtures of the diet today. These ingredients spawned a culture of quick and easy meals that shifted the diet of most CHamorus away from the seafood, fruit, and root vegetables that their ancestors might have eaten.

Today, less than 5 percent of seafood eaten in Guam comes from their seas, despite the presence of a variety of fish in local waters, such as parrotfish, mahi-mahi, and tuna. Ginger, which grows wild on Guam and is central to their cuisine, is not sufficiently cultivated and must be imported from Korea and Thailand. In part this is because the small island cannot produce sufficient food for its people, particularly when so much farmland was repurposed as military outposts. In addition, Guam is subject to the Jones Act—as is Puerto Rico and (perhaps surprisingly) Hawai'i—which stipulates that all international shipments must be delivered by ships owned by the United States, which significantly limits trade capacity and drives up the price of food.

However much the CHamoru diet has been impacted by colonization, that hasn't stopped them from developing a truly delicious cuisine that blends the flavors and ingredients of the region with those that are imported. Many traditional CHamoru dishes are rice-heavy, saucy, and meaty.

One thing many CHamorus are proud of is their barbecue. Cookout culture is fierce on Guam, where marinated meat is grilled and served alongside red rice and mayonnaise-heavy potato and macaroni salads.

But CHamoru barbecue is distinct from what we're used to in the United States, where meat is often dry-rubbed or bathed in sticky-sweet sauce. The secret to CHamoru barbecue is its marinade. Pork ribs and chicken are soaked overnight in a signature blend of garlic, ginger, onion or green onions, lemon, brown sugar, and lots of soy sauce. The marinade deeply penetrates the meat and boosts it with super savory umami. And even though ribs and chicken were introduced following US occupation, soy sauce marks Guam's broader connection to the region and Japanese influence, while the remaining ingredients are local and are the backbone of the cuisine.

People living on islands often struggle with limited resources and access to quality ingredients, and as such, marinating is a foundational technique and a foolproof way to infuse lesser-quality ingredients with intense flavor. This technique is the first step to many of the recipes in this book. Often stews, grilled meat, even whole fried fish such as Pescado Frito (page 219) begins with a marinade. Mastering this technique will serve you well when preparing island recipes, but it's also an excellent method for boosting the flavors of everyday dishes and weeknight meals. After a long day, you can throw together Sazón-Marinated Chicken Breasts (page 85), let them marinate while you decompress, then prepare as desired. Tofu and other plant-based proteins and vegetables really shine with a quick marinade, making this an incredibly adaptable method for preparing dishes. The recipes that follow bring together the flavors of the islands, while providing a road map to building a marinade that's right for you.

MARINATE

Marinating can turn tough cuts of meat and flavorless vegetables into dynamic, finger-licking dishes. The marinating process causes proteins to break down, subsequently tenderizing meat while injecting flavor. But there's an art to marinating, and choosing your base—vinegar, citrus, or yogurt—is key. The balance of aromatics and herbs—garlic, fresh or dried herbs—adds dimension. Fats impart richness. But above all, timing is crucial. An overnight marinade can truly transform a tough ingredient into something spectacular, while a quick marinade can impart bright, punchy flavors ideal for seafood and vegetables. This chapter will provide master recipes for marinades, with easy-to-follow graphs for creating the perfect blend for the ingredients you have on hand.

Because of the chemical process implicit in a marinade, most ingredients are interchangeable. This guide will help you decide on the best approach for your ingredients, and hopefully inspire you to create new dishes and flavor combinations of your own.

MARINATING TIMES

Chicken, pork, beef, or lamb	3–24 hours
Fish	20–30 minutes
Shellfish	15 minutes
Vegetables	30 minutes

ACIDS

Citrus juice (lemon, lime, sour orange, orange, calamansi)

Fruit (mango, papaya, pineapple)

Vinegar (apple cider, white or red wine, palm, coconut, rice)

Yogurt

AROMATICS

Citrus zest

Galangal

Garlic

Ginger

Onions (green onions, shallots, yellow and white onion)

Spices

OILS

Olive

Sesame

Vegetable

JUANITA BLAZ
GUAM

Juanita Blaz lives in Dededo Village, the most populous town on Guam. Situated on the northernmost tip, Dededo's shoreline is a spectacle of mountain cliffs, dense foliage, and jade waters peppered by submerged coral. Large rock formations sit along the coast, ancient faces chiseled by thousands of storms.

A mother of five who was born and raised on the island, Juanita has a broad face with pronounced cheekbones, often with a furrow in her brow alongside a sly smile that reflects an intensity, a toughness.

Juanita dedicated herself to raising a family soon after graduating from high school and worked hard to support them. Guam's economy is sparse, and few opportunities exist outside of tourism and military service. Twenty years ago, Juanita began volunteering to support local girls. Having four daughters herself, she wanted to keep girls safe and healthy and serve as a positive role model, because girls on Guam—as everywhere else on the planet—grapple with sexism and are

at greater risk for intimate partner violence. She began by starting a club, Island Girl Power, as a safe space in Dededo for girls ages seven to fourteen to go. On Saturdays, Juanita shows up at the clubhouse with activities, conversation starters, and an open mind and heart. For her, there's more to this than keeping girls physically safe. Connection to the CHamoru culture, CHamoru heritage, and nourishing their bodies is crucial.

The Island Girl Power clubhouse sits on a small compound of decommissioned US military family housing. Cookie-cutter homes sit atop a sea of gravel, up on the limestone forest that covers the northern part of the island. However austere, it provides a solid foundation for laying down raised boxes for planting crops. There, Juanita and other volunteers run a thrift store that receives donations and distributes vouchers to provide local women and families with clothing and other items free of charge. She also runs a community garden, where girls and other volunteers tend to flowers, fruits, and vegetables. Long beans and four-cornered beans climb up improvised trellises alongside taro, sweet potatoes, tomatoes, and basil, as well as garlic and cilantro, which are used in many CHamoru marinades and dishes. Moringa bushes and banana, cherry, and mulberry trees grow nearby, and girls grow flowers for mwarmwars—traditional floral headdresses worn during cultural celebrations.

Juanita uses the garden to teach girls about a different kind of self-defense: how to take care of their minds and spirits as well as their bodies. Among them is Sophie, a teenager who volunteers at the community garden, growing okra and tomatoes—the first things she's ever planted. She also grows marigolds, which serve as a natural insecticide. "They kept all my other plants alive!" she said. Sophie gets excited when she talks about her seedlings, full of hope and pride for what's coming. "I guess it just inspired me to keep on going. It just gave me a sense of motivation, something to look forward to," she said. "Nature always finds a way."

As a child, Juanita cherished her great-grandmother, who spoke very little English while Juanita spoke almost no native CHamoru. She watched as her great-grandmother grew medicinal herbs to protect and heal her family. These herbs included purslane, which is used to treat burns, headaches, digestive and upper respiratory illnesses, and arthritis; and tulsi or holy basil, which cures fevers and skin conditions. Juanita brings this same practice to the girls and other community members she works with—balms to heal the wounds of survivors of assault, of

ISLAS

neglect, of broken families. For Juanita, it's crucial that local girls learn and connect to ancestral practices, many of which have diminished in popularity.

Although it's not customary in Guam's male-dominant culture, Juanita is the grill master at her house, and her signature recipe is roasted breadfruit. But she also loves making Fina'denne' (page 43), a spicy soy-based dipping sauce that's a fixture on CHamoru tables. And in her mind, too often traditional CHamoru dishes are rice-heavy, saucy, and lacking in vegetables. This is something Juanita wants to change. "I want kids to know that fruit comes from trees, not from packages at the grocery store," she said.

She wants local girls to recognize ginger plants by their vibrant magenta and goldenrod blossoms, to detect their signature aroma—honeysuckle mixed with gardenia—from a distance, and to know that the foundation of their cuisine grows on their land. The girls motivate Juanita to show up several times a week to maintain and oversee their gardens.

For her, all of this serves a higher purpose. "The universe reacts to what you put into it. When you shoot out what you need and it's directly connected to the service of others, really wonderful doors open," she said. "And when you think you're about to give up and things can get more challenging . . . something comes along and reinforces that you should keep going."

RECENTS

CHAMORU BARBECUE CHICKEN WITH JUANITA'S FINA'DENNE'

This adaptation of a classic CHamoru marinade has become my go-to for grilling chicken and pork. It comes together quickly and packs a punch; soy sauce and lemon deeply penetrate the meat, which is then infused with abundant garlic and ginger. Start your marinade the morning of your cookout instead of the night before, as this soy-heavy marinade is potent. Once you begin cooking, baste the chicken with the remaining marinade several times to glaze and char, being sure to let the marinade cook before taking the meat off the grill.

MARINADE

10 to 12 large garlic cloves, minced

¼ cup [50 g] finely grated peeled fresh ginger

1 cup [240 ml] soy sauce

½ cup [120 ml] fresh lemon juice

¼ cup [60 ml] white wine vinegar

⅓ cup [65 g] light brown sugar

1 cup [104 g] finely chopped green onions, white and green parts

CHICKEN

3 to 4 lb [1.4 to 1.8 kg] bone-in skin-on chicken pieces, dark or white meat

Steamed white rice, for serving

Fina'denne' (page 43), for serving

To make the marinade: In a medium bowl, combine the garlic, ginger, soy sauce, lemon juice, vinegar, brown sugar, and onions and stir well to incorporate.

To make the chicken: Put the chicken pieces in a large resealable bag or airtight container, then pour the marinade over and seal the container. Marinate for at least 3 hours or up to 12.

Remove the chicken from the marinade and place the pieces on a rimmed baking sheet. Reserve the remaining marinade.

Bring a grill to medium heat, then cook the chicken for 25 to 40 minutes, turning often to avoid burning, and brushing with the reserved marinade a few times. Be sure to cook the last application of marinade before taking the chicken off the grill.

Tent the chicken with aluminum foil and let it rest for 5 to 7 minutes before eating. Serve with steamed rice and fina'denne' on the side.

TIP   If you don't have access to a grill, this recipe is easy to prepare in the oven. Preheat the oven to 350°F [180°C], then line a large rimmed baking sheet with foil. Arrange the chicken in an even layer, bone-side down. Cover with foil and bake for 35 minutes. To finish, brush with reserved marinade, turn the heat to a high broil, and place the baking sheet directly under the broiler. Watching carefully, and brushing with marinade a few more times, broil for 5 to 10 minutes until the chicken reaches your desired char.

TISA FAAMULI
AMERICAN SAMOA

If you walked barefoot into Tisa Faamuli's Barefoot Bar on Tutuila Island in American Samoa, you'd start off in the sand. Not the shifting, white, hot-hot-hot sand of a beach day, but the cool, damp sand of a shaded path packed down by many feet. You'd walk under a sign hanging from a rough-hewn archway of branches: Tisa's Bar and Grill. The little path branches right off an asphalt road, making the place feel more like a secret treasure than a popular tourist destination.

But Tisa's is much more than a bar. Every inch of Tisa Faamuli's eco-establishment is constructed from the surrounding beach and rainforest, as well as organic and inorganic materials collected around Alega Village. Her marine sanctuary, restaurant, and lodge is a love letter to the island and its people.

Overlooking protected waters, she runs a regenerative business inspired by her upbringing amid a family of farmers. "We lived in an open structure without walls, and would go to the stream, the ocean to collect our food," she said. "We gathered our firewood and built our own fires and cooked outdoors." On an island that has struggled with exploitation and colonization, Tisa is a fierce and stand-out advocate for her land. Recently, she was involved in a successful lawsuit against a wireless telecom company that was illegally dumping discarded cables and other waste in Alega Bay, polluting its waters.

Tisa's multifaceted business is centered around saving and protecting the environment. Much like the Samoan way of life, there's an emphasis on communion and fellowship during mealtime. Every Sunday, guests are invited to eat from a shared spread of slow-roasted pork, taro, banana, coconut, and fresh fish from the day's catch. This feast is wrapped in banana leaves and prepared in a traditional Samoan umu oven powered by hot stones. She also sustains poumuli and niu kuma trees on her property, used to build the thatched-roof, open-air huts called fales, or beach dwellings that sit atop the shoreline's shallow waters.

Tisa opened her business in 1980 with a cooler filled with beers and fresh coconut. Since then, she has aimed to keep that same casual vibe while using the space to promote land and ocean conservation. With its two wooden patios jutting out above the bay, the bar is reminiscent of a dock. Netting and several faded orange life preservers line the sides. Green plastic lawn chairs sit around tables with bright floral tablecloths, where diners can be found drinking piña coladas out of mason jars and munching on fresh fish caught on location. The water laps onto the shore ahead, and the rainforest rustles and breathes behind you. It may be a while before you make your way over the sand and back to the asphalt.

Island
Guam

Yield
4 to 6 servings

Active Time
1 hour

Total Time
At least 4 hours

CHAMORU BARBECUE PORK RIBS

The same marinade for Barbecue Chicken (page 60) can be used to make equally sumptuous pork ribs. They can be served as an appetizer or as a main course alongside steamed rice and dipping sauces such as Fina'denne' (page 43).

4 lb [1.8 kg] pork ribs, divided into individual ribs

1 recipe CHamoru Barbecue Marinade (page 60)

Put the ribs in a large resealable bag or airtight container, then pour the marinade over. Marinate for at least 3 hours or up to 12.

Remove the ribs from the marinade and place the pieces on a rimmed baking sheet. Reserve the remaining marinade.

Bring a grill to medium heat, then cook the ribs for 25 to 40 minutes, turning often to avoid burning, and brushing with the reserved marinade a few times. Be sure to cook the excess marinade before taking the ribs off the grill.

Tent the ribs with aluminum foil and let rest for 5 to 7 minutes before eating.

TIP   If you don't have access to a grill, this recipe is easy to prepare in the oven. Preheat the oven to 350°F [180°C], then line a large rimmed baking sheet with foil. Arrange the ribs in an even layer, bone-side down. Top with foil, then bake for 35 minutes. To finish, brush with reserved marinade, turn the heat to a high broil, and place the baking sheet directly under the broiler. Watching carefully, and brushing with marinade a few more times, broil for 5 to 10 minutes, until the ribs reach your desired char.

I
S
L
A
S

64

Island
Philippines

Yield
4 to 6 servings

Active Time
1 hour 30 minutes

Total Time
10 hours

BEEF TAPA
CURED BEEF

Typically eaten for breakfast, tapa is beef that is air-dried then roasted, forming a kind of tender beef jerky. It's eaten as a category of dish called tapsilog, formed from the words *tapa*, a salty protein; *sinangang*, garlic-fried rice; and *itlog*, a sunny-side-up egg. The tapa can be made ahead, although it will dry out after about 3 days. Thinly sliced green onions are a must for serving.

½ cup [120 ml] soy sauce

¼ cup [60 ml] calamansi juice (see Tip)

12 to 15 large garlic cloves, minced

2 Tbsp sugar

½ tsp kosher salt

¼ tsp freshly ground black pepper

3 lb [1.4 kg] beef sirloin or skirt steak, sliced into 2 to 3 in [5 to 7.5 cm] pieces ¼ in [6 mm] thick

1 Tbsp vegetable oil

Fried eggs, for serving

Garlic-fried or steamed rice, for serving

Thinly sliced green onions, white and green parts, for garnish

In a large nonreactive mixing bowl, combine the soy sauce, calamansi juice, garlic, sugar, salt, and pepper.

Add the beef and toss to coat fully with marinade, massaging to tenderize. Transfer to an airtight container or resealable bag and refrigerate overnight.

Preheat the oven to 200°F [95°C]. Line a baking sheet with parchment paper or aluminum foil and place a wire rack on top. Remove the beef from the marinade and arrange in an even layer on the wire rack.

Slowly dry the beef in the oven for 1 to 1½ hours, turning every 15 minutes, until the beef is mostly dry but still slightly moist in the center.

In a wide pan over medium-high, heat the oil. Add about half of the beef and sauté for 1 to 2 minutes on each side, until slightly crisp and caramelized. Remove the beef from the pan and cut into smaller pieces if desired. Repeat with the remaining beef.

Serve hot, with a fried egg and garlic-fried or steamed rice, and garnish with green onions.

TIP Calamansi juice is available frozen or bottled, typically in Asian grocery stores. If you can't find it, substitute half tangerine juice and half lime juice.

I
S
L
A
S

Island
Guam

Yield
4 to 6 servings

Active Time
30 minutes

Total Time
1 hour 35 minutes

KELAGUEN UHANG
CITRUS-MARINATED SHRIMP WITH COCONUT

Kelaguen is as much a technique as it is a dish. It combines proteins—particularly seafood and beef, but also venison and chicken—with lime, onions, and chiles. As a process, to kelaguen is to lightly pickle proteins in a spicy, citrusy marinade, with added fresh coconut and cilantro. This dish often starts with raw meat, but this version uses blanched fresh shrimp and can be served with steamed rice alongside a green salad or on a tostada for a quick snack.

1½ lb [680 g] fresh shrimp, peeled and deveined

2 cups [170 g] finely grated unsweetened coconut

1 cup [48 g] thinly sliced green onions, white and green parts

½ cup [120 ml] fresh lemon juice, plus more as needed

3 red bird's eye chiles, stemmed, seeded if desired to mitigate spiciness, and minced (optional)

½ tsp kosher salt, plus more as needed

Steamed white rice, tortillas, or tostadas, for serving

Bring 4 cups [945 ml] of water to a boil in a pot or kettle.

Meanwhile, finely chop the shrimp into small pieces.

Once the water is boiling, transfer the shrimp to a fine-mesh sieve, then pour the boiling water over the shrimp, shaking the sieve to ensure the shrimp are evenly heated. Shake a few times and let drain.

In a large nonreactive mixing bowl, combine the coconut, green onions, lemon juice, chiles (if using), and salt. Add the shrimp and toss well. Cover and transfer to the refrigerator. Chill for at least 1 hour before serving.

Toss again and add more salt or lemon juice as needed. Serve with steamed rice, tortillas, or on a tostada. Kelaguen uhang will keep in the refrigerator for several days.

ISLAS

OKA I'A
COCONUT CUCUMBER FISH CEVICHE

Refreshing but rich and deeply balanced, this classic Samoan dish blends fresh red snapper with lime, tomatoes, crunchy cucumber, and creamy coconut milk. Serve in individual bowls as an appetizer or snack, or pair with white rice for a more substantial meal.

½ lb [230 g] red snapper fillets, cut into bite-size pieces (see Tips)

½ cup [120 ml] fresh lime juice

2 green onions, white and green parts thinly sliced

2 medium tomatoes, finely chopped (about 1 cup [180 g])

1 small cucumber, peeled, seeded, and finely chopped (about 1 cup [130 g])

2 red bird's eye chiles, finely chopped

¾ cup [180 ml] canned full-fat coconut milk, well shaken and stirred

1½ tsp kosher salt, plus more as needed

In a deep nonreactive bowl, combine the fish and lime juice, cover, and refrigerate for 15 minutes.

Add the green onions, tomatoes, cucumber, chiles, coconut milk, and salt and stir well to incorporate. Return to the refrigerator and chill for an additional 20 to 30 minutes. Adjust salt as needed and serve chilled.

TIPS Sea bass, mahi-mahi, ahi tuna, or blanched shrimp can be substituted for red snapper.

This recipe doubles easily for larger portions, or to feed more people.

ISLAS

SHOYU AHI POKE
TUNA POKE

More earthy and umami-rich than similar raw fish dishes in this book, poke—which means to slice or cut crosswise into pieces—has deep ancestral roots in Hawaiʻi. Although it's well known and popular today, poke is believed to have been developed by native Polynesians many centuries ago, using sea salt and seaweed as a way of curing and preserving fresh fish. Be sure to use coarse alaea or Hawaiian salt for this recipe, as a finer grain would make the dish too salty. Serve alone, or with a side of steamed white rice or seaweed salad.

1 lb [455 g] fresh sashimi-grade ahi tuna steaks, cut into 1 in [2.5 cm] pieces (see Tip)

2 tsp finely grated peeled fresh ginger

½ cup [24 g] thinly sliced green onions, white and green parts

¼ cup [35 g] thinly sliced sweet yellow onion

4½ tsp soy sauce, plus more as needed

2½ tsp sesame oil

1 tsp honey

⅛ tsp aleppo pepper, Togarashi, or other spicy ground chile pepper

¾ tsp coarse alaea or Hawaiian salt, plus more as needed

1 Tbsp black sesame seeds

Steamed white rice or seaweed salad, for serving (optional)

In a large nonreactive bowl, gently toss together the tuna, ginger, green onions, yellow onion, soy sauce, sesame oil, honey, pepper, and salt. Taste and adjust the soy and other seasonings as needed.

Sprinkle with sesame seeds and serve immediately, with steamed rice or seaweed salad, if desired.

TIP The tuna for this recipe should be as fresh as possible. Be wary of tuna steaks that have dark brown streaks or are loose or separating along the streaks, which indicates that the tuna is not fresh.

KINILAW NA ISDA
FISH CEVICHE WITH GINGER AND VINEGAR

Like many of the marinated and pickled fish dishes in this book, kinilaw na isda is bright and refreshing—a cool snack that's perfect for a hot day. Part of a class of snackable dishes in the Philippines called pulutan that are typically enjoyed with a cold beer, it's often served family style in a large bowl, with each person choosing what toppings they want. It's great with mini tostadas or lettuce cups.

1 lb [455 g] tuna or mackerel steaks, cut into 1 in [2.5 cm] cubes (see Tips)

1 cup [240 ml] white sugarcane vinegar (see Tips)

2 tsp calamansi juice (see Tips)

2 Tbsp finely grated peeled fresh ginger

1 cup [140 g] minced red onion

2 Thai green chiles, thinly sliced on the diagonal

½ tsp kosher salt, plus more as needed

¼ tsp freshly ground black pepper

Lettuce cups or mini tostadas, for serving

Thinly sliced green onions (white and green parts), chopped fresh cilantro leaves, chopped red bell pepper, crispy fried shallots or garlic, and fish sauce, for garnish (optional)

In a large nonreactive mixing bowl, combine the fish, vinegar, calamansi juice, ginger, onion, chiles, salt, and pepper and toss gently to incorporate. Cover and marinate for 1 hour or up to 3 hours in the refrigerator, tossing occasionally to ensure the fish is evenly coated.

Adjust the seasoning as needed and serve immediately with lettuce cups or mini tostadas and desired garnishes.

TIPS The most common types of fish for kinilaw are yellowfin tuna and Spanish mackerel, but you can also use other firm-fleshed fish such as marlin, grouper, or mahi-mahi. Fresh shrimp, squid, and clams also work well with this recipe.

Datu Puti White Vinegar is a popular sugarcane vinegar.

Calamansi juice is available frozen or bottled, typically in Asian grocery stores. If you can't find it, substitute half tangerine juice and half fresh lime juice.

PERNIL
MARINATED ROAST PORK SHOULDER

Among the most coveted dishes from Puerto Rico, pernil is a positively sumptuous preparation for pork shoulder. It's marinated (ideally overnight) in garlic, citrus, and herbs, then slow-roasted at high heat to achieve a crisp chicharrón, or crispy pork skin. Traditionally, it's cut from a whole roasted pig or lechon, which can be found on the island year-round. This recipe is deeply inspired by chef Maricel Presilla and her pernil recipe in *Gran Cocina Latina*. Her method is a foolproof way to get that chicharrón as well as tender meat that falls off the bone. Serve with Tostones (page 213), Arroz con Tocino (page 292), Habichuelas Guisadas con Calabaza (page 145), or Yuca con Mojo (page 119).

ADOBO MARINADE

9 large garlic cloves, minced

8 tsp kosher salt, plus more as needed

3 Tbsp olive oil

5 tsp sour orange juice or equal parts fresh lime juice and orange juice

4 tsp dried oregano

1 tsp freshly ground black pepper

PORK

One 8 to 9 lb [3.6 to 4 kg] bone-in, skin-on pork shoulder, preferably with skin covering the entire top layer (see Tips)

1 tsp kosher salt

To make the adobo marinade: In a large pilón or mortar and pestle, combine the garlic and salt and grind into a thick paste. Add the olive oil, orange juice, oregano, and pepper and stir well to combine. Alternatively, combine the ingredients in a small bowl and mix well to blend.

To make the pork: Rinse the meat and dry well with a clean towel. Place the pork skin-side down on a large rimmed baking sheet. Poke 1 in [2.5 cm] holes in the fatty layer and into the meat with a paring knife, being careful not to pierce the skin. You can't have too many holes.

Pour the adobo marinade over the pork in batches, using your fingers to push adobo deep into the slits. If you're worried about your hands smelling like garlic—which they will!—wear gloves.

On a large work surface, place a long sheet of plastic wrap, layering with additional sheets as needed to ensure you can securely wrap the entire pork shoulder. Transfer the pork to the plastic wrap and wrap tightly, adding more sheets of plastic as needed to ensure the pork is wrapped airtight and the adobo is contained. Set on a clean baking sheet and place in the refrigerator to marinate overnight if possible, or for at least 2 hours.

continued

Preheat the oven to 400°F [200°C]. Working over the sink, carefully remove the pork from the plastic wrap, discarding any remaining adobo. Place the pork skin-side up in a deep roasting pan, and wipe the skin with a clean cloth. Sprinkle the skin with salt and rub it in.

Spray a piece of aluminum foil with cooking spray or brush it with oil and loosely tent it, oiled-side down, over the pork. (Ungreased foil will stick if it touches the pork.)

Roast for 1 hour, then carefully remove the foil and rotate the pan. Continue roasting for another 2 to 3 hours depending on the size of your pork shoulder, rotating every hour or so, and adding water to the pan to keep about ½ in [13 mm] of liquid in the pan as juices evaporate. The meat is done when the juices run clear and the thickest part of the leg registers 160°F [70°C] with a meat thermometer. The skin may take more time to crisp than the meat does to cook, so keep in the oven—watching closely so that it does not burn—until the skin makes a hollow sound when tapped with the back of a knife or metal spatula.

Remove the pork from the oven and let rest for 10 to 15 minutes, then transfer to a large cutting board. Remove the skin, or chicharron, from the roast by running a knife underneath the skin, starting from the bottom until loosened. Slice the meat off the bone, then use kitchen shears to cut the chicharron into serving pieces, trimming excess fat if desired. Rest both in the off but still-warm oven until ready to eat.

TIPS   If you use a smaller or larger pork shoulder, calculate your adobo accordingly by using the following formula: Per 1 lb [455 g] of meat, use 1 large garlic clove, 1 tsp olive oil, ½ tsp sour orange juice, ½ tsp dried oregano, 1 tsp kosher salt, and ⅛ tsp black pepper. If using a smaller pork shoulder, you may want to reduce the amount of salt slightly.

Use a pan that can handle char. You can line your pan with foil, but the foil may tear and make things even messier. When you're ready to clean the pan, combine ½ cup [90 g] baking soda and enough hot water to cover the burned spots, and let it soak for half an hour. The char should release easily with your abrasive tool of choice.

AKOHO SY VOANIO
LEMON-MARINATED COCONUT-BRAISED CHICKEN

Rich yet delicate, this simple dish is perfumed with lemon zest, ginger, and garlic, rounded out with sweet, acidic tomato. Like so many Malagasy dishes, this one transforms simple ingredients into a flavorful meal. And like so many other dishes in this book, this one is very similar to that from another region, the Philippines, where substituting vinegar for the lemon juice and adding soy and fish sauces would turn this dish into an adobo.

2 lb [910 g] boneless, skinless chicken breast, cut into bite-size pieces

2 Tbsp fresh lemon juice

1 tsp grated lemon zest (optional)

2 tsp kosher salt, plus more as needed

1 tsp freshly ground black pepper

1 tsp cayenne pepper

3 Tbsp coconut oil

1 large yellow onion, chopped (about 2 cups [280 g])

3 garlic cloves, minced

2 tsp finely grated peeled fresh ginger

2 small ripe tomatoes, chopped (about 1 cup [160 g])

1½ cups [360 ml] canned full-fat coconut milk, well shaken and stirred

Steamed white rice, for serving

In a large nonreactive mixing bowl, combine the chicken, lemon juice, lemon zest (if using), salt, black pepper, and cayenne and let marinate for at least 30 minutes at room temperature or up to 1 hour in the refrigerator.

In a large heavy-bottomed pot with a lid, heat the coconut oil over medium heat. Add the onion and sauté for 5 to 7 minutes, until starting to turn golden. Add the garlic, ginger, and tomatoes and sauté for 3 to 5 minutes, until the tomatoes become saucy.

Add the coconut milk, turn the heat to low, cover, and simmer for 20 minutes, stirring occasionally.

Increase the heat to high and add the chicken with the marinade, stirring well to incorporate. Once the mixture returns to a simmer, lower the heat and simmer for 10 to 15 minutes, until the chicken is cooked through and the sauce is thickened. Adjust the seasoning as needed, then serve over steamed rice.

Island	Yield	Active Time	Total Time
Mauritius	**4 servings**	**40 minutes**	**At least 9 hours**

VINDAYE POISSON
TURMERIC AND MUSTARD-MARINATED TUNA

This dynamic, flavorful dish, inspired by Selina Periampillai's recipe from *The Island Kitchen*, is an excellent thing to make ahead for busy weeks or special occasions. Fresh tuna is seasoned and quickly fried, then marinated in chiles, turmeric, garlic, and caramelized onion and chilled overnight. It can also be eaten immediately, but it's worth the wait. Serve alongside steamed rice with Trinidadian Cucumber Chow (page 107) for a refreshing island meal.

1½ lb [680 g] fresh tuna steaks (see Tip)

Kosher salt

Freshly ground black pepper

5 Tbsp [80 ml] vegetable oil

2 Tbsp ground turmeric

2 Tbsp black or brown mustard seeds

2 medium yellow or white onions, thinly sliced

4 large garlic cloves, minced

4 spicy chiles, such as long green or red bird's eye, seeded and finely chopped

3 Tbsp white wine vinegar

Steamed white rice, for serving

Season the tuna with salt and pepper on both sides. In a large, deep skillet or wide Dutch oven over medium-high, heat 2 Tbsp of the oil. Once shimmering, add the tuna and sear each side, flipping once or twice, until the tuna is just cooked through, 4 to 5 minutes total. Remove from the heat and let cool to room temperature. Once cooled, chop the tuna into bite-size pieces and set aside.

With a mortar and pestle, finely grind together the turmeric, mustard seeds, and a pinch of salt. Add a splash of cold water, and grind until the mixture forms a thick paste.

Return the pan to medium and heat the remaining 3 Tbsp oil. Add the onions and sauté for 7 to 10 minutes, until golden. Add the garlic and chiles and sauté for 2 to 5 minutes longer, until fragrant. Add the turmeric paste and fry for 30 seconds, stirring until fully blended.

Add the tuna and vinegar to the pan and stir gently to incorporate with the onions and spices. Transfer to an airtight container and let marinate in the refrigerator overnight. This is best served chilled the next day alongside steamed rice, but if you can't wait, you can enjoy it immediately.

TIP Mahi-mahi and mackerel steaks are good substitutes for tuna in this dish.

Island
Pan-Caribbean

Yield
4 servings

Active Time
1 hour 20 minutes

Total Time
**At least 11 hours
20 minutes**

STEWED OXTAIL

The brainchild of *Islas* recipe developer Brigid Washington, stewed oxtail is a dish she's been preparing and perfecting for decades. She says that when you're making oxtail, you have to pay attention, and the majority of the attention is needed at the beginning. Oxtail is gelatinous and fatty, not like a steak, and so it requires time and care. It should be marinated overnight and properly browned in order to develop its signature rich flavor. This is among the many island dishes that render the otherwise inedible edible, with the long marinade softening the nourishing tendon and forming a velvety gravy for the finished dish.

OXTAIL

1 large yellow onion, finely chopped

3 cups [144 g] thinly sliced green onions, white and green parts

10 medium garlic cloves, smashed

3 in [7.5 cm] piece fresh ginger, peeled and minced

1 fresh scotch bonnet chile, stemmed and chopped

½ cup [20 g] chopped fresh parsley leaves

1 cup [40 g] finely chopped fresh cilantro leaves and tender stems

2 tsp fresh thyme leaves

⅓ cup [65 g] light brown sugar

1 Tbsp Worcestershire sauce

2½ Tbsp kosher salt, plus more as needed

2 Tbsp ground allspice

1 Tbsp freshly ground black pepper

3 lb [1.4 kg] oxtails, cut into 2 in [5 cm] pieces

STEW

¼ cup [60 ml] vegetable oil

¼ cup [50 g] dark brown sugar

3 cups whole baby carrots

One 15.5 oz [439 g] can butter beans, drained

¼ cup [65 g] ketchup

2 tsp angostura bitters

Steamed brown or white rice, for serving

Fried sweet plantains, for serving (optional)

To marinate the oxtail: In a large container with an airtight lid, combine the yellow onion, green onion, garlic, ginger, chile, parsley, cilantro, thyme, light brown sugar, Worcestershire sauce, salt, allspice, and pepper and stir. Add the oxtails and toss well to incorporate. Cover and marinate the oxtails in the refrigerator for at least 8 hours or up to 12 hours.

To make the stew: Heat the vegetable oil in a large heavy-bottomed pot over medium-high. Sprinkle in the dark brown sugar and cook, undisturbed, until it is starting to sizzle and darken, 1 to 2 minutes. Continue to cook, stirring occasionally with a heatproof spatula, until the sugar is bubbling and the caramel is dark brown (but not black), 3 to 4 minutes more. (Note: The oil will not incorporate with the melted sugar.) Immediately add the oxtails with the marinade and stir to coat.

Cook the oxtails, turning occasionally, until evenly browned on all sides. Lower the heat to low and cook for 2 hours, turning every 30 minutes, until the meat is tender when pierced with a paring knife but not yet falling apart.

Add the carrots, butter beans, ketchup, bitters, and 3 cups [710 ml] water, and cook over low heat without stirring until the carrots are tender, the meat easily pulls away from the bone with a fork, and the sauce starts to thicken, about 45 minutes, skimming fat from the surface as needed. Gradually stir in up to an additional 1 cup [240 ml] of water as needed until the sauce reaches a gravy consistency. Serve with steamed rice and fried sweet plantains, if desired.

Island
Mauritius

Yield
4 to 6 servings

Active Time
20 minutes

Total Time
At least 7 hours

KALIA DE POULET

YOGURT-MARINATED CHICKEN WITH POTATOES AND SAFFRON

This is one of many outstanding curries from Mauritius, an island about 700 miles [1,125 km] east of Madagascar, whose dishes are a dynamic creole fusion of Indian, African, French, and Chinese cultures and flavors. Instead of citrus or vinegar, this dish uses yogurt as the foundation for the marinade. It's a balance of bright ginger, mint, and cilantro; warm garam masala and cinnamon; and floral saffron, all smothering rich chicken thighs and fried potatoes. As with most curries, it's incredibly adaptable, though this combination is truly sumptuous.

MARINADE

1 yellow onion, finely chopped

5 large garlic cloves, minced

1 tsp grated peeled fresh ginger

½ cup [6 g] chopped fresh mint leaves

½ cup [6 g] chopped fresh cilantro leaves

2 or 3 long green chiles, stemmed and seeded if desired to mitigate spiciness, minced

1 cup [240 ml] plain, full-fat yogurt

1 tsp kosher salt

CHICKEN

2 lb [910 g] bone-in chicken thighs, skin removed and trimmed of excess fat

2 Tbsp ground cumin

1 Tbsp garam masala

1 tsp ground cinnamon

½ tsp ground cloves

½ tsp freshly ground black pepper, plus more as needed

½ tsp freshly grated nutmeg

5 cardamom pods, seeds only, crushed, or ¼ tsp ground cardamom

1 Tbsp vegetable oil (see Tip)

Pinch of saffron threads

1 Tbsp hot water

2 ripe tomatoes, peeled and chopped

Kosher salt

POTATOES

⅓ cup [80 ml] vegetable oil (see Tip)

2 large Yukon gold potatoes, peeled and chopped into 1 in [2.5 cm] pieces

Steamed white rice, for serving

Additional fresh mint and cilantro leaves, for garnish

To make the marinade: In a blender or food processor, combine the onion, garlic, ginger, mint, cilantro, chiles, yogurt, and salt and pulse to form a paste.

To make the chicken: In a large nonreactive mixing bowl, combine the chicken, cumin, garam masala, cinnamon, cloves, pepper, nutmeg, and cardamon. Add the marinade. Gently toss to evenly coat, then cover and refrigerate for at least 6 hours, or overnight if desired.

When ready to cook, let the chicken come to room temperature on the counter, about 1 hour. Line a large plate with paper towels and set aside.

To make the potatoes: Meanwhile, in a large, deep skillet over medium-high, heat the oil until shimmering, 1 to 2 minutes. Add the potatoes and sauté for 7 to 10 minutes, stirring frequently, until evenly browned but not burnt. Remove from the oil with a slotted spoon and transfer to the prepared plate. Pour the oil into a heat-resistant container and set aside for another use.

To cook the chicken: Add the 1 Tbsp oil to the pan over medium heat. Pour in the chicken with all the marinade, and simmer for 3 to 4 minutes, stirring frequently, until the liquid is reduced and the sauce has thickened slightly.

Meanwhile, soak the saffron threads in the water. Once the liquid in the pan is entirely reduced, add the tomatoes and saffron threads in their water, then cover, lower the heat, and simmer for 15 to 20 minutes, stirring occasionally.

Return the potatoes to the pan, stir well, and cook for an additional 15 to 20 minutes, until the chicken is cooked through and the potatoes are tender. Season with salt and pepper as needed. Serve with steamed white rice and garnish with herbs.

TIP You can substitute ghee for the vegetable oil in any part of this recipe.

Island
Indonesia

Yield
4 servings

Active Time
25 minutes

Total Time
45 minutes

GARLIC TEMPEH

Today, tempeh is commonly found in grocery stores. But many don't realize that it's among the oldest soy-based foods on the planet. Originating in Indonesia one thousand years ago, it's produced by washing, pressing, and fermenting soybeans. This dish, inspired by a recipe from James Oseland's *Cradle of Flavor*, is an incredibly simple, quick, high-protein snack, with a mild flavor and satisfying texture that's perfect with Indonesian dipping sauces such as kecap manis (Indonesian sweet soy sauce), Sambal Oelek (page 49), and Coconut Peanut Sauce (page 43). It keeps for at least a week in the refrigerator and can be enjoyed cold or reheated in a toaster oven.

6 large garlic cloves, minced

1 Tbsp minced peeled fresh ginger

1 Tbsp soy sauce

1 Tbsp kecap manis or hoisin sauce

2 tsp kosher salt

1½ cups [360 ml] hot water

One 8 oz [225 g] package plain tempeh, cut into 8 pieces

Vegetable oil, for frying

In a deep lidded container just wide enough to fit the tempeh, combine the garlic, ginger, soy sauce, kecap manis, and salt. Stir in the hot water. Transfer the tempeh to the container and shake gently to toss in the marinade. Let sit at room temperature for 20 minutes.

Meanwhile, pour enough oil into a deep frying pan to reach ½ in [13 mm]. Heat over medium-high, adding a small piece of dry tempeh or ginger to test the temperature (it should rise to the top when ready).

Drain the tempeh and pat it dry with a paper towel. Line a baking sheet or large plate with paper towels.

Carefully add the tempeh to the oil piece by piece, using a splatter guard as needed and being careful not to crowd the pan. Fry the tempeh in batches for 2 to 3 minutes total, turning several times, until the tempeh is golden brown but not dark.

Carefully remove the tempeh from the oil with tongs and let drain on the paper towels. The tempeh can be eaten hot or at room temperature.

Yield
6 to 8 servings

Active Time
25 minutes

Total Time
**At least 3 hours
30 minutes**

CARNE GUISADA
STEWED BEEF

Carne guisada is pure comfort. It's a signature dish for Dominicans and Puerto Ricans alike, though it's comparable to other stewed meats in this book, such as Malagasy Romazava (page 170) and Filipino Adobong Puti (page 139). *Guisar* means "to stew" in Spanish, and here beef is slow cooked with aromatic Sofrito (page 38), with added tomatoes that produce a rich, velvety sauce. The key to a perfect carne guisada is taking your time at the beginning: Brown your meat well and give the aromatics space to meld into a silky gravy. Serve with plenty of steamed white rice and fried sweet plantains. Leftovers keep well in the refrigerator for several days or in the freezer for several months.

ADOBO

2 tsp olive oil

2 tsp white vinegar

2 large garlic cloves, minced

1 tsp dried oregano

1 tsp kosher salt, plus more as needed

½ tsp freshly ground black pepper

BEEF

2 to 3 lb [910 g to 1.4 kg] beef chuck roast or boneless short ribs (see Tips), trimmed of excess fat and cut into 2 in [5 cm] pieces

1 Tbsp vegetable oil

1 Tbsp olive oil, plus more as needed

1 cup [240 ml] Sofrito (page 38)

1 Tbsp store-bought or homemade Sazón Seasoning (page 39)

1½ cups [360 ml] low-sodium beef broth or water, plus more as needed

One 14½ oz [411 g] can whole peeled tomatoes, chopped, juice reserved

3 dried bay leaves

1 medium carrot, chopped

1 large celery stalk, chopped

1 lb [455 g] Yukon gold potatoes, peeled and chopped

Steamed white rice, for serving

Fried sweet plantains, for serving (optional)

continued

To make the adobo: In a small bowl, combine the olive oil, vinegar, garlic, oregano, salt, and pepper. Or grind the ingredients in a large pilón or mortar and pestle.

To make the beef: Pat the beef dry and place in a medium lidded container or a resealable bag. Evenly coat with the adobo and let marinate for at least 30 minutes at room temperature, or in the refrigerator overnight if possible, but not longer than a full day.

In a large lidded, heavy-bottomed pot over high, heat the vegetable oil. Working in batches as needed to prevent crowding, add the beef, shaking off excess adobo beforehand. Cook for 3 to 5 minutes, flipping often to brown evenly. Transfer the meat to a clean bowl and set aside.

Lower the heat to medium, add the olive oil, and pour in the sofrito, adding more olive oil if the pan is too dry. Sauté for 5 to 7 minutes, until any liquid has evaporated.

Add the sazón and sauté for 1 minute. Add the broth, tomatoes and their juice, and bay leaves, and scrape up any browned bits using a wooden spoon.

Nestle the meat into the sauce and bring to a simmer. Lower the heat to low, cover, and simmer for 1 hour, stirring occasionally.

Add the carrot and celery and cook, covered, for 1 hour more, adding more broth as needed to ensure the sauce remains just below the level of the meat. Check the tenderness of the meat: It should get close to falling apart when pressed with the back of a spoon.

Add the potatoes and cook, covered, for 30 minutes more, until the meat and potatoes are cooked through and tender.

Adjust salt as needed, and serve on a plate or in a shallow bowl over a mound of white rice, with fried sweet plantains, if desired.

TIPS If using short ribs, which tend to be fattier, you'll get a richer, darker, more velvety sauce. It's a matter of taste, and both yield delicious results.

You can also use this recipe to make pollo guisado, equally popular and common, simply by using bone-in or boneless chicken in place of beef and adjusting the cooking time by about half.

Island
Puerto Rico

Yield
4 to 6 servings

Active Time
35 minutes

Total Time
45 minutes

SAZÓN-MARINATED CHICKEN BREASTS

My culture influences my cooking continuously, making its way into my quick meals as much as my weekend projects. Sazón Seasoning (page 39)—a spice blend of cumin, coriander, oregano, garlic powder, black pepper, and annatto—is ubiquitous in Puerto Rican and Latin American cooking. This stovetop method of cooking Sazón-marinated chicken breasts produces juicy, fragrant, well-seasoned meat. The meat benefits from an overnight marinade, which will make the meat juicier and more flavorful, but the dish also comes together in about 45 minutes if you're short on time.

4 medium garlic cloves, minced

¼ cup [60 ml] fresh orange juice, preferably from 2 small mandarin oranges

2 Tbsp olive oil

2 Tbsp store-bought or homemade Sazón Seasoning (page 39)

½ tsp kosher salt

½ tsp freshly ground black pepper

4 medium boneless, skinless chicken breasts (about 1½ lb [680 g]), trimmed of excess fat (see Tips)

In a small food processor, combine the garlic, orange juice, olive oil, sazón, salt, and pepper and pulse to form a creamy marinade. Alternatively, you can mince the garlic super finely, then combine it with those same ingredients in a small bowl, stirring with a fork.

Pat the chicken breasts dry with a paper towel and transfer them to a large resealable bag. Pour in the marinade, seal, shake, then gently massage the seasoning into the meat. Let sit on the counter for at least 10 minutes, or refrigerate and marinate overnight. (If marinating overnight, bring the chicken to room temperature before cooking, about 1 hour.)

Heat a large nonstick skillet over medium-high. Add the chicken breasts, one by one, and pour over about half the marinade. Cook for 7 to 10 minutes, flipping frequently with tongs and being careful not to let them get too dark too fast. Lower the heat to medium and cook for another 10 minutes, flipping often. Lower the heat to low and continue cooking for 10 minutes more, flipping a few more times to ensure the meat is cooked through. Check for doneness by pressing the center of a breast with your tongs. If it's still squishy, continue to cook until the meat has a bit of resistance (though not rock hard) and measures 165°F [74°C] on a meat thermometer.

Let the chicken rest in the pan off the heat for a few minutes before serving.

TIPS   Thinner chicken breasts will take less time to cook, so monitor the color and texture of your meat as it cooks.

This recipe works great with boneless, skinless chicken thighs as well. Because they're often thinner and fattier, they may cook a little more quickly.

CHAPTER TWO

PICKLING + FERMENTATION

Seychelles

The flavors of Seychelles are a sensorial symphony: vanilla, nutmeg, cinnamon, pepper, pineapple, coconut, soursop, jackfruit, bilimbi (a miniature sour cucumber), abundant fresh greens, eggplant, yams, taro, cassava, fish, clams, mackerel, and shark. Salty, sweet, bitter, sour, and often quite spicy, the cuisine bears the marks of settlers, the enslaved, and migrants alike—including French, British, Spanish, African, Chinese, and Indian. Curry is abundant, as are chutneys, pickles, and peppery sauces. Lasos piman, known simply as "chili" to locals, is fiery and tangy: a blend of onions, tomatoes, lemon juice, bilimbi, and a ton of red-hot chiles.

Seychelles comprises 115 mountainous granitic and flat coralline islands. For much of their history they were deserted, uninhabited by humans until the 1500s, and even then largely a stopover for Arab and Maldivian seafarers—explorers such as Vasco da Gama—and a hub for pirates. Instead of humans, it was home to rare Aldabras—the second-largest tortoise in the world—as well as marine animals such as southern blue whales, giant clams, moray eels, eagle rays, and scalloped hammerhead sharks that still swirl among the coral reefs along the coast. Magpie robins, black parrots, and sheath-tailed bats also occupy the land.

This biodiversity is evident in the abundance of Seychelles. At least 50 percent of the plant and animal species on the island are endemic, meaning they're found nowhere else on earth. Trees hang heavy with breadfruit and other tropical fruits, and the air is perfumed by the leaves of cinnamon trees. Plus, its remote location in the Indian Ocean, a little less than halfway between Tanzania and Sri Lanka, leads to deeply hybridized cuisine that calls up East Africa, South India, and East Asia.

Pickles shine alongside traditional Seychellois dishes, particularly seafood and curries—by far the most common and beloved dishes on the island. Blending sweet, sour, spicy, and salty, some form of pickle, chutney, or chili—fiery fresh chiles, often simply crushed and combined with citrus juice—is served with every dish. Their tartness and crunch balances the heavily spiced, often rich dishes served over rice. This food group is abundant in Seychelles, as on many other islands, because tropical climates lead to long growing seasons where citrus and other fruits are so abundant they litter the ground. To add to the frequent availability of pickling ingredients, warm climates can cause fruit to ripen extra quickly, which nudges islanders to find innovative ways to quickly preserve the abundance of their ecosystem.

Seychellois culture is as vibrant as its cuisine. The French occupied the islands in 1756. Later came the British, who brought enslaved people from East Africa and Madagascar, forming the island's unique culture. The people of the Seychelles are creole, also spelled *kreyol* or *kreol* locally—a term that refers to a people, a culture, and a language. In many parts of the world, *creole* refers to the dozens of cultures that emerged when African, European, and often indigenous communities blended, forming fundamentally unique cultures that aren't found outside of their point of origin. While the term is most commonly associated with New Orleans in the United States, Seychellois kreol is deeply rooted in East African and Indian Ocean communities, with social structures and language that are heavily influenced by French colonization, and British influence that marks their current status as a member of the Commonwealth.

The diverse culture in Seychelles is also exceedingly musical. Sega and moutia are among the traditional forms of music with roots in early enslaved African communities and features flutes, hand drums, and rattles that swirl with a melodious hip-swinging rhythm. The capital, Victoria, is a rainbow of bright colors: the green, blue, red, and yellow of its flag; saturated purples mirroring the bougainvillea that cascade down walls and creep up the sides of structures; and the lively clothing worn by locals.

Much like other tropical islands, they are heavily reliant on tourism. Seychelles is challenging to get to and rather expensive, so it tends to attract travelers who are looking for an upscale, relaxing resort experience. You're more likely to encounter ecotourists interested in yoga and massage therapy than the partygoers of, say, Kingston, Jamaica. Tourism certainly sustains the island, but as is the case with many island nations, it's always a double-edged sword.

Annually, Seychelles receives about 300,000 tourists, in contrast to the 100,000 residents. These tourists produce approximately three times the amount of waste as locals, making waste management an urgent issue as their second landfill threatens to overflow. Marine waste—flowing from Asia due to ocean currents and the fishing industry—combined with local and tourist waste threatens to overwhelm existing resources.

Creativity and fortitude have always been critical to the Seychellois, but never more so than now. More than 90 percent of the population is concentrated on Mahe Island—a narrow coastal plateau with an average elevation of 6 ft [1.8 m] above sea level. Due to sea levels rising as a result of climate change, Seychelles and nearby Maldives could become uninhabitable as soon as the year 2100. That gives this small island nation little time to fortify and preserve an incredibly unique society and culture. But if their cuisine is any indication, the Seychellois are adept at adapting. The way they've blended ingredients and dishes from neighboring islands and colonizers alike, while still retaining a strong creole identity, suggests a society determined to survive.

PICKLE + FERMENT

Like the other techniques in this book, pickling is a way to make use of abundant local ingredients in ways that boost flavor and preserve them at their peak. Pickling, brining, and "cooking" proteins and vegetables in citrus and vinegar are among the oldest cooking methods on earth. Before refrigeration was widely available, acids—especially those produced by fermenting fruits and starches—enabled cooks to preserve ingredients, making them shelf stable to last through hurricanes and typhoons.

This technique will enable you to make condiments, salads, and more to pair with many of the dishes in *Islas*. The ingredients are often similar—a fruit or vegetable in vinegar or citrus juice with chiles and aromatics—which makes them particularly interchangeable. Filipino Pickled Green Papaya (page 106) makes an excellent companion to Poulet Boucané (page 261). Haitian Pikliz (page 99) is most often served with twice-cooked pork Griot (page 215), but also pairs well with the Malagasy pork belly, beef, and greens stew called Romazava (page 170). Beyond *Islas* recipes, these pickles can be a fun addition to a cookout: Lemon Lasary (page 96) tastes great on hot dogs, for example.

The process of pickling breaks down fruits and vegetables, and so it's best suited for firm ingredients. The chart on page 91 provides some building blocks for island pickles and beyond.

FERMENTATION VS. PICKLING

Both fermented and pickled foods contain beneficial microorganisms that promote mental and physical wellness. In particular, the probiotic elements of ferments and pickles fortify gut and digestive health, enabling the body to process foods more efficiently. Many island cuisines benefit from a side pickle, as they frequently combine a starch (root vegetable or rice) with protein (particularly fatty meat in the Caribbean) that needs a little extra help to be broken down in the body. Chiles and fiery spices such as peppercorns thrive in fermentation and pickling. Their flavors, and heat, deepen, as do the medicinal benefits they provide. While different, ultimately both processes are about balance—and a chemical balance leads to balanced flavor.

FRUITS AND VEGETABLES

Asparagus	Green onions
Beets	Green papaya
Cabbage	Jicama
Carrots	Okra
Cauliflower	Peas
Celery	Peppers
Chiles	Pineapple
Cucumbers	Radishes
Eggplant	Snap peas
Green beans	Tomatoes
Green mango	Zucchini

ACIDS

Citrus (calamansi, lemon, lime, sour orange)

Vinegars (coconut, palm, red wine, rice, white)

AROMATICS

whole spices are strongly encouraged over ground

Bay leaf

Cloves

Fresh whole chiles (bird's eye, habanero, jalapeño, scotch bonnet)

Garlic

Onions (pearl, red, white, yellow)

Peppercorns (black, green, pink)

Red pepper flakes

Star anise

Turmeric

Pickling is more about preservation than transformation. Typically, some type of sugar (brown or white) and acid (such as vinegar or citrus juice) are combined with vegetables or proteins, increasing the lifespan of the food being preserved. Pickling can lead to sharp sourness the longer it sits and is often a quicker process than fermentation.

Fermentation is a chemical process that creates a whole new ingredient as bacteria, yeast, or mold grows. In fact, vinegar, used in most of the pickles in this book, is itself produced by fermentation. The process tends to add a funky tang, which can deepen over time. Fermentation is an artful science, requiring careful measurement and temperature control, and beyond the scope of what we'll cover in this book. But there are a handful of recipes in this book that use simple forms of fermentation that are approachable regardless of skill level: Coco Bread (page 109), Ginger Beer (page 118), Black Cake (page 122), and Poi (page 121).

TIPS

• Pickles should always be stored in glass containers with airtight lids.

• Don't fill your container to the brim. The ingredients will release gasses over time, which could create an explosive (and messy) situation.

• Letting pickles sit at room temperature will speed up the pickling process and often add a bit of funkiness if desired. But left out for too long, quick pickles like many in this book can grow bad bacteria and mold. Unless you're properly canning your pickles in a sterile hot-water bath, which takes extra effort, transfer them to the refrigerator to extend their shelf life.

• Turn your container of pickles from time to time for the flavors to fully meld.

MARIE-MAY JEREMIE
SEYCHELLES

"We'd swim in rivers every afternoon, going around collecting fruits—mangoes were our favorite," Marie-May Jeremie said. A native Seychellois, Marie-May is a conservation biologist who has dedicated her career to the preservation of the island's endemic species and ocean ecosystems.

Her family has always been on Seychelles, though they've tracked their family tree back to an enslaved person from Mozambique. Marie-May grew up in a very loving home with humble means. She and her sister shared a room in a tiny two-bedroom apartment. Her parents, Marc and Jordana Jeremie, did not go to college but worked long hours at multiple jobs so she and her sister could have all they needed in order to excel in school. She had a happy childhood, and although they didn't have much, they always had enough to eat, especially because her mother is a very good cook. At nineteen, Marie-May went away to college in Sydney, Australia, where she studied science and conservation and was excited to live outside the boundaries of what she knew—a big city after a lifetime in a more remote area. But she missed her family, especially her mother, with whom she remains close, and longed for the sense of community she had taken for granted. Above all she missed the fresh fish and bright flavors of her homeland, and spicy pickles like Lasos Piman (page 48), which Marie-May says she always has on hand.

She attended graduate school in Australia through a Seychelles government scholarship, on the condition that she would return and contribute to her island. She's been working as a conservationist since 2015, focused on finding solutions for the litany of issues created by climate volatility. Although they experience heavy rains during cyclone season, historically Seychelles has not been heavily impacted by the annual cyclones that batter nearby Mauritius and Madagascar. But that's changing. Like tens of thousands of other islands in the tropics, storm systems are shifting their trajectories and becoming stronger and more destructive. In 2016, Seychelles was hit directly by Tropical Cyclone Fantala—the strongest known storm in the Indian Ocean—leveling buildings, flooding towns, and resulting in widespread coral bleaching. They've gotten hit by cyclones every year since, an urgent issue as Seychellois homes are very near to the coast, often made of wood with glass louver windows and corrugated metal roofs that are not built to withstand storms.

Thus, locals like Marie-May are scared. She is concerned that most of the local infrastructure is not built for impending cyclones. She worries about overfishing, which is diminishing the abundant marine life that is a daily source of food for the Seychellois, as well as the livelihood of its fishermen. Despite these challenges, Marie-May is tenacious and committed to finding solutions and preserving her beloved culture.

Among Marie-May's projects is the preservation of the rare coco de mer, the largest seed on earth. It's endemic to the island and endangered as a result of illegal harvesting and export, particularly to China, where the coco de mer is believed to increase virility. Between 2010 and 2021, Marie-May's agency planted 250 coco de mer seeds across the island. But instead of planting a grove, they provided a sapling for each willing household, with the hope that her fellow Seychellois would feel a deeper connection to the abundant land that provides them with so much.

This kind of intervention—educating people on the importance of native plants and animals, alongside creative methods for home-grown preservation—is Marie-May's mission. She loves her family and her island home, she loves dancing to the percussive rhythms of sega music, and she loves cooking big pots of rice over an open fire to serve alongside octopus curry. She can't imagine living anywhere else. Marie-May believes the Seychellois must all be stewards of the land, protecting and caring for its most vulnerable inhabitants, and ensuring the survival of their dynamic and unique creole culture.

RECESPES

PICKLING + FERMENTATION

JORDANA'S EGGPLANT CHUTNEY

When I visited Marie-May Jeremie's family home, her mother, Jordana, prepared this eggplant chutney. It's a family favorite she's prepared for decades, and it comes together quickly with ingredients that are common on the island but easily sourced in most places. It's a balance of sweet and sour, and she often serves it with Cari de Poisson et Potiron (page 151).

1 Tbsp vegetable oil

3 large shallots, peeled and chopped

1 large globe eggplant, peeled and chopped into 1 in [2.5 cm] cubes

4 bilimbi, or ½ cup [70 g] seeded and chopped star fruit

2 large roma tomatoes, chopped

2 Tbsp fresh lemon juice

2 red bird's eye chiles, crushed

2 tsp kosher salt

Freshly ground black pepper

Heat the oil in a saucepan over medium-high heat, then add the shallots and sauté for 3 to 5 minutes until softened. Add the eggplant and bilimbi, stir well to incorporate, then lower the heat and simmer, covered, for 5 to 7 minutes, until the eggplant begins to soften.

Add the tomatoes and stir well, using a wooden spoon to crush the eggplant pieces. Add the lemon juice, chiles, and salt and simmer, covered, on low for another 10 minutes, until the chutney is thick and fully combined. Season with pepper and adjust salt as needed. Serve warm or at room temperature as a condiment. Store in an airtight container in the refrigerator for up to 2 weeks, or in the freezer for up to 6 months.

Island
Seychelles

Yield
2 servings

Active Time
15 minutes

Total Time
15 minutes

SALAD PALMIS
PALM HEART SALAD

Palm hearts are among my favorite vegetables. I often eat them straight out of a salty brine from a jar. This salad balances the tanginess with a bit of sour and oil. For a little extra lift, add thinly sliced jalapeños.

2 green onions, white and green parts, thinly sliced on the diagonal

2 Tbsp olive oil

2 tsp Dijon mustard

3 Tbsp white vinegar

1 garlic clove, minced

1 tsp kosher salt

Pinch of sugar

Two 14 oz [400 g] cans hearts of palm

½ cup [80 g] halved cherry tomatoes

1 jalapeño, thinly sliced (optional)

In a medium nonreactive mixing bowl, combine the green onions, olive oil, mustard, vinegar, garlic, salt, and sugar. Whisk with a fork to incorporate and thicken the dressing.

Drain the hearts of palm and pat dry. Carefully slice into ½ in [13 mm] pieces and transfer to the bowl with the dressing. Add the tomatoes and jalapeño (if using) and gently toss. Serve immediately at room temperature, or refrigerate and serve cold. The salad will keep for 3 days in the refrigerator in a sealed container.

LEMON LASARY
LEMON CHILE PICKLE

Lasary is a whole category of spicy relishes in Madagascar. Much like the various chilis in Seychelles such as Lasos Piman (page 48), they add dimension to otherwise simple Malagasy dishes. Lemon lasary is particularly dynamic, and incredibly resourceful, making use of an entire lemon—fruit, peel, and all. It takes time and patience, but is worth the effort, as this condiment pairs well with all kinds of dishes. Serve it alongside Pescado Frito (page 219) or Haitian Griot (page 215), add a little haystack to a cheese plate, or use it as a condiment for sandwiches or hot dogs.

2 lb [910 g] lemons

1 large yellow onion, thinly sliced

2 Tbsp kosher salt

1 tsp finely grated peeled fresh ginger

1 tsp minced garlic

1 tsp mild curry powder

4 red or green jalapeños or red fresno chiles, thinly sliced

⅔ cup [160 ml] white vinegar

⅔ cup [160 ml] fresh orange juice

6 pequin peppers, crushed (optional)

Wash and dry the lemons. Using a very sharp knife or peeler, carefully remove the zest from the lemons, scraping off any of the bitter white pith on the peels. Cut the zest into very fine strips and place in a large nonreactive mixing bowl.

Cut the peeled lemons in half, remove the seeds, then carefully cut the lemon flesh away from the pith and chop it into chunks, adding the pieces and juice to the bowl with the lemon zest.

Stir the onion and salt into the lemon mixture, cover, and let sit at room temperature, loosely covered with a lid or cheesecloth, for 24 hours, stirring occasionally.

Add the ginger, garlic, curry powder, jalapeños, vinegar, and orange juice and stir well to fully incorporate. For a spicier lasary, crush and add the pequin peppers (if using).

Transfer the pickle to one or more jars or airtight glass containers and store in the refrigerator for up to a year. It can be eaten immediately, though it is better after at least 3 days, and is even better after 2 to 4 weeks.

Island	Yield	Active Time	Total Time
Curaçao	**2 cups [480 ml]**	**5 minutes**	**At least 8 hours**

PIKA
SPICY PICKLED ONIONS

Pika is a simple condiment made of finely chopped onions—very similar to what Dutch people eat atop raw herring—combined with scotch bonnet or habanero peppers and white vinegar. This funky, flavorful condiment is great on any number of dishes, but a warning: It is quite spicy. Reduce the number of chiles or deseed them for a milder version.

1 cup [140 g] diced yellow onion

2 or 3 habanero or scotch bonnet peppers, stemmed and finely chopped (see headnote)

1 whole star anise pod

4 whole cloves

2 cardamom pods, crushed

Pinch of freshly grated nutmeg

1 cup [240 ml] white vinegar

In a clean jar with a tight-fitting lid, combine the onion, peppers, star anise, cloves, cardamom, and nutmeg. Add the vinegar, topping with water if necessary so the ingredients are fully covered though not overflowing.

Tighten the lid on the jar, swirl it around a few times, then store in the refrigerator overnight.

Shake well before serving. Pika keeps for several weeks in the refrigerator.

TIP For a funkier flavor, let the pika sit on the counter for a day before refrigerating.

Island
Haiti

Yield
3 to 4 cups
[156 to 208 g]

Active Time
30 minutes

Total Time
At least 5 days

PIKLIZ
SPICY PICKLED VEGETABLE RELISH

When served with Griot (page 215), this crunchy pickle balances rich, twice-cooked pork with acid, spice, and texture. Apple cider vinegar is ideal, though white wine vinegar can add a bit of sweetness. Pikliz can be served the same day as a quick slaw, but ideally you should let it sit for several days to develop a more dynamic flavor.

2 cups [120 g] shredded green cabbage

1 cup [120 g] thinly sliced bell pepper (any color)

6 scotch bonnet peppers, seeded if desired to mitigate spiciness, thinly sliced into rings

1 small red onion, thinly sliced

2 green onions, white and green parts, sliced on the diagonal

1 large carrot, thickly grated

4 garlic cloves, minced

1 Tbsp black peppercorns

4 whole cloves

1 tsp kosher salt

2 cups [475 ml] apple cider vinegar, plus more as needed

2 Tbsp fresh lime juice

In a large mixing bowl, combine the cabbage, bell pepper, scotch bonnets, red onion, green onions, carrot, garlic, peppercorns, cloves, and salt and toss well with a pair of tongs to fully incorporate.

Transfer the mixture to a 2 qt [1.9 L] jar or other glass container with a nonreactive lid. Add the vinegar and lime juice, topping with more vinegar as needed until the vegetables are completely submerged, then tighten the lid and allow the mixture to pickle for 5 days at room temperature, then refrigerate. Pikliz can be stored at room temperature for several months, and in the refrigerator for up to a year. It will develop a deeper, funkier flavor the longer it sits.

TIP Pikliz is supposed to be quite spicy, and it will become even spicier as it ages. Reduce the number of peppers if you want a milder condiment.

MIKE YULO
HAWAIʻI

Mike Yulo, a Native Hawaiian beekeeper on Kauaʻi who harvests honey brimming with the flavors of local flora—cactus, coconut, plumeria, ginger, hibiscus—is harnessing the flavors of Hawaiʻi's westernmost main island. Kauaʻi has a strong history, which is a source of pride for locals. Among Native Hawaiians' core beliefs is "He Aliʻi Ka ʻĀina; He Kauwā ke Kanaka": The land is chief, and humans its servants. Mike embodies this philosophy and is dedicated to preserving the land through traditional Hawaiian beekeeping methods. He's so dedicated, in fact, that he once risked his life to save his bees. In April 2019, a heavy storm system battered the island, dropping a record 50 in [1.3 m] of rain. "Uncle Mike," as he's known locally, rushed to his beehouse, some distance from home, and loaded all his hives into his truck just minutes before the waters rose to wash them away. But just up the road, in a matter of minutes, the floodwater overwhelmed his truck, and he was forced to crawl out a window, where he used a honey bucket as a buoy until he could get to higher ground.

Tenacious and resilient, Mike rebuilt his beehouse and hives. Since then, he's been expanding and modernizing his business, moving beyond honey to create a series of products and vegetarian food businesses. He runs his business with his wife, Christine, who's Filipina. In fact, his grandmother was Puerto Rican—forming a family unit reflective of Hawaiʻi's mixed ethnic heritage. Like many tropical islands across the planet, Hawaiʻi was home to large sugar plantations, which were complex convening spaces for Native Hawaiians and immigrants from China, Japan, Portugal, Korea, and the Philippines. A unique local language known as pidgin emerged in these spaces, as did the truly hybridized cuisine of the island chain.

Mike embodies this hybridity through the products he makes with local ingredients. Hibiscus, lemongrass, and mint or basil ginger iced tea, sweetened with his honey, is his bestseller. He makes what he calls "sold-out salsa," because it goes so quickly at the market, using fresh garlic, onion, cilantro, and a local habanero variety that's sourced from nearby farms. He also makes Kalo Crumbles, a fermented plant-based protein source made of kalo (Hawaiian for taro), along with mung beans, moringa, and locally sourced Hawaiian salt.

Deeply committed to preserving the practices, ingredients, and dishes of his homeland, Mike also values modernizing and expanding in order to keep his island's culture alive. Like all islanders, he's concerned about the impacts of climate change—the worsening storms contrasted by unexpected droughts. He keeps his eyes keenly focused on the ancestral practices that do more than preserve culture—they preserve bodies to keep his fellow islanders healthy.

Island
Hawai'i

Yield
**6 to 8 cups
[1.4 to 1.9 L]**

Active Time
10 minutes

Total Time
40 minutes

TAKUAN
PICKLED DAIKON

Milder than red radishes, daikon are sweet and incredibly versatile. They can be pickled, stewed like a potato, or shredded and included in coleslaw or tucked into a Vietnamese banh mi. This side dish from Hawai'i is crunchy and funky, the rice vinegar and turmeric making an otherwise mild, white radish into a dynamic pickle that pairs well with rice dishes and salads, or as a snack.

4 lb [1.8 kg] daikon
radish (see Tips)

2½ cups [500 g]
granulated sugar

½ cup [120 ml] palm
vinegar, coconut vinegar,
or apple cider vinegar

2½ Tbsp kosher salt, plus
more as needed

1½ tsp ground turmeric

Scrub and peel the daikon, wiping with a towel or paper towel after peeling instead of rinsing with water. Cut the daikon into bite-size pieces or slices and transfer to a large jar or nonreactive container with a lid.

In a medium nonreactive mixing bowl, combine the sugar, vinegar, salt, and turmeric. Stir well until the sugar and salt are fully dissolved, then taste and adjust salt as needed.

Pour the vinegar mixture over the daikon. Tighten the lid, then swirl the jar several times to incorporate.

Let the daikon pickle sit at room temperature for at least 30 minutes, then transfer to the refrigerator. Takuan keeps in the refrigerator for several weeks—even months.

TIPS   When selecting daikon, choose radishes that are smooth and white, without brown spots. If you cannot find one without brown spots, remove the spots with a paring knife before slicing.

Takuan will get funkier the longer it sits in the refrigerator. It should be stored in an airtight, non-reactive container with a very tight lid; otherwise, the pungent aroma will overtake your refrigerator.

Island
Seychelles

Yield
7 to 8 cups [1.7 to 1.9 L]

Active Time
25 minutes

Total Time
2 days

ASAR
VEGETABLE PICKLE

Asar, also known as achard, is an everyday pickle and condiment in Seychelles, as well as other Indian Ocean islands. It's pungent, sour, and delightfully crunchy, and typically served alongside rice and curry.

½ cup [120 ml] vegetable oil

2 large red onions, thinly sliced

10 to 12 garlic cloves, thinly sliced

4 long green or bird's eye chiles, stemmed, seeded if desired to mitigate spiciness, and sliced crosswise into thin strips

2 Tbsp black mustard seeds

1 cup [60 g] finely shredded green cabbage

1 cup [140 g] julienned carrots

1 cup [110 g] green beans, thinly sliced on the diagonal

1 cup [105 g] finely chopped cauliflower

1 Tbsp ground turmeric

2 Tbsp white vinegar

In a large frying pan over medium-high, heat the oil. Add the onions and sauté for 3 to 5 minutes, until translucent. Add the garlic, chiles, and mustard seeds and sauté until fragrant, 1 to 2 minutes, lowering the heat as necessary to prevent the garlic from burning. Remove from the heat and let cool.

Meanwhile, in a large nonreactive mixing bowl, combine the cabbage, carrots, green beans, and cauliflower. Add the cooled sautéed aromatics, the turmeric, and the vinegar and toss well using a pair of tongs to ensure the vegetables are coated.

Transfer to a 2 qt [1.9 L] jar with a tight-fitting lid, or two jars with at least 4 cup [945 ml] capacity, and let sit in the refrigerator for at least 2 days before using. It will keep for at least 1 week in the refrigerator.

TIP   If you want a funkier flavor, let the asar pickle sit at room temperature on the counter for 2 days, then transfer to the refrigerator.

Yield	Active Time	Total Time
5 to 6 cups **[600 to 720 g]**	**30 minutes**	**2 hours 30 minutes**

ASINAN
FRUIT PICKLE

Fruits are abundant and beloved across the tropics, where most islands have long growing seasons and a wide variety of fruits with exciting flavors and textures. Firmer fruits lend themselves best to pickling, and this crunchy, spicy, refreshing fruit pickle brings together pineapple and mango with jicama and cucumber. It's also a little funky with the addition of the shrimp paste, and the toasted peanuts make it dynamic.

**1 small pineapple,
2 to 3 lb (0.9 to 1.3 kg)**

1 small jicama

1 green mango

1 medium cucumber

3 red bird's eye chiles

**½ tsp kosher salt, plus
more as needed**

**½ tsp prepared shrimp
paste (optional; see Tips)**

**1 cup [190 g] jaggery or
demerara sugar**

**⅓ cup [80 ml] white
vinegar**

**½ cup [120 ml] fresh
lemon juice**

**Roasted or fried salted
peanuts, for garnish**

Wash and peel the pineapple, jicama, and mango, then chop into small pieces (see Tips) and mix in a large nonreactive mixing bowl. Chop the cucumber into small pieces (do not peel) and add to the bowl.

In a small food processor or mortar and pestle, combine the chiles, salt, and shrimp paste (if using) and grind into a fine paste.

In a medium pot, combine the sugar, vinegar, and chile-shrimp paste with 4 cups [945 ml] of water. Bring to a boil, then lower the heat and simmer for about 10 minutes, until the sugar is fully dissolved.

Meanwhile, transfer the pineapple mixture to a 1½ qt [1.4 L] container or jar with a tight-fitting lid, or separate jars with a total of 5 to 6 cups [1.2 to 1.4 L] capacity.

Strain the sugary liquid through a fine-mesh sieve into a large container, then add the lemon juice. Let cool to lukewarm, then pour over the pineapple mixture, cover with a lid, and transfer to the refrigerator.

Let cool for at least 2 hours, then garnish with roasted peanuts. Asinan keeps for 2 to 3 days in the refrigerator.

TIPS Shrimp paste can be found in most Asian grocery stores. Filipino or Indonesian brands of roasted shrimp paste are ideal for a balanced flavor.

If desired, the fruit can be cut into thin slices so the pickling liquid can more fully permeate the fruit, creating a more concentrated flavor and a different look.

For a stronger, more fermented flavor, let the mixture sit at room temperature on the counter for 4 to 8 hours before refrigerating.

Island
Guam

Yield
4 to 6 servings

Active Time
15 minutes

Total Time
9 hours

PICKLED GREEN PAPAYA

Among the many quick pickles in this book, this one is delightfully crunchy and refreshing on a hot summer day. It's also a great addition to a pickle plate, alongside rich curries, or as a condiment for sandwiches.

1 medium green papaya

2 Tbsp kosher salt

2 large garlic cloves, thinly sliced

2 Thai red chiles, seeded if desired to mitigate spiciness, finely chopped

1 cup [240 ml] rice vinegar

2 cups [475 ml] hot water

Wash the papaya, cut it in half, and use a spoon to scrape out the seeds and the soft pith. Peel and thinly slice the flesh (see Tip), then place the pieces in a colander set over a large bowl. Toss the papaya with the salt and let it sit in the colander for at least 30 minutes to soften the flesh.

Meanwhile, in a small nonreactive bowl, combine the garlic, chiles, vinegar, and water.

Rinse the papaya to remove as much excess salt as possible and then squeeze gently with a clean, dry cloth or paper towels to dry.

Place the papaya in a resealable bag or a glass container with a lid and pour over the vinegar mixture. Seal and refrigerate overnight. The pickled papaya will keep in the refrigerator for several weeks.

TIP   For extra-thin slices of papaya, use a mandoline or sharp peeler.

Island
**Trinidad/
Jamaica**

Yield
4 servings

Active Time
5 minutes

Total Time
20 minutes

CUCUMBER CHOW

A recipe to add to your weekly rotation, cucumber chow comes together in seconds, and is so easy that you can make just enough for the meal you're about to have. It's crunchy and refreshing—and because it's quick and adaptable, it's a perfect side dish for CHamoru Barbecue Chicken (page 60) or Pork Ribs (page 64), or to add balance alongside rich stews such as Haitian Soup Joumou (page 173).

2 large cucumbers, peeled and chopped

3 medium garlic cloves, minced

⅓ cup [20 g] finely chopped fresh culantro leaves

1 small scotch bonnet pepper, seeded and chopped

Juice of 1 lime

2 Tbsp kosher salt

In a medium bowl with a lid, combine the cucumbers, garlic, culantro, pepper, lime juice, and salt. Cover and chill for at least 15 minutes, then serve. Cucumber chow will keep for up to 2 days in the refrigerator.

MANGO CHOW

This lively little snack from *Islas* contributor Brigid Washington's childhood remains a staple in her home. Made with fresh mangoes—both green and ripe work—it comes together quickly, and like other chows is best made and eaten the same day.

2 large unripe, firm, green-skinned mangoes, peeled, pitted, and sliced lengthwise into thick strips

½ cup [120 ml] fresh lime juice, plus more as needed

1 Tbsp kosher salt

4 small garlic cloves, minced

½ scotch bonnet pepper, seeded and minced

¼ cup [10 g] roughly chopped fresh cilantro leaves

Place the mangoes in a medium nonreactive mixing bowl.

Add the lime juice, salt, garlic, pepper, and cilantro. Toss to combine using a fork and serve immediately. Mango chow keeps for several days in the refrigerator.

Island
Jamaica

Yield
6 to 8 servings

Active Time
20 minutes

Total Time
2 hours

COCO BREAD

Coco bread is a Jamaican staple and, according to recipe developer Brigid Washington, "it nourishes islanders of all stripes." It is rich and fluffy, with a delightful subtle sweetness, and as its name suggests, the inclusion of coconut milk imparts warm nutty notes. As with all yeasted breads, light fermentation is what causes the dough to rise. Coco bread is eaten at all times of day and sold in store-front bakeries in Jamaica, where these handheld pockets are oftentimes served with Cheddar cheese or stuffed with a beef patty.

6 Tbsp [90 ml] unrefined coconut oil, plus more for greasing and brushing

1 cup [240 ml] canned full-fat coconut milk, well shaken and stirred

¼ cup [50 g] sugar

1 tsp kosher salt

1 envelope active dry yeast (about 2¼ tsp, ¼ oz [7 g])

1 egg, gently whisked, at room temperature

3½ cups [490 g] all-purpose flour, plus more for dusting and rolling

Lightly grease a large bowl with melted coconut oil and line a large rimmed baking sheet with parchment paper.

In a large microwaveable bowl, combine the coconut oil, coconut milk, sugar, and salt. Microwave on high until the sugar is dissolved and the oil is melted, about 1 minute. Alternatively, heat the mixture in a small saucepan over low heat for 1 minute and stir to combine. Let cool slightly, then stir in the yeast and egg. Add the flour and stir together to form a soft dough.

Transfer the dough to a lightly floured surface and gently knead until the dough is smooth and well combined, about 2 minutes. Resist the urge to add more flour—the softer the dough, the lighter and more tender the coco bread. Place the dough in the greased bowl, cover lightly with a clean kitchen towel, and let rise in a warm place (75°F [24°C]) until doubled in size, about 1 hour.

Place a rack in the middle position and preheat the oven to 350°F [180°C]. Punch down the dough, flattening to about 1 in [2.5 cm] thick, and transfer to a lightly floured surface. Using a bread knife or bench scraper, cut the dough in half, then cut each half into four equal portions. Shape each portion into a ball and roll it out with a rolling pin to a 6 to 7 in [15 to 18 cm] oval, about the size of your hand, and ¼ in [6 mm] thick. Brush the top of each oval with melted coconut oil, and fold in half crosswise to form a semicircle. Brush the tops with more melted coconut oil. Place the folded dough semicircles 1 to 2 in [2.5 to 5 cm] apart on the prepared baking sheet and let rest at room temperature for 15 minutes. Bake for 17 minutes, until light brown. Let cool 5 minutes and serve warm.

Island
Puerto Rico

Yield
4 to 6 servings

Active Time
5 minutes

Total Time
2 hours

GANDULES EN ESCABECHE
FIELD PEAS IN ESCABECHE

Among Puerto Rico's indigenous plants, gandules, or pigeon peas, are a native field pea with an unmistakably earthy flavor. Arroz con gandules (rice with field peas) is a staple of holiday meals on the island, but this preparation is fresh and bright, highlighting the unique flavor of gandules. Inspired by my friend Berto's recipe, this refreshing side dish pairs well with Carne Guisada (page 83) or can be enjoyed on its own with steamed white rice.

1 cup [240 ml] olive oil

½ cup [120 ml] white vinegar

2 dried bay leaves

1 small white onion, finely chopped

1 medium red, orange, or yellow bell pepper, seeded and finely chopped

½ tsp freshly ground black pepper

1½ lb [680 g] canned or frozen gandules, drained and rinsed if canned, cooked according to package instructions if frozen (see Tip)

2 Tbsp chopped fresh cilantro leaves

1 tsp kosher salt, plus more as needed

In a large nonreactive mixing bowl, combine the olive oil, vinegar, bay leaves, onion, bell pepper, and black pepper and let sit for 10 to 15 minutes.

Add the gandules, cilantro, and salt and toss to combine. Taste and season with additional salt and pepper as needed. Refrigerate until ready to serve. The peas can be eaten cold or at room temperature and keep well in the refrigerator for several days.

TIP   Canned gandules can be found in the international section of many standard groceries; both canned and frozen can be sourced from Latin American and Caribbean specialty markets.

Yield	Active Time	Total Time
6 to 8 servings	**15 minutes**	**1 hour 15 minutes**

CUCUMBER, MANGO, AND PINEAPPLE SALAD WITH TAMARIND AND CHILE

Inspired by Selina Periampillai's recipe in *The Island Kitchen*, this crunchy, sweet and sour fruit salad will easily become a favorite for cookouts. This salad pairs beautifully with a number of dishes in this book, such as Poulet Boucané (page 261) and Pwason Griye (page 251), because it's a perfect balance of salty and sweet. It keeps for a couple of days in the refrigerator and is also a great topping for salads or tacos.

1 red bird's eye chile, stemmed and thinly sliced (see Tips)

1 Tbsp kosher salt

1 tsp light brown sugar or honey

2 tsp tamarind pulp or paste

1 large cucumber, peeled, seeded, and chopped

1 ripe mango, peeled, pitted, and chopped

1 large pineapple, peeled, cored, and chopped

Fresh finely chopped mint or cilantro leaves, for serving (optional)

Using a mortar and pestle, grind the chile and salt together.

In small bowl, combine the brown sugar and tamarind pulp, mixing well with a fork until the sugar is mostly dissolved.

In a large nonreactive mixing bowl, combine the cucumber, mango, and pineapple and toss well.

Sprinkle the chile salt over the fruit, then add the tamarind mixture. Toss well to fully incorporate. Cover and let it sit in the refrigerator for at least 1 hour before serving. Add finely chopped fresh mint or cilantro leaves before serving for a more savory approach. This salad will keep for 3 to 4 days in the refrigerator.

TIPS This salad is very adaptable. You can finely dice, coarsely chop, or even slice the fruit, depending on how you want it to look. The overall flavor will be the same, but a smaller dice allows the fruit to soak up more tamarind flavor.

If you have trouble sourcing fresh chiles, substitute crushed red pepper flakes.

For a stronger tamarind flavor, use tamarind paste.

Jicama is a great addition or substitution for cucumber.

Island
Seychelles

Yield
4 servings

Active Time
30 minutes

Total Time
40 minutes

SALAD LALO KREOL
OKRA SALAD

Okra is among the most significant plants brought to the Americas during the transatlantic slave trade. Its origins are disputed, as it's featured prominently in traditional dishes across Africa and Southeast Asia. But its prominence in African cuisines is undeniable. Most often fried, stewed, or used as a thickener for vegetable dishes like Callaloo (page 143) or soups like Giambo (page 167), it is also controversial, as many dislike its sliminess. But this light, refreshing salad showcases the flavor and texture of okra. It's also beautiful and a great addition to a cookout.

2 tsp kosher salt

1 red onion, thinly sliced

⅓ cup [80 ml] fresh lime juice

½ tsp freshly ground black pepper

2 Tbsp olive oil

2 lb [910 g] fresh okra, washed and stems trimmed

2 green onions, white and green parts, thinly sliced on the bias

Fill a medium pot with water, add 1 tsp of the salt, and bring to a boil.

Meanwhile, in a large nonreactive mixing bowl, combine the onion, lime juice, pepper, and remaining 1 tsp salt, and mix well. Add the olive oil and massage the mixture with your fingers for several minutes, until the onions have softened.

Once the water is boiling, add the okra and cook for 3 to 4 minutes, until crisp-tender. The okra will be bright jade green, not olive.

Drain the okra in a colander and shock with cold water. Shake the colander, then transfer the okra to a clean towel or paper towels to fully dry. Transfer to the bowl with the dressing and gently toss.

Sprinkle with green onions and serve at room temperature, or chill and serve cold if desired.

Island
Philippines

Yield
4 to 6 servings

Active Time
45 minutes

Total Time
1 hour

SINIGANG SA MANGGA

SOUR SEAFOOD STEW

This brothy, healing sour soup, adapted from Yasmin Newman's *7000 Islands*, is among the Philippines's best-known dishes. Green mango can be difficult to source, but tamarind paste or purée is a good substitution. Note that the flavor will be different—more puckering—with the tamarind, but it's commonly used in sinigang recipes. Serve with steamed jasmine rice.

2 lb [910 g] green mangoes, peeled, pitted, and chopped

2 large shallots, quartered

1½ Tbsp kosher salt, plus more as needed

1 large Japanese eggplant (about ½ lb [230 g]), sliced into rounds

½ lb [230 g] whole fresh okra pods, sliced into rounds

1 daikon (about ½ lb [230 g]), peeled and sliced into rounds

1 lb [455 g] fish fillets, such as milkfish or tilapia, cut into serving pieces

1 lb [455 g] green beans, trimmed and snapped in half

1 lb [455 g] whole head-on shrimp, deveined, whiskers trimmed

½ lb [230 g] baby bok choy, rinsed well and quartered

1 cup [160 g] cherry tomatoes

1 Tbsp fish sauce

Steamed jasmine rice, for serving

Additional fish sauce, calamansi juice (see Tips), lemon wedges, or Sinamak (page 48), for serving

Place the mango in a large, deep saucepan and cover with 2 qt [1.9 L] of water (see Tips). Bring to a boil over medium-high, then cook for 20 to 30 minutes, mashing with a wooden spoon to help break apart the flesh. Strain through a fine-mesh sieve into a large nonreactive mixing bowl, pressing the pulp with the back of the spoon to get all the juice.

Discard the pulp and transfer the liquid to a large heavy-bottomed pot. Add the shallots and salt and bring to a boil over high heat. Lower the heat to medium, then add the eggplant, okra, and daikon, adding 1 cup [240 ml] of water at a time as necessary to ensure the ingredients stay covered. Simmer for 5 minutes, then add the fish, nestling it among the vegetables, and cook for 2 minutes.

Carefully shake the pot a few times to gently stir without breaking the fish apart. Add the green beans and cook for 2 minutes more, then add the shrimp, bok choy, and tomatoes. Shake the pot to incorporate all the ingredients. Cook until the vegetables are tender but not falling apart and all the seafood is opaque but still tender, 2 to 3 minutes longer.

Stir in the fish sauce, taste, and adjust seasoning. Serve with steamed jasmine rice and sprinkled with calamansi juice, lemon juice, additional fish sauce, and/ or sinamak.

TIPS   Calamansi juice is available frozen or bottled, typically in Asian grocery stores. If you can't find it, substitute half tangerine juice and half fresh lime juice.

For richer flavor, use fish stock in place of the water.

I
S
L
A
S

Island
Jamaica

Yield
4 to 6 servings

Active Time
20 minutes

Total Time
2 to 3 days

GINGER BEER

Distinct from most commercially available canned or bottled ginger beers, this popular fermented beverage, typically served during the Christmas season in Jamaica, is refreshing and invigorating—and it gets even better the longer it ferments. While it can be enjoyed within 1 or 2 days, I strongly encourage you to let it sit for at least 1 week in the refrigerator, or longer if possible. It makes a huge difference. Serve over ice with a squeeze of lime if desired.

1 lb [455 g] fresh ginger

3 cups [710 ml] warm water

½ cup [100 g] cane sugar, plus more as needed

Zest of 1 lime, grated

1 Tbsp brown rice

1 tsp whole cloves

1 cinnamon stick

½ tsp vanilla extract (optional)

1 Tbsp rum (optional)

Splash of angostura bitters (optional)

Scrub the ginger well, then coarsely chop. In a blender, purée the ginger with the water.

Transfer the puréed ginger to a pitcher or extra-large jar with an airtight lid and add the sugar, lime zest, rice, cloves, and cinnamon stick. Close the container and leave to ferment on the countertop for at least 1 day, then transfer to the refrigerator and ferment for at least 1 more day (see headnote).

Strain the mixture through a cheesecloth or fine-mesh sieve into another pitcher. Add 5 cups [1.2 L] of water. Taste and adjust the sugar 1 tsp at a time as needed, then add the vanilla (if using), rum (if using), and bitters (if using). Refrigerate overnight and serve over ice.

TIPS Ginger beer keeps for several weeks in the refrigerator and will develop a stronger, spicier ginger flavor over time.

Always make sure to store ginger beer in an airtight container. It lasts longer and stays fresher.

If you don't care for sediment, which forms naturally with this recipe, strain again before serving.

Island
Puerto Rico

Yield
4 to 6 servings

Active Time
15 minutes

Total Time
45 minutes

YUCA CON MOJO
CASSAVA WITH WARM PICKLED ONIONS

Yuca is among the most commonly eaten viandas—the local Puerto Rican word for starchy fruits and vegetables, such as plantain and taro. It's also among the most common root vegetables across the tropics, a fixture as much in Madagascar as in Vanuatu. It's believed to have been among the principal foods of the indigenous Taínos of the Caribbean. This is my grandmother's recipe. She never wrote it down, but my mother had it deep in her memory, and we cooked it together for this version. The onions are not traditionally pickled per se, but the vinegar gives them a similar tanginess. The mojo will keep for several weeks in the refrigerator, and is also delicious on Tostones (page 213), roasted vegetables, and fish.

YUCA

2 lb [910 g] yuca (see Tip)

¼ cup [60 g] kosher salt

MOJO

1 cup [240 ml] olive oil

1 large white onion, sliced into thin rounds

5 large garlic cloves, minced

1 tsp black peppercorns

2 dried bay leaves

½ tsp kosher salt, plus more as needed

¼ cup [60 ml] white vinegar

To make the yuca: Fill a large pot with water and bring to a boil over high heat.

Fill a large bowl with water. Peel the yuca with a sharp peeler or paring knife, then chop it into 2 in [5 cm] pieces, tossing them in the bowl of water as you go to avoid discoloration.

To make the mojo: In a deep skillet over medium, heat the olive oil. When the oil is shimmering, add the onion, garlic, peppercorns, bay leaves, and salt, stirring well to incorporate. Cook until the onions are translucent and soft, stirring often and being careful not to let the onions brown, 5 to 7 minutes. Remove from the heat and add the vinegar. Add more salt as needed. Set aside and keep warm.

Once the water is at a rolling boil, add the ¼ cup [60 g] salt, then carefully add the yuca. Boil for 20 to 30 minutes, until a sharp knife goes through easily, being careful not to let the yuca overcook and become mushy.

Drain the yuca and transfer to a serving dish. Pour the warm mojo sauce over and serve.

TIP   Fresh cassava, or yuca as it's often called in Latin America, can be found at most African, Asian, and Latin American grocery stores year-round. The roots are sealed in wax; when selecting one, look for cracks or signs of mold. You can break off the end to inspect and ensure the flesh is white (with the vendor's permission, of course). Once peeled, inspect closely for black spots, green veins, or discoloration. If they don't run throughout, you can just cut off those pieces. If dark veins run throughout, do not eat— it can be poisonous.

POI
MASHED FERMENTED TARO

Poi is an ancestral Hawaiian dish, made by peeling, boiling, pounding, and then fermenting taro root. It's a bit chewy and mildly sweet, and is meant to be eaten with your hands to sop up sauces and accompany grilled meat. Traditionally, it's made using a basalt stone mortar and pestle, but this version, which I've adapted from Alana Kysar's *Aloha Kitchen*, utilizes a food processor for ease. Hawaiians take pride in how they prepare their poi, because it's believed to have been among the first foods to sustain the early Polynesian settlers when they arrived on the islands. Poi is no longer eaten as commonly as it once was, but it will always have an important place in Hawaiian culinary history.

2 lb [910 g] taro root, scrubbed well and trimmed of roots (see Tip)

Hawaiian salt, demerara sugar, or soy sauce, for serving (optional)

Bring a large pot of water to a boil over high heat. Add the taro, lower the heat to medium-low, and simmer until the root is very tender, about 1 hour. The taro is done when you can easily pierce it with a fork. Drain and let the taro rest until it is cool enough to handle, about 30 minutes.

Wearing disposable gloves and using the side of a spoon, peel all the skin from the taro. Chop the taro into 2 in [5 cm] pieces.

Transfer the taro to a food processor and add ½ cup [120 ml] of water. Process on high speed for 3 minutes, then scrape down the sides of the bowl. Process for an additional 2 minutes, adding water as needed to achieve a thick, smooth consistency.

The poi can be served immediately or allowed to ferment in the refrigerator. To ferment, transfer the mashed poi to an airtight container with extra room and pour in a shallow layer of filtered water to prevent a skin from forming. Allow the poi to age in the refrigerator for 2 to 3 days; pour off the water when ready to serve. Add salt, soy sauce, or sugar to taste if desired.

TIP Taro is inedible in its raw form and must be cooked. Be sure to wear gloves when handling raw taro, as its calcium oxalate crystals can irritate the skin.

BLACK CAKE

This iconic Jamaican and Trinidadian dessert is a holiday staple that requires precision, patience, and practice. A dense, boozy, pitch-dark cake, it's made by fermenting raisins, dried plums, dried cherries, and prunes in a combination of rum and fruit-based brandy or, at times, Manischewitz, which is a popular substitute. This recipe comes from *Islas* contributor Brigid Washington, who continues to prepare the cakes in the manner similar to three matriarchs before her every Christmas.

14 to 16 [100 g] pitted prunes (about ¾ cup)

3½ oz [105 g] raisins (about ¾ cup)

3½ oz [100 g] dried currants (about ¾ cup)

3½ oz [100 g] unsweetened dried cherries (about ¾ cup)

2½ cups [600 ml] white rum

1½ cups [360 ml] Manischewitz wine

1 cup [226 g] unsalted butter, at room temperature, plus more for the pans

2½ cups [500 g] dark brown sugar

4 eggs

2 tsp grated lime zest

2 tsp vanilla extract

1 Tbsp almond extract

1½ cups [210 g] all-purpose flour, plus more for the pans

2 tsp baking powder

1 Tbsp ground allspice

2 tsp ground nutmeg

¼ cup [60 ml] plus 1 Tbsp dark unsulfured molasses

1 oz [30 g] sliced raw almonds (about ¼ cup)

In a large container with a tight-fitting lid, combine the prunes, raisins, currants, dried cherries, 1½ cups [360 ml] of the rum, and the Manischewitz. Stir to combine, cover, and set aside for at least 2 days (and up to 6 months for a stronger flavor).

When you're ready to bake, preheat the oven to 250°F [120°C]. Lightly butter two 9 in [23 cm] round cake pans and line their bottoms with parchment paper. Lightly butter the parchment, then dust the interior of the cake pans with flour and tap out the excess.

Transfer the fruit and soaking liquid to a food processor. Pulse into a rough paste, with some larger fruit pieces remaining.

In a stand mixer, beat the butter and brown sugar on medium speed until fluffy, about 8 minutes. Add the eggs one at a time, beating after each addition. Beat in the lime zest, vanilla, and almond extract.

In a large mixing bowl, whisk together the flour, baking powder, allspice, and nutmeg. Working in two batches, gently beat the dry ingredients into the butter mixture on the lowest speed. Add the fruit mixture and molasses and beat to combine. Fold in the almonds.

Divide the batter between the prepared cake pans and smooth the tops. Bake for 1 hour, then lower the oven temperature to 225°F [110°C] and bake until a cake tester inserted into the center comes out clean, 2½ to 3 hours more. Set the pans on a wire rack to cool for 10 minutes, then brush the tops with some of the remaining 1 cup [240 ml] rum. Let the cakes rest for another 10 minutes, brushing until all of the rum is absorbed.

Invert the cakes onto plates, then wrap each plate in wax paper and aluminum foil. Let sit at room temperature for at least 1 day, and up to a month before serving.

CHAPTER THREE

BRAISING + STEWING

Madagascar

Madagascar conjures magic. Celestially iridescent panther chameleons, indigo-feathered blue couas, bug-eyed aye-ayes, and aptly named tomato frogs call the island home, as do otherworldly colossal baobab trees and star-shaped orchids—resembling a fictional Pandoran biosphere.

The concentration of endemic species, particularly the iconic ring-tailed lemurs that hint at the origins of humanity, alongside local vanilla—prized the world over for its highly concentrated sweet, warm, creamy flavor—give the island an almost mythical allure. Its bountiful ecosystem produces an abundance of natural resources, microcosms of lush woods, and 3,000 miles of coastline brimming with species of fish that can be traced back 420 million years.

And yet, unlike the other islands prominently featured in this book—notably Seychelles, a close neighbor and also home to a host of endemic species—Madagascar is not heavily touristed. Less than 2 percent of the economy is based on tourism. Curiously, locals and researchers alike struggle to define its cuisine. Most often, it's described as bland and even dull, surprising due to the relative abundance of the island. This contradiction—distinctive and enchanting, yet somehow indescribable—is what makes Madagascar a confounding and complex place.

Located at the southernmost boundary of the tropics, with a shape that suggests it was once a part of neighboring Mozambique, this Indian Ocean island conjures a world before humanity. It's the fourth largest island on the planet, and the wonders of this precious landscape also appear on the faces of the Malagasy. Made up of twenty distinct ethnic groups, the Malagasy, or Malgache in French, trace their ancestry to seafaring people from the archipelago of Indonesia and descendants of East Africans from across the Mozambique Channel.

Part of what makes Madagascar so complex stems from how its land and people have been exploited. European powers, who coveted the lush island for its resources and proximity to Western-controlled parts of the Indian Ocean, first arrived in the 1600s. Pirates ruled the island for much of that era. There were subsequent attempts from Europeans to conquer the land, but it wasn't until 1896 that Madagascar was officially colonized by France. They ultimately pulled tens of thousands of Malagasy into World War II, leading to decades of resistance. In 1960 Madagascar won its independence, though the new republic was plagued by coups and civil unrest. Today, the government continues to struggle with corruption and political and economic instability. It's estimated that three-quarters of Malagasy live below the international poverty line, and citizens are often aggressively repressed by the local government, prevented from holding public demonstrations, and lack basic resources. Despite the riches coursing through its veins, Madagascar remains one of the most vulnerable places on earth.

In addition to the island's economic struggles, endemic droughts, and food scarcity, it is plagued by cyclones of mythic proportions that threaten residents with landslides, severe flooding, the destruction of power grids and communication systems, and mangled buildings. Consistent with other islands across the tropics, climate change is making natural disasters worse.

Climate change is also visible on the island's shores. Madagascar boasts a complex, interconnected water system that begins at Maramokotro mountain, the country's highest peak, down to the mangrove forests. The animated bushes grow in shallow waters of tropical climates. Characterized by their entangled, protruding roots, mangroves often appear to be standing afloat in still waters. The forests are crucial to the island's coastal villages that depend on them for building material, firewood, food, and protection against shore erosion. Residents of Marohata, a southwest province accessible only by boat, are closely monitoring a fluctuating fish population and the health of its once ample mangrove forests.

And yet, the Malagasy find a way to make do, stretching available resources to make nourishing dishes. Above all, Malagasy cuisine is exceedingly simple. The cornerstone: stews served with rice. And in keeping with the principles of good stews and braises, theirs start with aromatics—onion, garlic, ginger, peppers, chiles—paired with proteins such as zebu, a local cattle species, or fish, and rice or root vegetables such as cassava. Food found in the populous capital of Antananarivo, "Tana" for short, differs from what one may eat in Madagascar's bush, a dry coastal region that relies predominantly on surrounding water systems for nourishment. Tana is nestled in Madagascar's highlands, filled with congested, winding roads, remnants of French colonial rule, and three-wheeled tuk taxis whizzing by. The air is hot, heavy, and perfumed with diesel. In Tana you'll find street food such as deep-fried locust, Masikita—beef skewers marinated in papaya juice and Coca-Cola (page 245)—and Koba—a banana, peanut, and glutinous rice tamale steamed in banana leaves (page 286)—as well as colonial holdovers like French bread. In contrast to the northern forests and savanna landscapes, Madagascar's south is arid and desertlike and prone to severe drought and prolonged periods of extreme heat. Access to water defines how people eat. Rice and vegetables—often paired with curry-scented braised beef, goat,

or chicken when available—are staples. Ranovola, a beverage made from scorched rice, is quite popular on the island and can be enjoyed hot or cold. Cassava, breadfruit, yams, cabbage, zebu meat, and of course seafood such as crab, rainbow lobsters, and oysters found in the waters where rivers and oceans converge are fundamental to the Malagasy way of life.

One of the principal reasons that stews are so popular in Madagascar, and across the tropics, is that it's a way to make a lot with a little, and enough to share with an entire village. The Malagasy are a tribal people, who forge close bonds with their families and village communities. There, food is made to be shared. This is true across island communities, where flavorful stews

are served with white rice in homes across the tropics. Malagasy dishes, such as Romazava (page 170)—a remarkably rich combination of pork belly and beef that's balanced by ginger, tomato, and leafy greens—exemplify the stewing approach. You could say the same for Stewed Oxtail (page 78), which takes an ingredient that would be otherwise inedible due to the toughness of the meat and transforms it into a nourishing, sumptuous, velvety braise. Stews can also be delicate in flavor, as with Comoros' M'tsolola (page 164), where tender white fish, cassava, and green bananas are layered with onions and garlic and slowly simmered in coconut milk. Across island cuisine the goal is the same—to be nourishing, satisfying, and full of flavor—and stewing accomplishes that goal perfectly.

BRAISE + STEW

Despite their warm climates, soups and stews feature prominently in island cuisines. This cooking technique is a critical way to stretch ingredients and is exceedingly adaptable, lending itself to different vessels and heat sources—from cast-iron pots set over open fires to Dutch ovens on a conventional stove. It's a way to use up bits of ingredients that on their own wouldn't make a meal. And because you can taste and adjust as it cooks, each individual cook can put their stamp on their dish. Above all other techniques, braises and stews define island cooking.

In particular, this method is among the best for tenderizing tough cuts of meat and creating flavorful one-pot meals. Island nations often struggle with food access due to complex trade agreements and import-export policies that increase food costs. That means that meat can be pricey, making more affordable, fattier dark meat more popular. (Think pork country ribs instead of tenderloin, or bone-in chicken thighs over skinless breast.) And while lean meats may be preferred for certain dishes, fattier cuts are absolutely the best for stewing, as the process infuses meat with intense flavor. I mean, there's nothing like pork ribs that are literally falling off the bone.

Typically, stews and braises begin with a blend of aromatics and spices that are then slow-cooked in a liquid—sometimes simply water, but often flavorful broth, stock, beer, or wine. These types of dishes can have a "kitchen-sink" approach, layering ingredients such as tough cuts of meat, carrots and onions, local root vegetables such as cassava or taro, and then more tender vegetables and herbs. Sometimes the aromatics are ground into a paste as with Puerto Rican Sofrito (page 38) or Haitian epis (see pages 173 and 215). But more often these ingredients are chopped and layered—onions, carrots, celery, then garlic, ginger, or chiles, then spices. The timing forms a flavor foundation to build upon, and is just as applicable to seafood, legumes, and vegetable dishes as it is to meat.

Mastering stewing and braising will ensure that you and your family never go hungry. Some of the following recipes come together quickly, as with Maldivian Mas Riha (page 148)—a heavily perfumed tuna and coconut milk curry—or Puerto Rican Pollo en Fricasé (page 146), chicken thighs tenderized in wine and tomato sauce, punctuated by briny olives. Others are project meals, such as Haitian Soup Joumou (page 173), a dish developed to celebrate the island's independence from France, made of slow-cooked pumpkin and meat. It's perhaps not surprising that many of these dishes, as with Maldivian Mas Riha and Malagasy Romazava (page 170), are their country's national dishes. No matter the ingredients, they are all layered with history and meaning and exemplify quintessential home cooking.

BRAISING VS. STEWING

These methods are very similar, with one main distinction: Braising is a convection method, where ingredients—typically meat—are slowly steamed within a shallow pool of braising liquid, as with Filipino Adobong Puti (Pork White Adobo) (page 139). Stewing, on the other hand, involves submerging ingredients fully in a flavorful liquid. What connects the processes is developing the flavor foundation of your sauce or liquid.

BRAISING LIQUIDS

Water: neutral, adaptable

Chicken broth: low-sodium chicken broth is the most adaptable choice, as the flavor melds well with most others while adding body to the broth.

Pork broth: imparts a strong flavor that's ideal for simmered greens, legumes, or pork-based dishes

Beef broth: has a decidedly meaty flavor and is most appropriate for beef dishes

Seafood: typically lighter colored, seafood broth can be incredibly flavorful and a great foundation for coconut curries, seafood stews, or rice porridge.

ORDER OF OPERATIONS

Onions: across the tropics and beyond, saucy dishes start with onions. The way you cook your onions is, potentially, the most important step in the process. Burnt onions will make your dish bitter; undercooked onions will stay crunchy and have a raw taste.

> **For more delicate dishes (2 to 3 minutes):** Sauté over medium heat, stirring frequently, until they become translucent.

> **For most dishes (5 to 7 minutes):** Sauté over medium heat, stirring frequently, until they begin to turn golden; good timing for carrots and celery as well.

> **For richer, more robust dishes (7 to 10 minutes):** Sauté over medium heat, stirring often and watching carefully to prevent onions from burning. If onions get dark too quickly, lower the heat to medium-low.

Carrots, celery, and peppers: these ingredients can be cooked along with onions, ideally in the middle range of 5 to 7 minutes.

Ginger, garlic, and chiles: these ingredients should be added as a near-final step before adding the remaining stew ingredients.

Ground spices and dried herbs: typically, I fry my spices for about 30 seconds once my garlic becomes aromatic.

Fresh herbs: fresh parsley, thyme, oregano, and bay leaf can be added earlier in the cooking process, depending on the dish. More delicate herbs like cilantro and chives should be added just before finishing, or simply as a garnish.

• Use only as much oil as you need to prevent vegetables from sticking, as your ingredients are likely to release fat as well. Using too much oil at first can lead to a greasy, oily dish.

• It's always a good idea to deglaze the pan with a liquid, such as broth or wine, or tomatoes in the form of fresh tomatoes or sauce. This brings together the flavor foundation and also serves to loosen any browned bits that may have stuck to the bottom of your pot. If using wine, simmer for 2 to 3 minutes to cook off the alcohol. For this step, use your nose, smelling often while it simmers until the sharp alcohol smell dissipates. If using tomatoes, simmer for 2 to 3 minutes to cook off the liquid.

PERLINE ERNESTINE
MADAGASCAR

By Stephanie Rodriguez

Fisherman Perline Ernestine presides over Marohata—a coastal village in southwestern Madagascar where fresh and saltwater ecosystems converge, brimming with green sea turtles, shrimp, crab, and tentacled sea cucumber. As a child growing up by the sea, she'd eagerly watched fishermen return home from their expeditions. Today, the mother of four is a leader within the Marohata fisher's association, an alliance of local villagers dedicated to protecting their way of life. She is the only female president of the association's nine villages.

Perline regularly wears her hair in neatly twisted knots or in thick black and fire-red strands braided then wrapped into a perfect spiral behind her neck. It's not common for the women of Marohata to fish in the open waters, but ocean diving always felt liberating, making her stronger and more confident. Ndrema, Perline's youngest son, often follows his mother around, his small hands gripping the fringes of her traditional lambahoany skirt tied securely around her waist. The family's home, a small, thatched dwelling just steps away from the shore, sits behind a row of lakanas—slim canoes hollowed from a single tree trunk, their sails fashioned from recycled fabric such as blankets, banners, and flags.

Perline and Ndrema are the bearers of the Vezo legacy, an ancient seafaring people facing new threats to their way of life. *Vezo* means "people who live with the sea." They are a semi-nomadic tribe occupying the island's western coast, and their children learn to swim and sail at a young age, their lungs adjusting to intense dives, navigating the waters with the ease of an expert diver. Fishing is the primary source of revenue and trade for these ocean-reliant villagers. Perline and her family depend on the coastal bush for sea creatures, both for nourishment and a modest income, but diminishing catches push fishermen farther out to sea—a worrisome effect of overfishing and climate change.

Like many women in her tribe, Perline visits the mangroves almost daily. Beforehand, she applies a clay-like paste made from ground sandalwood bark to her face to protect her skin from the tropical sun—a warrior's mask for an arduous task. She harvests mackerel or prawns, then divides the bounty, providing both her family's nourishment and goods to be sold. Back in her kitchen, Perline utilizes timber harvested from surrounding mangrove forests to build two fires. She carefully assembles the small pieces of wood into sturdy pyramids, then tops each with a lightweight metal pot—one filled with fresh water for cassava, the other with onions and curry. As the fire gets going, she runs the sharp edge of a knife across the skin of the mackerel, removes the scales,

then skillfully runs the knife through the belly, gutting the fish before rinsing it in salt water and adding it to the onions. She calls this dish Cassava with Fish (page 136), a daily staple for her family and similar to that enjoyed by millions of islanders across the planet.

Sourcing food can be a challenge in isolated coastal areas. Perline and her husband both fish, harvesting sea cucumbers, mackerel, trevally, crabs, and other seafood three times a week. Through trade and foraging, they also have access to root vegetables such as taro and cassava, as well as plantains, bananas, and rice. Perline's cooking style is a signature of Malagasy cuisine. It's exceedingly simple. Each dish uses a handful of ingredients: oil (coconut or vegetable), aromatics (garlic, ginger, onions, chiles), proteins (most often beef, chicken, or fish), curry spices, starches (root vegetables, rice, or fried breads), and greens, which might be paired with fiery condiments such as Lemon Lasary (page 96) when ingredients are available. These meals reflect both a deep resilience and boundless creativity among people who do what they can to make delicious food under challenging circumstances.

On some days, the radio transmits troubling news about Marohata's coastline, much of which confirms what Perline already knows: mangroves ceasing to regenerate, pockets of lush canopy now stumps in the mud; a diminishing catch; once-vibrant reefs now suffering at the hands of desperate villagers who often resort to exploitative fishing practices in order to feed their families, disrupting a delicate, ancestral balance of exchange between humans and ocean. Perline aims to help villagers develop healthier fishing habits, eliminating a destructive culture of using seine nets—made of fine mesh that scrapes coral and otherwise disrupts fragile ecosystems—along with other illegal tools responsible for degrading the ocean. Together with members of her community, she safeguards designated preservation zones so they can be restored.

Because she is descended from sea voyagers, Perline feels ocean threats perhaps more acutely than others. That she is a woman in this role is no small matter in a society that is still deeply stratified by sex. She wants to be an example for other women in her tribe, but more so for her daughters, who will carry the torch after she's gone. Because while Perline may be breaking barriers with her presence on the fishing council, as well as her efforts to ensure that members of her community are literate, to her this is not new. It is her legacy—the strength she draws from the sea and pours back into it. For her, connection to ancestry is about preservation and a responsibility to finding a way forward in a changing world.

RECITES

Island
Madagascar

Yield
4 to 6 servings

Active Time
15 minutes

Total Time
45 minutes

PERLINE'S CASSAVA WITH FISH

This recipe is inspired by the simple, nourishing dish Perline Ernestine makes for her family. Over improvised burners directly on the sand, she boils peeled cassava root (yuca) and cooks fresh-caught lanora, or bluefin trevally, with oil, onions, and curry powder. She serves the fish atop the cassava, or rice when available. Fish or vegetable stock can be substituted for water for an extra boost of flavor.

FISH

2 tsp Seychellois Massalé (page 40, see Tips)

1 large garlic clove, minced

1 Tbsp minced peeled fresh ginger

1 Tbsp vegetable oil

1 tsp kosher salt

2 lb [910 g] fatty fish steaks, such as mackerel, kingfish, or salmon, rinsed and patted dry

CASSAVA

2 lb [910 g] cassava (see Yuca con Mojo [page 119] for Tips)

¼ cup [60 g] kosher salt

CURRY

2 tsp ground coriander

1 tsp ground cumin

1 tsp sweet paprika

1 tsp ground turmeric

¼ tsp ground cardamom

¼ tsp chili powder

¼ tsp ground cinnamon

⅛ tsp ground allspice

2 tsp kosher salt, plus more as needed

1 Tbsp vegetable oil

1 small yellow onion, finely chopped

2 large garlic cloves, minced

1 Tbsp minced peeled fresh ginger

To make the fish: In a large nonreactive bowl, combine the massalé, garlic, ginger, oil, and salt and whisk to combine. Add the fish and toss, then cover and let marinate at room temperature for at least 30 minutes.

To make the cassava: Meanwhile, fill a large pot with water and bring it to a boil over high heat.

Fill a large bowl with water. Peel the cassava with a sharp peeler or paring knife, then chop it into 2 in [5 cm] pieces, and transfer to the bowl of water.

Once the pot of water is at a rolling boil, add the salt, then the cassava. Boil for 15 to 20 minutes, until a knife goes through easily; don't let the cassava become mushy. Drain and transfer to a serving dish.

Meanwhile, make the curry: In a small bowl, combine the coriander, cumin, paprika, turmeric, cardamon, chili powder, cinnamon, allspice, and salt.

In a saucepan over medium-high, heat the oil. Add the onion and sauté for 5 to 7 minutes, until just beginning to turn golden, then add the garlic and ginger and cook for 1 minute or so, until fragrant. Add the spice blend and fry for another minute, stirring frequently.

Add the fish and marinade to the pan, then add 3 cups [710 ml] water (or stock) to cover, and more for desired sauciness. Increase the heat to medium-high and cook the fish for 7 to 9 minutes, until the fish is fully opaque but not overcooked.

Serve the fish and curry over the cassava.

TIPS   You can substitute garam masala for massalé.

Skin-on fish fillets can be substituted for steaks but will cook slightly faster.

See Yuca con Mojo (page 119) for tips on sourcing yuca or cassava, and for a flavorful alternative to boiled cassava.

Island
Dominican Republic

Yield
4 servings

Active Time
15 minutes

Total Time
50 minutes

CORNED BEEF CASERA
HOMESTYLE STEWED CORNED BEEF

Shelf-stable canned meats, such as Spam, Vienna sausages, and corned beef, have long been part of island cuisines, particularly in Puerto Rico, Hawai'i, Guam, and the Philippines—places colonized by the United States. That's due in part to US trade policies and because of the ingredients' capacity to withstand storms. Countless variations on these recipes have emerged, a marker of islanders' resilience and creativity. And while canned meats are high in both fat and salt, this also makes them quite delicious. This is the corned beef recipe I grew up eating, and the smell of it is deeply nostalgic and comforting to me; my father always served it with ketchup. It is also very rich and heavy and will definitely stick to your ribs. Pair it with fried sweet plantains or Arroz con Tocino (page 292).

1 Tbsp olive oil

¼ cup [60 ml] Sofrito (page 38)

One 8 oz [227 g] can tomato sauce

¼ cup [40 g] pimento-stuffed olives

1 Tbsp store-bought or homemade Sazón Seasoning (page 39), plus more as needed

½ tsp freshly ground black pepper

One 12 oz [340 g] can corned beef (see Tips)

1 medium russet potato, peeled and diced into 1 in [2.5 cm] cubes

Kosher salt, plus more as needed

Steamed white rice and fried sweet plantains, for serving

In a large, deep skillet with a lid over medium, heat the olive oil. Add the sofrito and sauté for 3 to 5 minutes, stirring frequently, until the liquid is almost entirely reduced. Add the tomato sauce, olives, sazón, and pepper and sauté for 5 to 7 minutes, until the sauce has thickened and begins to darken.

Scoop the corned beef into the skillet and mix well with the sauce, breaking up the corned beef with a wooden spoon.

Add the potato and ¾ cup [180 ml] of water and bring to a simmer over medium-high. Lower the heat to medium-low, cover, and simmer for 15 to 20 minutes, until the potatoes are fork-tender but not falling apart. Let sit off the heat for 5 to 7 minutes before serving, and adjust seasoning as needed. Serve over steamed white rice with fried plantains on the side.

TIPS   There are many brands of corned beef, but my family always used Libby's.

This dish is naturally quite salty, so taste before adding any additional salt or sazón.

For breakfast, serve over plain white rice with a yolky fried egg on top.

Island
Philippines

Yield
6 servings

Active Time
30 minutes

Total Time
1 hour 30 minutes

ADOBONG PUTI
PORK WHITE ADOBO

Most adobo today is made with a mix of soy sauce and vinegar, but this older recipe harkens back to traditional Filipino cooking, before soy sauce was so commonly used. Making abundant use of vinegar, a flavorful souring agent and preservative, this recipe is among the most ancestral preparations: The use of vinegar and braising tenderizes the meat and balances the fattiness of the pork.

2 Tbsp canola oil

10 to 12 garlic cloves, minced

3 lb [1.4 kg] pork belly or boneless pork shoulder, cut into 1 in [2.5 cm] pieces (see Tip)

1 cup [240 ml] white vinegar

1 Tbsp kosher salt

3 dried bay leaves

1 tsp black peppercorns

1 tsp demerara sugar

Steamed white rice, for serving

In a wide, heavy-bottomed pan over medium, heat the canola oil. Add the garlic and cook, stirring frequently, until softened, 3 to 5 minutes.

Add the pork and brown lightly for 7 to 10 minutes, then add the vinegar and bring to a boil. Cook, uncovered, without stirring, for 3 to 5 minutes.

Add 1½ cups [360 ml] of water, the salt, bay leaves, and peppercorns and stir to combine. Bring to a boil. Continue to boil for 3 to 5 minutes, skimming any scum off the surface.

Lower the heat, cover, and simmer for 40 to 50 minutes, until the meat is fork-tender and the liquid is reduced by half. If the meat is not yet tender, add ½ cup [120 ml] of water and simmer for 5 minutes more.

Add the sugar and stir to combine. Cook, uncovered, for 5 to 10 minutes longer, until the sabaw (Tagalog for *soup*) thickens. Serve with steamed white rice.

TIP Bone-in chicken legs, thighs, or quarters can be substituted for pork belly if desired.

Island
Guam

Yield
4 servings

Active Time
15 minutes

Total Time
45 minutes

KÅDUN PIKA

HOT PEPPER–BRAISED CHICKEN

Reminiscent of Filipino Adobong Puti (page 139), this recipe from neighboring Guam comes together easily and is flavorful and satisfying. For a spicier take, add more chiles; if you'd like a completely mild dish, you can omit the chiles altogether.

2 Tbsp vegetable oil

1 small white onion, finely chopped

3 garlic cloves, minced

2 lb [910 g] bone-in chicken legs and thighs

1 tsp kosher salt

1 tsp freshly ground black pepper

¼ cup [60 ml] soy sauce

2 Tbsp coconut vinegar or apple cider vinegar

2 red bird's eye chiles, stemmed and finely chopped

1½ cups [360 ml] canned full-fat coconut milk, well shaken and stirred

Steamed white rice, for serving

In a large, heavy-bottomed pot over medium-high, heat the oil until shimmering, 1 to 2 minutes. Add the onion and sauté for 3 to 5 minutes, until golden, then add the garlic and sauté 1 minute more, until fragrant.

Add the chicken, salt, pepper, soy sauce, and vinegar and cook for 10 to 15 minutes, stirring often.

Lower the heat to low, add the chiles, and stir well to incorporate. Cover and cook for an additional 10 to 15 minutes, stirring often, until the chicken is tender. Add the coconut milk and simmer, uncovered, for 5 minutes more. Serve with steamed white rice.

Island
Trinidad

Yield
4 servings

Active Time
15 minutes

Total Time
30 minutes

STEWED CURRY EGGPLANT

Islas contributor Brigid Washington grew up eating this stewed eggplant. The recipe developed from her mother's preparation, and it's one she continues to prepare for her family today. It's quick, simple, and nourishing, and a vegan side dish that can be enjoyed on its own with white rice or paired with Callaloo (page 143) and Cucumber Chow (page 107) for a hearty vegetarian meal.

3 Tbsp vegetable oil

2 tsp Chief or Madras curry powder

1 medium globe eggplant (about 14 oz [400 g]), peeled and cubed

7 garlic cloves, finely chopped

1 tsp kosher salt, plus more as needed

¼ tsp Tabasco or other hot sauce, plus more as needed

Steamed brown or white rice, for serving

In a large skillet over medium, heat the oil for about 30 seconds, then add the curry powder and stir to combine. Lower the heat to medium-low and add the eggplant, stirring to coat in the oil. Add ¼ cup [60 ml] of water, stir again, and cover the pan. Cook until the eggplant is tender but not falling apart, 7 to 9 minutes.

Uncover the pan and pour in another ¼ cup [60 ml] of water. Stir, cover, and cook for 7 minutes, or until the eggplant is semi-translucent. Mash the eggplant with a fork (it should be soft enough to be mashed easily). Mix in the garlic, salt, and Tabasco and cook, uncovered, until the garlic mellows and the flavors have come together, about 3 minutes. Remove from the heat. Taste and season with more salt and hot sauce as needed. Serve with rice.

CALLALOO
COCONUT-BRAISED GREENS

Callaloo is a native West African dish that, like many of the dishes in this book, made its way to the Caribbean during the transatlantic slave trade. Depending on where you travel in the Caribbean, *callaloo* may refer to the green leafy vegetable—typically the heart-shaped leaves of the taro plant—or the actual, finished dish. In this recipe, from Brigid Washington, greens are combined with okra, aromatics, spices, and coconut milk, then lightly cooked and puréed into a creamy, hearty vegetarian side dish. Traditionally, it was whipped with a swizzle stick, a simple tool made of a stick with protruding branches at the bottom, like an ancient frother. It can be easily transformed into a soup by adding more coconut milk and water, and it's exquisite paired simply with steamed white rice. Serve alongside Poulet Boucané (page 261) or with Fijian Lamb Barbecue (page 257).

8 large okra pods, stemmed and cut into 1 in [2.5 cm] rounds

1 medium yellow onion, finely chopped

4 green onions, white and green parts, finely chopped

8 cups [160 g] baby spinach, roughly chopped

2 cups [480 ml] canned full-fat coconut milk, well shaken and stirred, plus more if serving as a soup

1 Tbsp kosher salt

1½ tsp freshly ground black pepper

½ tsp allspice berries, crushed

3 large garlic cloves, finely chopped

2 fresh thyme sprigs, leaves removed

3 whole cloves, crushed

1 scotch bonnet or orange habanero pepper

1 Tbsp unsalted butter

Steamed white rice, for serving

In a large stockpot over medium-high heat, bring 2 cups [480 ml] of water to a boil. Add the okra, onion, green onions, spinach, coconut milk, salt, pepper, allspice, garlic, thyme, and cloves. Stir to combine and cover the pot. Cook for 7 to 10 minutes, until the spinach is wilted.

Add the chile pepper, cover the pot, and lower the heat to medium-low. Simmer for 20 minutes. Remove and discard the pepper. Stir in the butter.

Using an immersion blender, purée the mixture until smooth. (If you don't have an immersion blender, use a regular blender, working in batches.)

Serve hot over steamed white rice. Or serve as an alternative to spinach dip. To serve as a soup, add 2 to 3 cups [480 to 720 ml] of warmed coconut milk or boiling water after the callaloo has been puréed, or to the desired consistency (adjust the salt and pepper as needed).

Island
Puerto Rico

Yield
4 to 6 servings

Active Time
15 minutes

Total Time
45 minutes

HABICHUELAS GUISADAS CON CALABAZA
STEWED RED BEANS WITH PUMPKIN

Across the Caribbean, rice and beans are sometimes cooked together—as with Jamaican Rice and Peas (page 160)—or prepared separately but served together, like several spoonfuls of beans atop white rice. I've been making beans for my family since I was a kid. They are one of the first dishes I learned to make, and my preparation has evolved quite a bit over time. As in many other island families, mine was heavily reliant on frozen and canned foods and premade seasonings. I began by using jarred sofrito, a packet of sazón, a couple cans of red kidney beans with their liquid, tomato sauce, olives, and potatoes cut into large pieces. Eating with other Puerto Ricans, though, both in the States and on the island, I discovered more traditional preparations, including starting with dried beans, using homemade Sofrito (page 38), and adding calabaza—a winter squash commonly found throughout the Caribbean and Latin America, similar to pumpkin but with a slightly sweeter, milder flavor. Calabaza is typically sold precut in Latin American and Asian grocery stores. I always make a big batch of this dish, because it's hearty and filling and keeps for at least a week in the refrigerator or several months in the freezer. It's the perfect side dish for any of the Puerto Rican or Caribbean dishes in this book.

2 Tbsp olive oil

½ cup [68 g] diced jamón de cocinar or smoked ham steak, finely chopped (see Tips)

½ cup [120 ml] Sofrito (page 38) (see Tips)

1 Tbsp store-bought or homemade Sazón Seasoning (page 39)

1 Tbsp tomato paste

One 8 oz [227 g] can tomato sauce

3½ cups [920 g] cooked red kidney beans (about two 15½ oz [439 g] cans, drained and rinsed)

½ lb [230 g] chopped calabaza (about 2½ cups) (see Tips)

½ cup [75 g] pimento-stuffed olives

1 dried bay leaf

2 small (3.7 g) chicken bouillon cubes, or 2 tsp powdered chicken bouillon

2 tsp red wine vinegar, plus more as needed

1 tsp kosher salt, plus more as needed

¼ tsp freshly ground black pepper, plus more as needed

In a large pot over medium, heat the olive oil. Add the jamón and cook for 3 to 5 minutes, until browned. Add the sofrito and sauté 5 to 7 minutes, stirring often, until the liquid is absorbed and it develops a rich aroma.

Add the sazón and tomato paste and sauté for 30 seconds or so, until it begins to darken in color, then add the tomato sauce and deglaze the pan.

Add the beans, calabaza, olives, bay leaf, bouillon, and 4 cups [945 ml] of water. Bring to a simmer, then cover, lower the heat, and simmer for 25 to 30 minutes, until the calabaza is fork-tender but not falling apart. Add the vinegar, salt, and pepper, stir well to incorporate, then taste and adjust seasoning as needed.

TIPS Jamón de cocinar can be found in most Latin American grocery stores, but smoked ham steak is a perfect substitute.

Homemade sofrito is preferable, but you can use commercially available sofrito—just be sure to taste before adding the salt and vinegar.

Peeled kabocha or butternut squash are good substitutes for calabaza.

POLLO EN FRICASÉ
CHICKEN FRICASSEE

The ultimate comfort food, this dish bears the mark of Spanish and French colonial influence but takes a decidedly Puerto Rican approach. Bone-in chicken thighs are braised to perfection in a rich, oniony, garlicky tomato-based sauce, balanced with white wine and vinegar and punctuated by briny olives and capers. Potatoes are added toward the end for a satisfying meal. Like so many Puerto Rican dishes, this one is highly adaptable. Some people brown the chicken first, adding sofrito and other aromatics later. Some add carrots, or use beer or red wine instead of white wine. My take is pared down and incredibly simple, making it an easy weeknight meal that can be prepared while you're getting your house in order after work. This recipe is adapted from Carmen Valldejuli's *Cocina Criolla*, which has remained the island's best-known and most popular cookbook for more than sixty years.

2 to 3 lb [910 g to 1.4 kg] bone-in, skin-on chicken thighs, skin removed

One 8 oz [227 g] can tomato sauce

1 medium yellow onion, finely chopped

10 garlic cloves, minced

¼ cup [60 ml] white wine vinegar

2 Tbsp olive oil

2 tsp sweet paprika

½ tsp ground cumin

3 dried bay leaves

1½ Tbsp kosher salt

¼ tsp freshly cracked black pepper

1 cup [240 ml] dry white wine

¼ cup [40 g] pimento-stuffed olives

1 Tbsp capers, drained

1 lb [455 g] Yukon gold potatoes, peeled and sliced into ½ in [13 mm] rounds

Steamed white rice, for serving

Chopped fresh cilantro leaves, for garnish

Pat the chicken dry, then place the thighs in a lidded, heavy-bottomed pot or Dutch oven.

In a medium nonreactive mixing bowl, combine the tomato sauce, onion, garlic, vinegar, olive oil, paprika, cumin, bay leaves, salt, and pepper and whisk together with a fork. Pour the sauce over the chicken.

Bring the mixture to a boil over high heat, then lower the heat, cover, and simmer for 45 minutes, stirring occasionally.

Add the white wine, olives, capers, and potato slices, stirring well to incorporate. Bring back to a boil, then lower the heat, cover, and simmer for 30 to 40 minutes, until the potatoes are tender but not falling apart. If your sauce is thinner than you'd like, transfer the cooked chicken and potatoes to a serving bowl using tongs or a slotted spoon, then simmer the sauce for 5 to 7 minutes more over medium-high heat until thickened.

Serve over steamed white rice with plenty of sauce, and garnish with cilantro.

Island
Fiji

Yield
4 servings

Active Time
5 minutes

Total Time
45 minutes

CURRIED GREEN JACKFRUIT

Reminiscent of chicken tikka masala, this recipe is inspired by the in-ground, or lovo, cooking of Fiji. There, meats, tubers, jackfruit, or breadfruit are seasoned, doused in coconut milk, then wrapped in banana leaves and slow-cooked. This simple vegan dish is rich and satisfying, drawing on the Indo-Fijian flavors of the island, with aromatic spices and a bit of a kick. Serve with white rice and sautéed veggies, with naan, or alongside your favorite curries.

One 20 oz [565 g] can green jackfruit, drained

One 13½ oz [400 ml] can full-fat coconut milk, well shaken and stirred

1 Tbsp soy sauce

2 tsp kosher salt, plus more as needed

1 tsp ground coriander

1 tsp sweet paprika

1 tsp garlic powder

1 tsp ground ginger

1 tsp ground turmeric

½ tsp ground cumin

½ tsp cayenne pepper

Preheat the oven to 450°F [230°C].

Using your fingers, shred the jackfruit into bite-size pieces and place in a large nonreactive mixing bowl.

Add the coconut milk, soy sauce, salt, coriander, paprika, garlic powder, ginger, turmeric, cumin, and cayenne, and stir carefully with a rubber spatula to incorporate.

Transfer the jackfruit mixture to a shallow 2 qt [1.9 L] baking dish. Place in the oven and roast for 25 minutes.

Turn the oven to broil and roast for 5 to 7 minutes more, until the top chars a bit. Let rest for 5 to 7 minutes before serving.

TIPS This recipe can easily be doubled, using a 9 by 13 in [23 by 33 cm], 3 qt [2.8 L] baking dish.

You can substitute your favorite curry powder for the coriander, paprika, garlic powder, ginger, turmeric, cumin, and cayenne. Instead, use 2 Tbsp of no-salt curry powder, and continue with the recipe as written.

Island
Maldives

Yield
2 to 4 servings

Active Time
15 minutes

Total Time
30 minutes

MAS RIHA
TUNA CURRY

Mas riha, the national dish of the Maldives, comprises fresh tuna nestled in a vibrant, fragrant, surprisingly complex coconut curry sauce. It's a beautiful dish, and delicious when served with steamed basmati rice.

1 lb [455 g] fresh tuna steaks, cut into 1½ in [4 cm] pieces

Kosher salt

Freshly ground black pepper

1 Tbsp coconut oil

1 medium white onion, chopped

4 large garlic cloves, finely chopped

1 Tbsp finely grated peeled fresh ginger

1 to 2 long green chile peppers, thinly sliced

5 fresh or frozen curry leaves, finely chopped

2 green cardamom pods, crushed

1 tsp ground turmeric

½ tsp garam masala

½ tsp ground cumin

1½ cups [360 ml] canned full-fat coconut milk, well shaken and stirred

1 cinnamon stick

¼ cup [10 g] chopped fresh cilantro leaves, for garnish

Steamed basmati rice, for serving

Pat the fish dry, then lightly salt and pepper all sides.

In a large, deep saucepan or Dutch oven over medium, heat the coconut oil until shimmering. Add the onion and cook until softened, 5 to 7 minutes. Add the garlic, ginger, chiles, and curry leaves and sauté for 1 minute or so, then add the cardamom, turmeric, garam masala, cumin, and ½ tsp pepper and sauté for 30 seconds more, until deeply fragrant.

Add the coconut milk, cinnamon stick, and 2 tsp salt and bring to a simmer over medium-high. Gently nestle the fish in the sauce and cook for 5 to 7 minutes, turning halfway through, until the fish is opaque but still tender. Serve immediately, garnished with cilantro and alongside steamed basmati rice.

Island
Seychelles

Yield
4 to 6 servings

Active Time
20 minutes

Total Time
1 hour 20 minutes

KADON GAMSON
SEYCHELLOIS OCTOPUS CURRY

Octopus is plentiful in Seychelles's waters, making it a common seafood ingredient in salads, soups, and curries. This traditional dish, among the most popular and best-known on that island, is extremely flavorful, spicy, and unique. The creaminess of the octopus blends with the silky coconut curry sauce that's heavy with cardamom and cinnamon. It's incredibly rich and warming, and it should always be eaten with rice.

2 to 3 lb [910 g to 1.4 kg] octopus tentacles, cleaned and cut into bite-size pieces

3 tsp kosher salt, plus more as needed

2 Tbsp coconut oil

1 yellow onion, chopped

3 garlic cloves, minced

One 2 in [5 cm] piece fresh ginger, peeled and minced

1 or 2 red Thai bird's eye chiles, seeded if desired to mitigate spiciness and chopped

2 Tbsp Seychellois Massalé (page 40, or store-bought) or mild curry powder

1 Tbsp ground turmeric

3 green cardamom pods, crushed

1 large dried bay leaf

2 cinnamon sticks

Two 13½ oz [400 ml] cans full-fat coconut milk, well shaken and stirred

2 medium Japanese eggplants, chopped

Steamed white rice, for serving

In a deep saucepan, combine the octopus and 2 tsp of the salt, then cover with cold water until at least 1 in [2.5 cm] above the octopus. Bring to a boil, then lower the heat to medium and simmer, covered, for 30 to 40 minutes, until the octopus is tender and easily pierced with a fork. Set a colander over a large bowl, then strain the octopus, reserving the liquid.

In a heavy-bottomed pot or Dutch oven over medium, heat the coconut oil. Add the onion and sauté for 5 to 7 minutes, until starting to turn golden. Add the garlic, ginger, and chiles and sauté for 1 minute or so, until fragrant. Add the massalé, turmeric, cardamom, bay leaf, cinnamon sticks, and the remaining 1 tsp salt. Add the reserved octopus and a ½ cup of the reserved octopus braising liquid, then stir once more to coat.

Add the coconut milk and increase the heat to medium-high, stirring well. Once simmering, lower the heat to medium-low, cover, and simmer for 15 to 20 minutes, until the octopus has become more tender and the sauce has thickened.

Add the eggplant, stir well, and simmer for 7 to 10 minutes, until the eggplant is fork-tender.

Let rest for 5 minutes off the heat before serving so the flavors can meld. Serve with steamed white rice.

Island
Seychelles

Yield
6 to 8 servings

Active Time
15 minutes

Total Time
45 minutes

CARI DE POISSON ET POTIRON

PUMPKIN FISH CURRY

Rich, flavorful coconut curries are popular in Seychelles, and this one is inspired by Jordana Jeremie, the mother of Marie-May Jeremie, who is profiled on page 92. Jordana's recipe is richer and simpler, using flavorful fatty trevally, onions, and spices for a comforting dish that's Marie-May's favorite. Serve with Jordana's Eggplant Chutney (page 94), Lasos Piman (page 48), Mint-Cilantro Chutney (page 44), or Sambal Oelek (page 49). Pair with basmati rice or naan, or try it with funchi (see page 167) from Curaçao. For an extra boost of flavor, substitute fish or vegetable stock for the water.

1 Tbsp vegetable oil

1 large yellow onion, finely chopped

3 large garlic cloves, minced

2 Tbsp finely grated peeled fresh ginger

3 Tbsp Seychellois Massalé (page 40; see Tips)

1 tsp ground turmeric

2 Tbsp tomato paste

One 13½ oz [400 ml] can full-fat coconut milk, well shaken and stirred

3 Tbsp tamarind purée (see Tips)

1 dried bay leaf

2 fresh thyme sprigs

2 tsp kosher salt, plus more as needed

2 lb [910 g] firm-fleshed fish, such as grouper, snapper, or swordfish

¼ tsp freshly ground black pepper

1 lb [455 g] fresh whole pumpkin, peeled, seeded, and chopped into 2 in [5 cm] cubes (about 3 heaping cups) (see Tips)

¼ cup [3 g] fresh cilantro leaves, for garnish

Lime wedges, for garnish

In a heavy-bottomed pot or Dutch oven with a lid over medium, heat the oil. Add the onion and sauté for 5 to 7 minutes, until starting to turn golden. Add the garlic and ginger and sauté for a minute or so, until fragrant. Add 2 Tbsp of the massalé and the turmeric, and sauté 1 minute more, then add the tomato paste and stir to deglaze the pan.

Add 2 cups [475 ml] of water (or stock) and the coconut milk, tamarind, bay leaf, thyme, and 1 tsp of the salt. Bring to a boil, then lower the heat and simmer for 15 minutes.

Meanwhile, dry the fish with paper towels and toss in a bowl with the remaining 1 Tbsp massalé, remaining 1 tsp salt, and the pepper.

Taste the sauce and adjust the seasoning as needed, then add the pumpkin and cook for 10 to 15 minutes more, until just barely tender.

Fold the fish into the curry, then cover and simmer for 5 to 7 minutes, until the fish is completely opaque but not tough. Remove from the heat and let rest for a couple minutes, removing the bay leaf and thyme sprigs. Garnish with the cilantro leaves and lime wedges.

TIPS The spice blend recipe yields about twice what you will need for this recipe. Store the remaining blend in an airtight container for a future meal.

Tamarind purée is thinner and blends better with other ingredients than tamarind paste. But for a tangier flavor, you can use only 1 Tbsp or less of tamarind paste.

Kabocha or butternut squash can be substituted for pumpkin.

Island
Hawai'i

Yield
4 to 6 servings

Active Time
**3 hours 30 minutes to
4 hours**

Total Time
5 hours

CHICKEN JOOK

Whole roast chicken remains in heavy rotation at my house. I make one at least every other week, often eating the wings plus a leg and thigh as soon as it's cool enough to handle. The rest will go into salads or be carved up for snacks and tacos throughout the week. This recipe from Hawai'i was originally made popular as a way to use up leftover Thanksgiving turkey, forming a rice congee that's infused with deep roasted meat and bone flavors, reflecting the US cultural influence on the island state. While you can make this recipe using a leftover poultry carcass, you can also use a leftover roast or premade rotisserie chicken and your favorite broth. While it may seem similar to Arroz Caldo (page 155), it's quite different. The flavor profile of arroz caldo is much lighter and the texture is brothier, whereas jook is more like grits or oatmeal.

One 3 lb [1.4 kg] roast chicken, meat pulled from bones and carcass reserved, or 6 cups [800 g] leftover roast chicken and its carcass

One 2 in [5 cm] piece fresh ginger, peeled and chopped

6 large garlic cloves, peeled

1 small yellow onion, quartered

4½ qt [4.2 L] chicken broth

2 tsp kosher salt, plus more as needed

2 cups [400 g] short-grain rice

Freshly ground black pepper

Thinly sliced green onions (white and green parts), fried shallots, soy sauce, and/or hot sauce (optional), for garnish

In a large pot, combine the chicken carcass, ginger, garlic, onion, broth, and salt. Bring to a boil, cover, then lower the heat and simmer for 1½ hours, until the broth develops a rich flavor. Taste along the way and add additional salt as needed.

Strain the broth into a separate large pot. Add the chicken meat and rice to the broth, then bring to a boil. Lower the heat to medium-low and simmer for 20 minutes, stirring often, then lower the heat to low and cook for 1 to 1½ hours, stirring often to prevent the rice from sticking to the bottom. The jook is ready when it resembles a thick porridge or grits.

Taste and season with salt and pepper as needed. Scoop into separate bowls and add garnishes as desired.

Island
Puerto Rico

Yield
4 to 6 servings

Active Time
30 minutes

Total Time
45 minutes

ARROZ CON JUEYES
STEWED CRAB RICE

Best when eaten at a beachside kiosko, especially La Comay in Piñones, arroz con jueyes is traditionally made with small land crabs whose shells can be soft enough to eat. It's a great example of a recipe that is quick and easy but also incredibly flavorful. For ease, this recipe uses lump crab meat.

3 Tbsp olive oil

1 small yellow onion, chopped

¼ cup [60 ml] Sofrito (page 38)

¼ cup [40 g] chopped pimentos

2 garlic cloves, minced

3 Tbsp whole pimento-stuffed olives

3 fresh cilantro sprigs, finely chopped

3 fresh culantro leaves, finely chopped

1½ tsp ground cumin

2 dried bay leaves

2 tsp store-bought or homemade Sazón Seasoning (page 39)

½ tsp dried oregano

½ cup [120 ml] tomato sauce

¼ tsp freshly ground black pepper

1 tsp kosher salt

1 lb [455 g] lump crab meat

2 cups [400 g] short-grain white rice

2½ cups [600 ml] fish stock, chicken broth, or water

1 ripe plantain, sliced, for garnish (optional)

1 large ripe avocado, sliced, for garnish (optional)

In a deep, heavy-bottomed pot or Dutch oven over medium-high, heat the oil until shimmering, 1 to 2 minutes. Add the onion and sofrito and sauté until the mixture begins to darken in color and emits a strong aroma, 5 to 7 minutes.

Add the pimentos, garlic, olives, cilantro, culantro, cumin, bay leaves, sazón, oregano, tomato sauce, pepper, and salt and mix well. Sauté for 2 to 3 minutes, until the mixture thickens and becomes fragrant. Gently fold in the crab meat and cook, uncovered, until the crab absorbs most of the liquid.

Add the rice and stock and cook, uncovered, for 5 to 7 minutes, until the liquid is mostly absorbed, shaking the pot gently every few minutes to prevent the rice from sticking.

Once the liquid is mostly absorbed, lower the heat to low and stir the rice gently, then put on the lid and cook for 20 minutes. Remove the lid and cook for another 15 to 20 minutes, gently stirring the rice every 5 to 10 minutes, until the rice is tender and fully cooked through. Serve with plantain and avocado on the side, if desired.

Island
Philippines

Yield
6 servings

Active Time
50 minutes

Total Time
1 hour

ARROZ CALDO
CHICKEN RICE PORRIDGE

This dish is Filipino comfort food, one your mom or auntie might prepare to cure a cold. As *Islas* contributor Jenn de la Vega says, for Filipinos, this is like chicken or matzo ball soup. Translated, *arroz caldo* means "brothy rice," and while the term is a nod to the country's history of Spanish colonization, it's been adapted with island techniques and flavors, like many other recipes in this book.

RICE

1 Tbsp vegetable oil

1 yellow onion, chopped

4 Tbsp minced peeled fresh ginger

3 garlic cloves, minced

One 3 to 4 lb [1.4 to 1.8 kg] whole chicken, cut into 8 pieces (see Tips)

2 Tbsp fish sauce

1 cup [190 g] jasmine rice (see Tips)

1 tsp ground turmeric

2 small [3.7g] chicken bouillon cubes, crushed, or 2 tsp powdered chicken bouillon

Kosher salt

Freshly ground black pepper

TOPPINGS

3 hard-boiled eggs, peeled and halved

¼ cup [30 g] homemade or store-bought crispy fried onions or shallots

2 or 3 green onions, white and green parts, thinly sliced on the diagonal

Lemon wedges, for serving

Fish sauce, for serving

To make the rice: In a large, heavy-bottomed pot with a lid over medium, heat the oil. Add the onion, ginger, and garlic and sauté for 3 to 5 minutes, stirring frequently, until softened and aromatic.

Add the chicken and cook, stirring frequently, for 5 to 7 minutes, until lightly browned and the juices are released. Add the fish sauce and cook for 1 minute more.

Pour in the rice and turmeric and cook, stirring frequently, for a couple of minutes, until the rice is lightly toasted. Add 6 cups [1.4 L] of water and the bouillon cubes and bring to a boil, stirring frequently and skimming any scum that floats to the top.

Lower the heat, cover, and simmer, stirring occasionally and skimming as needed, for 20 to 30 minutes, until the rice has broken apart and comes to the desired thickness, resembling porridge or congee. Using tongs, transfer the chicken to a large bowl. You can either shred the meat using two forks, discarding the bones (see Tips), or serve with whole chicken pieces.

Season the arroz caldo with salt and pepper. Ladle it into serving bowls, then top with some chicken. Garnish each portion with half a hard-boiled egg and some fried onions and green onions. Serve hot, with lemon wedges and fish sauce on the side.

TIPS You can substitute 4 lb [1.8 kg] bone-in chicken legs and thighs for a whole chicken. Dark meat will be more tender and has a richer flavor.

If shredding your chicken and it's too steamy, let it cool for at least 5 minutes.

You can replace jasmine rice with long-grain white rice.

Island
Cuba

Yield
6 to 8 servings

Active Time
1 hour 30 minutes

Total Time
2 hours 30 minutes

ARROZ CON POLLO
RICE WITH CHICKEN

Variations on arroz con pollo exist throughout Latin America, and it is a staple for home cooks across the region. There are countless variations—some folks use whole chicken legs, others prefer chunks of chicken breast. I like a lot of flavor in my arroz con pollo, which is reflected in this recipe. But the process lends itself to simpler preparations using store-bought powdered adobo in place of fresh, or a simple packet of sazón seasoning along with rice, olives, and frozen peas. The key to great arroz con pollo is to avoid stirring once the rice is in the pot, as it will make your rice gummy. Instead, carefully shake the pot during the cooking process to prevent the rice from sticking too much to the bottom. Although, a little pegao or concon—the toasted rice that sticks to the bottom of composed rice dishes—is welcome.

CHICKEN

3 large garlic cloves, minced

1 Tbsp kosher salt

1 Tbsp olive oil

2 tsp white vinegar

1½ tsp dried oregano

¼ tsp freshly ground black pepper

3 lb [1.4 kg] bone-in, skin-on chicken drumsticks and/or thighs (see Tip)

RICE

3 Tbsp olive oil

5 cups [1.2 L] low-sodium chicken broth

1 large yellow onion, diced

1 medium red bell pepper, seeded and diced

3 dried bay leaves

1 tsp ground annatto (achiote) or sweet paprika

1 cup [240 ml] tomato sauce

3 cups [600 g] medium-grain white rice, rinsed well

1 tsp kosher salt, plus more as needed

½ tsp freshly ground black pepper

¾ cup [115 g] medium pimento-stuffed olives, drained (optional)

2 cups [240 g] frozen peas, thawed

Avocado and tomato, sliced and salted, for serving

Lime wedges, for garnish

continued

To make the chicken: In a bowl, a small food processor, or a pilón (mortar and pestle), combine the garlic, salt, olive oil, vinegar, oregano, and pepper to make the marinade.

Pat the chicken dry, then place the pieces in a large container or resealable bag. Pour the marinade over the chicken. Toss well to combine, then cover or seal the bag and let the chicken marinate in the refrigerator for at least 30 minutes. If you have the time, marinate for several hours or overnight to make the chicken extra tender and flavorful.

To make the rice: In a large, heavy pot or Dutch oven over medium-high, heat the olive oil until it is shimmering. Working in batches if necessary, add the chicken pieces in a single layer and brown for 7 to 10 minutes per batch, turning several times to brown evenly. Transfer the pieces to a plate.

Meanwhile, in a medium saucepan, bring the broth to a boil. Lower the heat to keep at a simmer until ready to use.

Return the chicken to the pot, then add the onion, bell pepper, bay leaves, and annatto and stir well. Lower the heat to medium and sauté the vegetables for 7 to 10 minutes, until they begin to caramelize.

Add the tomato sauce and cook, stirring, for 3 to 5 minutes, until the sauce darkens. Add the rinsed rice, salt, and pepper, and fold in to ensure that the rice is fully coated and the chicken is evenly distributed.

Pour in the hot stock and olives (if using), then simmer, uncovered, over medium heat for about 15 minutes, stirring only two or three times and shaking the pot every few minutes to keep the rice level. (The liquid surrounding the rice will lower by about 1 in [2.5 cm].)

Once you start to spot lots of little bubbles on the surface but see no more pronounced liquid on top, cover with the lid, lower the heat to low, and cook until the rice is al dente, 15 to 20 minutes, shaking the pot a few times. Watch the rice very closely: The window between just right and overcooked is small and difficult to predict, but you'll become an expert at this over time. Once the liquid is almost entirely absorbed, sprinkle the peas on top.

To finish, gently stir the rice, bringing grains from the bottom to the top. Return the lid and let rest for 10 to 15 minutes before serving.

Serve with avocado and tomato slices and garnish with lime wedges. The dish keeps well in the refrigerator for 3 to 5 days.

TIP Boneless, skinless chicken thighs can be substituted for bone-in, skin-on chicken, but chicken breasts are not ideal, as white meat will dry out.

Island
Seychelles

Yield
4 servings

Active Time
45 minutes

Total Time
1 hour 30 minutes

BOUYON BRED
FRIED FISH SOUP WITH GREENS

This simple soup makes use of Seychelles's abundant fish and greens. Moringa, which also grows in the Philippines, is a staple leafy green on Indian Ocean islands. It can be difficult to source, though, and challenging to work with. If you can't find moringa, arugula is a good substitute, as is baby spinach—though the latter should be barely wilted once the soup is complete, so it still has some texture. And while this recipe calls for kingfish, mackerel, or salmon, any fatty fish makes a delicious swap. For a lighter approach, fresh tuna, swordfish, or mahi-mahi also work well.

2 bunches moringa, arugula, or spinach (about 4 cups [80 g]; see Tips)

1½ lb [680 g] fish fillets, preferably kingfish or mackerel, cut into bite-size pieces

Kosher salt

Freshly ground black pepper

Vegetable oil, for frying

1 medium white onion, thinly sliced

2 garlic cloves, smashed

1 tsp finely grated peeled fresh ginger

Steamed basmati rice, for serving

If using moringa leaves, pick them from their stems (see Tips). Place in a large bowl and cover with cold water until ready to use.

Season the fish with salt and pepper.

In a large, deep skillet over medium-high heat, pour enough oil to reach ½ in [13 mm] depth. Heat the oil to 375°F [190°C]. Add the fish pieces, working in batches so as not to overcrowd the skillet, and fry for 5 minutes, turning frequently, until golden brown. Remove from the oil with a slotted spoon and drain on paper towels.

In a large pot over medium, heat 1 Tbsp oil. Add the onion and sauté for 2 to 3 minutes, until translucent, then add the garlic and ginger, sautéing for 1 minute more, until fragrant. Add 4½ cups [1 L] of water (see Tips) and bring to a boil.

Meanwhile, drain and rinse the moringa. Add the leaves to the simmering broth along with the fried fish and stir gently to incorporate. Lower the heat and simmer for 10 to 15 minutes, until the moringa leaves become dark green and are fully wilted. Season with salt and pepper as needed and serve with steamed rice.

TIPS   Arugula and spinach do not need to be soaked before cooking.

Picking moringa leaves from their stems can be tedious. Employ a helper with this step.

Fish stock can be substituted for the water.

RICE AND PEAS

Among the most popular side dishes across the Caribbean is rice and legumes. Sometimes it's called rice and beans, sometimes moros y crisitanos, arroz con habichuelas, or arroz con gandules. In Jamaica, peas *are* beans, and this classic side is a standard accompaniment for Stewed Oxtail (page 78). The flavors of rice and peas are iconic to the island's dishes, blending coconut milk with thyme, scotch bonnet chiles, and allspice. This dish is also substantial enough to stand on its own.

1 cup [160 g] dried red kidney beans, rinsed and soaked overnight

2 tsp kosher salt, plus more as needed

1 cup [140 g] finely chopped yellow onion

4 garlic cloves, minced

2 green onions, white and green parts, finely chopped

4 whole allspice berries

6 fresh thyme sprigs

1 scotch bonnet pepper, stemmed, seeded to mitigate spiciness if desired, and chopped

2 dried bay leaves

1 tsp grated peeled fresh ginger

¼ tsp freshly ground black pepper, plus more as needed

1½ cups [360 ml] canned full-fat coconut milk, well shaken and stirred

2 cups [400 g] long-grain white rice

In a deep saucepan over medium-high, combine the beans and salt. Cover with water and bring to a boil.

Add the onion, garlic, green onions, allspice, thyme, scotch bonnet, bay leaves, ginger, pepper, and coconut milk and stir well to incorporate. Cover and lower the heat, then simmer for 45 minutes to 1 hour, stirring often, until the beans are tender.

Add the rice, stir well, then cover and simmer on medium-low until most of the liquid is absorbed and the rice is cooked through, 25 to 30 minutes. Do not stir while the rice is cooking, or it will become mushy. Remove from the heat and let sit for 7 to 10 minutes, covered, before serving.

Fluff the rice and peas with a fork, discarding the thyme stems, bay leaves, and allspice berries. Adjust seasoning as needed and serve hot.

Island
Puerto Rico

Yield
4 to 6 servings

Active Time
45 minutes

Total Time
50 minutes

ARROZ NEGRO CON PULPO Y CALAMARES
BLACK RICE WITH OCTOPUS AND SQUID

No doubt inspired by Spanish black paella, this distinctly humbler, quicker dish comes together with all shelf-stable ingredients and packs a lot of flavor. A deep, purply black, it's beautiful as a side dish or main. Replacing the tinned octopus ink with fresh squid ink brightens this dish, and the alcaparrado—a jarred blend of pimento-stuffed olives and capers, sold at most Latin American grocery stores—balances the fishy brininess.

1 Tbsp olive oil

One 6 oz [170 g] tin squid in ink, ink reserved

Two 4 oz [115 g] tins octopus in olive oil, drained

¼ cup [60 ml] jarred squid ink (see Tips)

½ cup [120 ml] alcaparrado (see Tips)

2½ cups [500 g] short-grain rice

5 cups [1.2 L] chicken broth or water

2 tsp kosher salt

1 tsp freshly ground black pepper

In a saucepan with a tight-fitting lid over medium, heat the olive oil. Sauté the squid and octopus for 5 minutes.

Add the reserved and jarred squid ink, alcaparrado, rice, broth, salt, and pepper. Increase the heat to medium-high and bring the liquid to a boil, then lower the heat to medium and simmer until the liquid has mostly evaporated. Stir the rice once, cover, and cook over very low heat for 30 minutes more, shaking the pot every 10 minutes.

Remove the pot from the heat and let sit for an additional 5 minutes. Fluff with a fork and serve.

TIPS Squid ink can be challenging to source in grocery stores but can be found in specialty or Italian grocery stores or purchased online.

If you can't source alcaparrado, substitute equal parts green pimento-stuffed olives and capers in brine.

Yield	Active Time	Total Time
6 to 8 servings	**1 hour 10 minutes**	**1 hour 10 minutes**

M'TSOLOLA

FISH, CASSAVA, GREEN BANANA, AND COCONUT STEW

This recipe, inspired by Hawa Hassan's adaptation of Ma Mariama's recipe from *In Bibi's Kitchen*, is simple to prepare, and despite having few ingredients, is surprisingly rich and flavorful. Fresh cassava and green banana are thinly sliced while the fish soaks in a quick citrus-lime marinade. Half the starches are layered, topped with marinated fish and red onions, then layered with more starches and smothered in coconut milk. M'tsolola will keep for several days in the refrigerator and also keeps very well in the freezer for several months.

2 to 3 red bird's eye or long green chiles, stemmed

1 Tbsp kosher salt, plus more as needed

3 large garlic cloves

⅓ cup [80 ml] fresh lime juice

2 lb [910 g] marlin or ahi tuna steaks (see Tips)

4 green bananas (see Tips), peeled and sliced into ½ in [13 mm] rounds, submerged in water until ready to use

2 lb [910 g] cassava, peeled and sliced into ½ in [13 mm] rounds, submerged in water until ready to use

Freshly ground black pepper

2 or 3 large shallots, diced (about ½ cup [26 g])

One 13½ oz [400 ml] can full-fat coconut milk, well shaken and stirred

Steamed white rice, for serving

In a mortar and pestle (or a food processor), combine the chiles and salt and grind to a paste. Add the garlic, one clove at a time, and grind it into the paste. Stir in the lime juice.

Place the fish in a large bowl or on a plate and rub it all over with the chile paste. Cover and set aside for 30 minutes at room temperature while you prepare the remaining ingredients.

Drain the green bananas and cassava, and place half of each in the bottom of a large Dutch oven. Sprinkle with salt and pepper and layer on the fish. Add the shallots, then cover with the remaining green bananas and cassava.

Pour the coconut milk into the pot, adding a bit of water if the coconut milk doesn't fully cover the ingredients. Bring to a boil, then lower to a medium simmer. Cover and cook for about 20 minutes, until the vegetables are soft but the fish is not overcooked.

Let sit for a few minutes off the heat before serving with steamed white rice.

TIPS Swordfish or halibut are good substitutes for the fish in this recipe.

Green bananas are distinct from unripe bananas. They are much closer in flavor and texture to green plantains, but with a more delicate flavor.

GIAMBO
OKRA FISH SOUP

This thick, luscious soup is deeply indebted to West African ingredients and cooking techniques, adapted to a uniquely Curaçaoan context. Aromatics such as onion and garlic, along with fresh thyme sprigs, are combined with whatever fresh seafood is available. This pared-down version starts with a simple, adaptable fish stock. The signature aspect of this dish is the abundant okra, which creates a one-of-a-kind broth that strings up like melted cheese when scooped out of the pot. And like so many other saucy dishes and stews in Curaçao, this one is served with funchi, the island's traditional semi-firm polenta cake.

FISH STOCK

1 lb [455 g] bone-in fish steaks, such as mahi-mahi or swordfish (see Tips)

1 Tbsp white vinegar

4 small shallots, halved

3 large garlic cloves

2 fresh thyme sprigs

1 celery stalk, snapped into three pieces

1 Tbsp Old Bay seasoning

1 tsp kosher salt

TIPS You can replace the fish steaks in the stock with 1 lb [455 g] mixed reserved seafood, such as fish heads and bones, or shrimp shells.

Use a ceramic-coated, cast-iron, or stainless-steel pot. Other metals can change the okra's color and flavor.

FUNCHI

3 cups [710 ml] cold water

1½ cups [210 g] fine cornmeal

1½ tsp kosher salt

GIAMBO

2 lb [910 g] whole okra, rinsed, dried, and sliced into 1 in [2.5 cm] rounds

½ lb [230 g] shrimp, peeled and deveined

8 to 10 oysters, removed from shells if fresh (liquid reserved), or jarred

1 tsp kosher salt, plus more as needed

½ tsp freshly cracked black pepper

To make the fish stock: In a medium nonreactive pot over high heat, combine the fish steaks, vinegar, shallots, garlic, thyme, celery, Old Bay, salt, and 2 qt [1.9 L] of water. Bring to a boil, then lower the heat and simmer for 30 to 45 minutes, until the broth has a deep, rich fish flavor.

To make the funchi: Butter an 8 in [20 cm] pie plate or square casserole dish just big enough to hold the funchi and set aside. In a medium saucepan over high heat, combine the water, cornmeal, and salt, whisking well to incorporate. Bring to a boil, stirring fairly continuously, and cook for 3 minutes. Lower the heat to medium-low and stir vigorously with a wooden spoon. Once the funchi is stiff and pulls away easily from the sides of the pot, remove from the heat. Transfer the funchi into the prepared dish, spreading gently into an even layer.

To make the giambo: In a large pot, place the okra. Strain the fish stock directly into the pot using a fine-mesh strainer, discarding the solids. Bring the stock to a simmer over medium-low heat and cook for 15 to 20 minutes, until the broth becomes thick and stringy. Increase the heat to medium-high, then add the shrimp and cook for 3 to 5 minutes, until the shrimp are cooked through but still tender. Add the oysters, salt, and pepper, stir well, then remove from the heat and let cool for 5 minutes.

Taste and adjust seasoning as needed. Pour into separate bowls. Slice the funchi into wedges and add a piece to each bowl.

Yield	Active Time	Total Time
4 servings	**30 minutes**	**1 hour 25 minutes**

PAPAYA STOBA
BRAISED GREEN PAPAYA STEW

A staple of Curaçao cuisine, this dish reflects layers of ancestral knowledge and island wisdom. Enzymes from papaya are nature's tenderizer, which resilient native communities have used for generations for a number of culinary and medicinal purposes. For papaya stoba, meat and vegetables are combined with papaya and slow-cooked into a stew. This Curaçaoan take on a classic beef stew is inspired by Kris Kierindongo, a native chef, artist, and farmer, and the founder of Vittle Art—an innovative, sustainable farm and restaurant space with a focus on celebrating Curaçaoan artists and cuisine. Be sure the papaya is very green, as green and ripe papayas taste and behave very differently.

1 small red onion, peeled and chopped

6 large garlic cloves, peeled

1 Tbsp fresh thyme leaves

1 Tbsp fresh cilantro leaves

2 tsp kosher salt, plus more as needed

1 Tbsp honey

2 Tbsp olive oil

1 lb [455 g] beef stew meat, cut into 2 in [5 cm] cubes

1 lb [455 g] green papaya, peeled, seeded, and cut into 2 in [5 cm] cubes

½ tsp freshly ground black pepper, plus more as needed

Steamed white rice or funchi (see page 167), for serving

Combine the onion, garlic, thyme, cilantro, and salt in a small food processor and chop into a loose paste. Add the honey and 1 Tbsp of the olive oil and pulse a few times to incorporate.

Transfer the paste to a large mixing bowl, then add the beef cubes and toss well with your hands to cover the meat.

Heat the remaining 1 Tbsp olive oil in a large, heavy-bottomed pot over medium-high heat. Add the beef and its marinade and cook for 7 to 10 minutes, turning the meat to ensure it is browned on all sides.

Add the papaya, lower the heat to low, cover, and simmer for about 1 hour, stirring occasionally, until the meat is tender and the papaya has partly broken down, forming a thick sauce. Add the pepper. Serve with steamed white rice or funchi.

Island
Madagascar

Yield
4 to 6 servings

Active Time
2 hours 30 minutes

Total Time
3 hours

ROMAZAVA

STEWED BEEF AND PORK BELLY WITH GREENS

This national dish of Madagascar epitomizes the simplicity and signature ingredients of the region. Fatty stew beef and pork belly are browned, then slow-simmered in a simple ginger and garlic–laced tomato sauce, with greens added at the end to balance the richness. Romazava is a very filling, stick-to-your-bones dish, typically paired with steamed white rice. While it might feel like a winter dish to those of us outside the tropics, rich, filling stews like this one are common across the region year-round—a way to make the most of tough meat, and a deeply nourishing meal for people relegated to hard work. It keeps for at least 1 week in the refrigerator and will deepen in flavor as it sits. It will keep in the freezer for at least 6 months.

1 lb [455 g] pork belly

1 lb [455 g] beef chuck roast, cut into 1 in [2.5 cm] pieces

Kosher salt

Freshly ground black pepper

2 Tbsp vegetable oil

1 large yellow onion, diced

5 garlic cloves, minced

2 Tbsp finely chopped peeled fresh ginger

1 or 2 jalapeños or serrano chiles, stemmed, seeded if desired to mitigate spiciness, and finely chopped

1 lb [455 g] ripe tomatoes, peeled and roughly chopped

1½ cups [360 ml] beef broth, plus more as needed

3 cups [60 g] leafy greens such as spinach, kale, or arugula

Steamed basmati rice, for serving

In two separate bowls, season the pork belly and beef with salt and pepper.

In a large, heavy-bottomed pot or Dutch oven over high heat, heat the oil until it is shimmering. Add the pork belly and sear both sides until browned and lightly caramelized, about 7 minutes total. Remove with a slotted spoon and set aside.

Add the beef pieces to the pot and sear in batches until browned on all sides. Remove with a slotted spoon and set aside. Add the onion to the pot and sauté for 5 to 7 minutes, until translucent, scraping up any bits of meat from the bottom with a spoon.

Add the garlic, ginger, and chiles and sauté for 1 minute more, until fragrant. Add the tomatoes and deglaze the pot, scraping up any browned bits stuck to the bottom. Return the beef and any accumulated juices to the pot. Pour in the broth and bring to a boil. Lower the heat, cover, and simmer for 1 hour.

Meanwhile, once the pork belly is cool enough to handle, cut it into 1 in [2.5 cm] pieces. Once the stew has simmered for 1 hour, stir in the pork belly, then cover and cook for 30 minutes. Remove the lid and cook for an additional 30 minutes, stirring occasionally, and adding additional stock or water as needed.

Cook for 2 hours, until the meat falls apart easily when pressed against the side of the pot with a wooden spoon. Add the greens and cook uncovered for 5 to 7 minutes, until fully wilted but still green. If you'd like your greens to be more tender, cook a little longer. Serve with steamed basmati rice.

Island
Haiti

Yield
6 to 8 servings

Active Time
30 minutes

Total Time
At least 3 hours

SOUP JOUMOU

Soup joumou is known as freedom soup for Haitians, who prepare it on January 1 to commemorate their independence from France in 1804. Inspired by author and cook Cindy Similien and adapted by *Islas* contributor Brigid Washington, this version is a hearty, flavorful stew of puréed squash brimming with beef and vegetables, seasoned with scotch bonnet chiles and epis (itself similar to Puerto Rican Sofrito [page 38]). Before independence, Haitians were forbidden to eat this stew, though they were forced to prepare it for their overseers. Today, it's a tradition that marks resilience, survival, and justice.

EPIS

1 yellow onion, chopped

10 to 12 garlic cloves, chopped

2 green onions, white and green parts, chopped

10 fresh thyme sprigs, left whole if stems are tender

2 cups [100 g] fresh parsley, stems and leaves coarsely chopped

1 scotch bonnet pepper, chopped

1 cup [240 ml] fresh orange juice

¼ cup [60 ml] fresh lime juice

1 Tbsp white sugarcane vinegar or white wine vinegar

1 Tbsp kosher salt

¼ tsp freshly ground black pepper

SOUP

1½ lb [680 g] boneless beef chuck or goat, cut into 1 in [2.5 cm] pieces

2 Tbsp vegetable oil

2 Tbsp tomato paste

2 large carrots, cut into ½ in [13 mm] pieces

1 large yellow onion, finely chopped

2 celery stalks, cut into ½ in [13 mm] pieces

2 lb [910 g] calabaza, pumpkin, or butternut squash, peeled and roughly chopped

3 fresh parsley sprigs, chopped

1 scotch bonnet pepper, stemmed, seeded if desired to mitigate spiciness, and minced

1 Tbsp kosher salt, plus more as needed

¼ tsp freshly ground black pepper

6 cups [1.4 L] water or low-sodium chicken broth

2 large Yukon gold potatoes, peeled and cut into 1 in [2.5 cm] chunks

½ small savoy cabbage, thinly shredded (about 3 cups [210 g])

2 green onions, white and green parts, sliced

1 tsp fresh thyme leaves

Lime wedges, for serving

Fresh bread and steamed white rice, for serving

continued

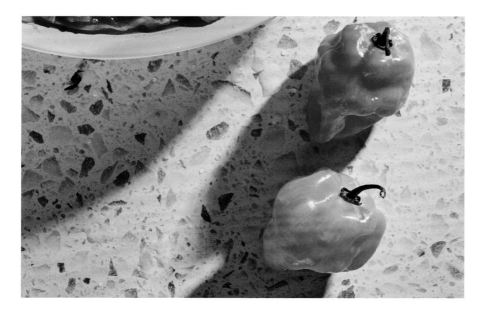

To make the epis: In a food processor, combine the onion, garlic, green onions, thyme, parsley, scotch bonnet, orange juice, lime juice, vinegar, salt, and pepper and grind into a loose paste.

To make the soup: In a large mixing bowl, combine ½ cup [120 ml] of the epis and the beef, mixing to evenly coat the meat. Cover and transfer to the refrigerator, marinating for at least 1 hour, or overnight if possible.

In a large, heavy-bottomed pot over medium-high, heat 1 Tbsp of the oil. Add the meat, including the marinade, and sauté for 3 to 5 minutes, turning often to brown. Add the tomato paste, lower the heat to medium, and cook for 5 minutes more, stirring often to evenly coat and caramelize the meat. Use a slotted spoon to transfer the beef to a medium mixing bowl.

Add the remaining 1 Tbsp oil, then add the carrots, onion, and celery and sauté for 2 to 3 minutes, until the onion becomes translucent. Add the calabaza, parsley, scotch bonnet, salt, pepper, beef and accumulated juices, and water or chicken broth, stirring well to incorporate and gently scraping the bottom to release

any browned bits. Bring to a boil, then cover, lower the heat, and simmer for 40 to 50 minutes, stirring often, until the beef starts to become tender.

Add the potatoes, cabbage, green onions, and thyme. Replace the lid and simmer for 25 to 30 minutes more, until the potatoes are fork-tender. Let sit off the heat for 5 to 10 minutes, then taste and adjust seasoning as needed. Serve with lime wedges and fresh bread or steamed white rice.

TIP   If desired, double the epis recipe and keep some in the freezer or refrigerator for a future meal. Leftover epis will keep in the refrigerator for up to 6 weeks or in the freezer for several months.

RADO AMBININTSOA
MADAGASCAR

By Sophia Ramirez

Wednesdays and Sundays are market days in Rado Ambinintsoa's village in Madagascar. That's when she prefers to do her shopping; it's cheaper, plus all kinds of vegetables are available on market days—carrots, cauliflower, pumpkins, leeks, peas, and leafy greens called anana—depending on the season. But regardless of what produce she brings home, all her meals have one thing in common: rice.

"My family and I eat rice thrice a day," she explains. "We eat rice with dried seeds, leafy greens . . . vegetables with beef or not, sauced or watery." Rice for breakfast, or for lunch with a salad; the list went on. She sent photos of her lunch that day: mutton stew served over rice with salad greens.

Rice is a staple food in many countries, but it's central to the national culture of Madagascar. The massive island has the highest per-capita consumption of rice in the world, and the crop is the subject of multiple festivals and rituals. *Mini-ham-bary* is the Malagasy verb literally meaning "to eat rice." But rice is so ubiquitous that the colloquial meaning has become "to eat a meal."

In Sandrandahy, the southern village where Rado lives, rice paddies dot the surrounding countryside, along with fields of peanuts, beans, cassava, and sweet potatoes. The community comes together to share their bounty on special occasions, she said. Some big ones are marriage, anniversaries, circumcisions, and famadihana, a funerary tradition where the dead are taken from their tombs to join their living relatives for a few hours of merriment. The remains are rewrapped in white cloths and mounted joyously on the shoulders of dancing family members.

"During the celebration of exhumation, people kill fat pigs and/or oxen and . . . feed their friends and neighbors greasy meats with huge quantities of rice," she said. "We call that food vary be menaka; *vary* means rice, *menaka* means grease." Rado works as an English language teacher at a public high school and often sprinkles translations from Malagasy into her messages.

When she was pregnant with her first child, Rado grew self-conscious about her diet. She had miscarried three times before and was worried that a meat-heavy routine was affecting her health. She said she's seen a lot of people who ended up sick because they ate a lot of meat, especially red meat. She even tried to change her diet for a time. "My husband and I have tried to be vegetarian," she said, "but we can't resist the smell of fried or cooked meat."

Alluring aromas aside, there's little flexibility within the Malagasy diet. More than a third of households lack adequate food at any given time. And most people depend on farmers' markets for fresh fruit and vegetables, as ongoing droughts make it difficult for people to cultivate their own vegetable gardens.

But rice will always sustain them, as it does millions of islanders across the planet. Rado often prepares the popular beverage ranon'apango. It looks like tea and has a bitter, earthy taste. But the root of this beverage is the rice left at the bottom of the pot after a meal. The Malagasy let a half-inch layer of rice toast until it's burnt and crispy, and then they pour boiling water over it. The result is a flavorful, caramel-colored liquid—and not a grain gone to waste. It's believed to have curative properties in addition to being a particularly effective form of hydration.

Despite the challenges faced by Rado and the Malagasy of her region, their cooking inspires a close look at what we actually need to sustain ourselves. In a place with such limited resources, burnt-rice tea is a symbol of ingenuity and a capacity to survive.

Yield	Active Time	Total Time
8 to 10 servings	**30 minutes**	**1 hour 30 minutes**

SANCOCHO
MEAT AND ROOT VEGETABLE STEW

Sancocho, a word often used as slang to mean "a big ol' mix of things," is an iconic stew eaten across the Caribbean with every imaginable combination of proteins and vegetables. In my family, my father made his with beef, corn, and noodles; my mom with chicken breasts, lean pork, and sweet plantains; my grandmother with beef and pork on the bone and yautía (taro). This recipe comes from Francisca Goris, a Dominican auntie (and *Islas* contributor Stephanie Rodriguez's mother), who lives in Queens, New York.

1 medium cassava (see Tip)

1 medium white yautía (taro root) (see Tip)

1 green plantain

1 green banana

2 large carrots

10 oz [280 g] peeled white potatoes, cut into 1 in pieces

10 oz [280 g] calabaza, pumpkin, or butternut squash

2 ears fresh sweet corn

1 lb [455 g] pork stew meat, trimmed of excess fat and cut into 2 in [5 cm] pieces

1 lb [455 g] beef stew meat, trimmed of excess fat and cut into 2 in [5 cm] pieces

1 lb [455 g] bone-in goat stew meat, trimmed of excess fat and cut into 2 in [5 cm] pieces

1 lb [455 g] boneless, skinless chicken thighs, trimmed of excess fat and cut into 2 in [5 cm] pieces

1 Tbsp kosher salt, plus more as needed

1 tsp freshly ground black pepper

1 Tbsp olive oil, plus more as needed

½ cup [120 ml] Sofrito (page 38)

10 cups [2.4 L] pork or beef stock

3 dried bay leaves

1 Tbsp Sazón Seasoning (page 39, or store-bought)

2 small [3.7 g] chicken bouillon cubes, or 2 tsp powdered chicken bouillon

Fresh bread or steamed white rice, for serving

Peel and cut the cassava, yautía, plantain, green banana, carrots, and potatoes into 1 in [2.5 cm] pieces. Scrape out the seeds, then chop the calabaza with its skin into 1 in [2.5 cm] pieces. Place each ingredient in a separate bowl, covering with water to prevent them from turning brown while you prepare the rest of the soup.

Husk the corn, then slice the cobs into 2 in [5 cm] segments; set aside.

Season the pork, beef, goat, and chicken with 2 tsp of the salt and ½ tsp of the pepper.

In a large pot over medium-high, heat the olive oil. Add the pork, beef, and goat in batches, and brown on all sides for 5 minutes. Transfer to a clean bowl with a slotted spoon, then add the chicken to the same pot and brown on both sides for 5 minutes, adding more oil as needed if the pot gets dry. Transfer with a slotted spoon to the same bowl as the other meat.

Lower the heat to medium and add the sofrito, scraping up any browned bits on the bottom of the pot with a wooden spoon. Cook for 5 to 7 minutes, until the liquid has evaporated and the mixture darkens in color.

Return all of the meat and any accumulated juices to the pot. Add the stock, bay leaves, sazón, bouillon, and the remaining salt and pepper and bring to a boil over high heat. Once simmering, lower the heat to medium-low and cook, uncovered, for 15 minutes, stirring occasionally.

Add the vegetables in order of firmness, cooking each for 5 minutes before adding the next. Begin with the cassava, then the yautía, green plantain, green banana, carrot, calabaza, potatoes, and corn;

the cassava will cook for 30 minutes and the corn for 5 minutes.

Cook for an additional 10 to 15 minutes over medium-low heat until the meat and vegetables are tender and break easily with a fork. Because of all the starches and meat in this dish, this stew tends to be thick and rich. Some of the vegetables will fall apart, giving it a porridge consistency. This is a good thing.

Adjust the seasoning as needed and serve with fresh bread or steamed white rice.

TIP   Cassava and yautía can be difficult to find in basic supermarkets, though you may be able to find them in the freezer section. Farmers' markets or Latin American, Caribbean, or Asian grocery stores are your best bet. There's no real substitute for the rich, earthy flavor of these tubers, but potatoes can be used. Reduce the cooking time by half if using potatoes.

Island
Curaçao

Yield
10 to 12 servings

Active Time
1 hour

Total Time
2 hours 30 minutes

KESHI YENA
STUFFED CHEESE

It's believed this dish emerged during the first Dutch colonial period in Curaçao, when enslaved cooks used the rinds of cheese their masters discarded, stuffed them with a blend of meat scraps and other ingredients, and baked it. The dish is still served in Curaçao, though prepared more simply by lining a round container with cheese and stuffing it with seasoned beef or chicken as well as raisins and olives.

FILLING

1 Tbsp olive oil

1 large yellow onion, chopped

1 red bell pepper, seeded and chopped

1 garlic clove, minced

1 Thai red chile, minced

2 lb [910 g] ground beef

3 ripe roma tomatoes, about 8 oz [227g], peeled and chopped

1 Tbsp capers (optional)

¼ cup [35 g] raisins (optional)

¼ cup [40 g] pimento-stuffed olives

1 Tbsp tomato paste

2 Tbsp ketchup

2 tsp Worcestershire sauce

1 Tbsp finely chopped fresh parsley

4 eggs

STUFFED CHEESE

2 Tbsp unsalted butter, at room temperature

2 lb [910 g] sliced Gouda (not smoked), Havarti, Muenster, or Monterey Jack cheese

TIP   Keshi yena should be enjoyed warm but keeps well in the refrigerator for up to 1 week, and in the freezer for up to 6 months. Reheat in the oven at 350°F [180°C] for 15 minutes for best results, fully defrosting first if frozen.

To make the filling: In a heavy-bottomed pot over medium, heat the olive oil. Sauté the onion and bell pepper for 3 to 5 minutes, until the onion is translucent, then add the garlic and chile and sauté for 1 minute longer. Add the beef and sauté for 5 minutes over medium heat, or until evenly browned. Add the tomatoes, capers (if using), raisins (if using), olives, tomato paste, ketchup, Worcestershire sauce, and parsley. Simmer for 20 minutes, then set aside and let cool.

To make the stuffed cheese: Meanwhile, butter ten to twelve oven-safe ramekins. Line each ramekin with enough cheese slices to fully cover the bottom and sides.

Preheat the oven to 350°F [180°C]. Prepare a water bath by putting 1 to 2 in [2.5 to 5 cm] of water in a deep rectangular casserole dish, and set aside.

When the filling is cool, beat the eggs and add to the mixture, stirring well to incorporate. Fill a cheese-lined ramekin with egg filling until there is about ½ in [13 mm] of room at the top, then cover the top with another piece of cheese, breaking apart slices as needed to cover completely but not fall over the top. Repeat for each ramekin.

Place the ramekins in the water bath, cover with foil, and bake for 1 hour. Carefully remove the pan and let sit for at least 5 minutes. Carefully remove each ramekin with tongs and transfer to a heat-proof surface. Let rest for at least 10 minutes before serving. Keshi yena can be eaten straight out of the ramekin or inverted onto a plate using a knife to separate the cheese from the edges of the ramekin.

ISLAS

Island
Martinique

Yield
6 servings

Active Time
20 minutes

Total Time
1 hour 20 minutes

LAMB COLOMBO

Lamb curries are a staple in many cultures, and this dish from Martinique features Colombo powder, a mild curry blend carried to the Caribbean by Sri Lankan laborers who were brought to work sugar plantations. Colombo powder, named for Sri Lanka's largest city, is widely used in Martinique, Guadalupe, and other French Caribbean islands. The spice blend traditionally includes toasted ground rice (which thickens as it flavors), brown mustard seeds, and fenugreek. This pared-down version uses allspice as well as cumin, coriander, turmeric, and black pepper. Most curry powders benefit from toasting and then grinding the seeds, but that's not necessary for this dish, where the subtlety of the spices is lost in the fatty gaminess of the lamb.

1½ lb [680 g] leg of lamb, trimmed of fat and cut into 1 in [2.5 cm] cubes

1 Tbsp kosher salt

1 tsp freshly ground black pepper

2 Tbsp vegetable oil, plus more as needed

1 yellow onion, finely chopped

1 bunch green onions, white and green parts, finely chopped

6 large garlic cloves, minced

2 Tbsp minced peeled fresh ginger

1 recipe Colombo Seasoning (page 40) (see Tip)

2 Tbsp tomato paste

1 Tbsp chopped fresh thyme leaves, or ½ tsp dried thyme

4 cups [945 ml] chicken broth, vegetable broth, or water, plus more as needed

1 lb [455 g] Yukon gold potatoes, peeled and cut into 1 in [2.5 cm] pieces (about 2 cups [475 ml])

1 lb [455 g] calabaza, pumpkin, or butternut squash, peeled, seeded, and cut into 1 in [2.5 cm] pieces (about 2 cups)

¼ cup [10 g] chopped fresh cilantro leaves, for garnish

Lime wedges, for serving

Steamed brown or white rice, for serving

TIP   Colombo powder is also available premade from various online vendors or at specialty Caribbean grocery stores.

Line a rimmed baking sheet with paper towels.

In a large mixing bowl, place the lamb and sprinkle 2 tsp of the salt and the pepper over, tossing well to ensure the meat is fully seasoned.

In a heavy-bottomed pot or Dutch oven over medium-high, heat 1 Tbsp of the oil, then brown the lamb in batches, turning every 2 to 3 minutes to brown evenly on all sides, adding more oil as needed between batches. Using a slotted spoon, transfer the browned meat to the lined baking sheet and allow to drain.

Lower the heat to medium, add the remaining 1 Tbsp of oil to the pot, and use a wooden spoon to scrape any browned bits from the bottom. Add the onion, green onions, garlic, and ginger and sauté, stirring frequently, for about 3 minutes, until the vegetables are softened but not browned. Add the Colombo powder and fry for about 1 minute, until fragrant.

Add the tomato paste and thyme and stir well to incorporate, then return the lamb to the pot and add the broth. Bring to a boil, then lower the heat and simmer uncovered for 1 hour, until the meat is starting to become tender.

Add the potatoes, calabaza, and the remaining 1 tsp salt. Stir well, cover, then increase the heat to medium and cook for 25 to 30 minutes, until the vegetables are easily pierced with a knife but not falling apart. If your stew is thicker than you'd like, add more broth to reach your desired consistency.

Garnish with cilantro and serve with lime wedges and steamed rice on the side.

Island
Madagascar

Yield
10 servings

Active Time
20 minutes

Total Time
45 minutes

VARY AMIN'ANANA
RICE WITH GREENS AND BEEF

When combined, rice, greens, and protein make for a perfectly satisfying meal. Among the flavorful, simple, and approachable recipes from Madagascar, this classic dish is filling, satisfying, and adaptable. Although not traditional, you can substitute ground pork, lamb, or venison if desired, adjusting the oil and cook time as needed.

1 Tbsp vegetable oil

1 large yellow onion, chopped

1 lb [455 g] ground beef

1½ tsp grated garlic

1½ tsp grated peeled fresh ginger

1 Tbsp kosher salt

½ tsp freshly ground black pepper

1 cup [180 g] diced fresh or canned tomatoes

1 lb [455 g] mixed greens (such as collards, spinach, and watercress), finely chopped

2 cups [400 g] long-grain white rice

Hot sauce, such as Lemon Lasary (page 96) or Pique (page 49), for serving

In a large pot over medium, heat the oil. Add the onion and sauté for 3 to 5 minutes, until it becomes translucent. Add the beef, garlic, ginger, 1 tsp of the salt, and pepper and cook, stirring, until the meat is fully cooked.

Add the tomatoes and greens, then lower the heat and simmer for 10 minutes, stirring constantly, until the greens are wilted.

Add the rice, 8 cups [1.9 L] of water, and the remaining 2 tsp salt and bring to a boil. Once boiling, cover, lower the heat, and simmer for 20 to 30 minutes, until the rice is cooked through but still slightly saucy, not fully reduced. Serve hot, with hot sauce on the side. This keeps well in the refrigerator for up to a week.

CHAPTER FOUR

FRYING

Curaçao

On the outskirts of the Caribbean Sea, closer to Venezuela than to Cuba or Jamaica, Curaçao lacks nothing for beauty, with coastlines and beaches, hidden coves and coral reefs. But its history has been defined by what it did not have when the Spanish first arrived in 1499: gold, jewels, or adequate conditions for cultivating sugar plantations. Because of this, the Spanish declared that Curaçao (and nearby Aruba and Bonaire) was useless—an *isla inutile*.

That's because Curaçao is a desert. While white-sand beaches and stunning bright blue seas are its trademark, the interior looks more like New Mexico than neighboring Caribbean islands. Much of the landscape is dusty, the color of toasted wheat, and instead of lush rainforests the foliage is a muted olive or hunter green, peppered with bursts of hot red flamboyant and delicate pink plumeria flowers. It's hot and dry, making irrigation a tremendous challenge.

Still, nature finds a way. Cacti abound, particularly native datu and kadushi—tall, cylindrical, and extremely spiny—which are commonly used to create natural fences but also in traditional dishes. Nopal cactuses also thrive, bursting with magenta prickly pears, alongside towering papaya and nispero (loquat) trees. Curaçao liqueur, perhaps the most iconic flavor of the island, stems from this environment. Spanish colonizers sought to grow Valencia oranges, but the arid climate turned the fruit small and exceedingly bitter. The fruit came to be known as laraha; peeled, dried, and blended with other spices it imparts warm orange notes with a subtle bitter finish to the island's namesake liqueur.

When Dutch settlers arrived in Curaçao, on the other hand, they were undaunted by this barren landscape. What they saw was a vast natural port—a resource they were quite skilled at exploiting—and by 1662 they had transformed the island into one of the primary hubs for the transatlantic slave trade. It served primarily as a trading post, where enslaved people would disembark and be redirected to their final destinations in the Americas. Approaching the capital of Willemstad by sea today, the tangerine and baby pink of its buildings ricochet off cerulean waters, marking the Dutch colonial culture that would come to dominate Curaçao's history and remains a governing body to this day.

The influence of African culture is incredibly visible and celebrated on the island, particularly in its most traditional dishes. Nothing is perhaps as exciting for locals than a plate piled high with whole fried fish: lionfish, parrotfish, triggerfish—whatever is fresh, typically dusted with flour and deep-fried in plenty of oil. Most traditional restaurants offer similar sides: avocado salad, rice and beans (arros moro), fried plantains, and funchi or tutu. Funchi is fine cornmeal that's vigorously whipped with hot water then set into a round mold. It's similar to fufu—the African staple made of pounded starch. Tutu starts like funchi, but is then blended with stewed black-eyed peas, often with added sugar, and sometimes cinnamon. This combination of fried fish and cornmeal follows African communities across the globe, from fish and grits in the American South to Fish and Fungi (page 210) in St. Croix.

And while African culture is prominent, many more communities call Curaçao home, leading to the formation of their distinct language, Papiamento, which contains elements of Portuguese, English, Spanish, French, Dutch, and Arawak Indian and African languages. The faces of Curaçaoan people are equally diverse, the embodiment of centuries of complex history. They are deeply proud of their island's culture—and its food.

Curaçao's signature dishes read like a history book. Papaya Stoba (page 168) is reminiscent of a classic British or German beef stew, but with added green papaya—reflecting what grows on the island, and a natural tenderizer. Giambo (page 167), an okra-rich seafood soup, is an evolution of kadushi—a layered salted beef and seafood stew developed by African workers, which utilized plentiful local cadushi (or kadushi) cactus before okra could be grown. Today both are treasured by Curaçaoans from all walks of life (in part because it's believed to increase . . . stamina). And then there's Keshi Yena (page 179), a dish many attribute to the first Dutch colonial period, when enslaved cooks used the rinds of Gouda and Edam cheeses their enslavers discarded as a creamy casing for meat scraps, then baked them. Even Pika (page 98) is fiery hot, a blend of raw onions—beloved by the Dutch—and the scotch bonnet and habanero chiles that are plentiful across the Caribbean. These dishes can all be found in local eateries, from the sneks to high-end restaurants today.

FRY

Deep-frying has diminished in popularity in recent years, as nutritionists often attribute high cholesterol and other health issues to a diet high in fried foods. But deep-frying is an age-old cooking technique with deep roots on the African continent and a way of cooking that enslaved people brought to many islands in the Caribbean. In that way, it will always be a marker of African culture in the region, and an important one, because deep-frying is incredibly adaptable, and always (when done properly) delicious. Oil—especially that extracted from peanuts, corn, seeds, coconuts, or palms—can be heated to extremely high temperatures, critical for generations of island cooks who had only open fires to cook with, which makes temperature control difficult. And if you've ever eaten a leftover piece of fried chicken, you know it's also an excellent method for preserving food. In addition, oil can be reused many times—adding another layer of flavor to what's being fried.

Many of the recipes in this chapter reflect the profound influence of African culture throughout the tropics, notably in the Caribbean, which bore the brunt of the transatlantic slave trade. But it's far from exclusive to that region, and frying is used to different ends across the tropics. Deep-frying in lots of oil is essential for fried doughy snacks, such as Jamaican Festival (page 196), Samoan Panikeke Lapotopoto (page 199), and Malagasy Mofo Anana (page 202), as well as frying whole fish (page 219) and chicken wings (page 194). Frying is also used to add dimension to braised meat, as in Haitian Griot (page 215) and Filipino Lechon Kawali (page 223). It's also a great method for preparing starchy vegetables, such as Maldivian Fried Yams (page 212) and Cuban green plantain Tostones (page 213). The key to good frying is timing and attention, and it typically involves more oil than you think. Fried food is beloved—and addictive. In Puerto Rico, I'm guaranteed to burn my mouth on steaming-hot Alcapurrias de Jueyes (page 220) out of sheer impatience.

However common and beloved fried food is, it can be daunting to prepare at home. It requires a lot of oil, which you must let cool and then store for re-use or dispose of. And it will make your house smell like fried food for days, particularly with fish. But with the right tools, and a plan for oil disposal and odor control, this may become your favorite way to prepare delicious, crispy snacks and dishes.

CHOOSING THE RIGHT OILS

The most crucial decision when choosing the right kind of oil for frying is the smoke point, which is the temperature at which the oil itself starts to burn. If you've ever left olive oil in a pan on high heat for too long, you may have noticed it smoking and developing a bitter, burnt aroma. Most commercial vegetable oils have a smoke point of at least 400°F [200°C] and are fairly interchangeable.

Vegetable and canola oil • Smoke point: 400°F [200°C]—Easily the most widely available varieties, these oils are equally good for most basic cooking and are also used for preparing baked goods.

Corn, peanut, and soybean oil • Smoke point: 450° F [230°C]—These oils are commonly used across the tropics, though they are perhaps less popular in the United States. They are ideal for deep-frying, particularly ingredients that cook more quickly at a higher heat.

Grapeseed oil • Smoke point: 450°F [230°C]—This oil is ideal for high-heat stir-frying, as it's light-bodied and has a neutral flavor. It is typically much costlier than other vegetable oils.

Ghee • Smoke point: 475°F [245°C]—Ghee, which is clarified butter, is a staple for frying onions, spices, and other ingredients for curries, which abound on Indian Ocean islands. It has a very distinct flavor that's a bit funkier than regular butter and adds a velvety richness to dishes. It's also excellent for frying potatoes.

FRYING TOOLS

Having the right tools takes a lot of the anxiety out of frying. You don't necessarily want to use your best pans or utensils, because you're working with high heat and greasy oil, which can damage delicate implements. In my kitchen, I have a wok and several tongs dedicated exclusively to frying, which, in addition to protecting my tools, ensures consistent timing for my fried dishes.

Deep fryers: There are many affordable home deep fryers on the market. They are excellent tools for keeping your oil at a consistent temperature.

Woks: Nonstick wide woks are perfect tools for deep-frying. A wok is my preferred tool for frying whole fish. A wok can be challenging to fit on the stove with other pots, particularly once you start frying. Unless you buy a large one, though, it's typically best suited for cooking in small batches.

Candy thermometer: This little tool is critical for testing your oil temperature, which can mean the difference between something being quickly burnt, undercooked, or just right.

Splatter guard: This is a must, as oil frequently sputters and pops when introducing ingredients.

Metal tongs: Useful for stirring, adding ingredients to a pot of hot oil, and pulling things out of the oil.

Spider: This handheld strainer enables you to move things around in the oil and drain them as you scoop them out.

Paper towels: Have plenty on hand for cleaning up spills and letting fried foods drain.

Small fine-mesh strainer and funnel: Use these to transfer used oil to a storage or disposal container.

GOOD THINGS TO FRY

Hearty vegetables: cauliflower, corn, eggplant, mushrooms, okra, peppers, zucchini

Starches: potatoes, cassava, breadfruit, sweet potatoes, yams, pumpkin

Aromatics: onions, shallots, garlic

Fritters: doughy and stuffed snacks

Bone-in chicken: especially wings

Fatty meat: such as pork belly

Seafood: most seafood, including fish, shrimp, and oysters

TROUBLESHOOTING

• Be confident when you introduce an ingredient to your oil. Always gently place or slide food into simmering oil, using tongs or a fork if you're worried about burns. People often get scared, which leads to dropping things in the oil, causing splatters and burns—or, worse, spills that can cause a grease fire.

• Keep your splatter guard handy. Even one drop of water or the sweat from your brow can make your oil get wild.

• Line a baking sheet or plate with paper towels to drain and rest your ingredients. This is important (even when you're adding fried ingredients to a dish such as Bouyon Bred [page 159]), as it prevents the ingredients from overcooking in hot oil and drains off excess oil so your dish is not too greasy.

• Have a vessel ready to transfer your oil into after you're done cooking and the oil has fully cooled. Never pour oil down the drain, as it will clog your pipes.

• Fry oil can be reused multiple times. For breaded items and fritters, three or four times is the maximum recommended, as small amounts of sediment can accumulate after multiple uses and may burn. Otherwise, depending on the seasoning used, it's safe to reuse fry oil eight or nine times. Personally, I let my nose indicate if my fry oil is still good: If it has a funky or rancid smell, don't use it.

• There's no real way to fully avoid the lingering smell of fried food in your home. But I recommend closing doors to other rooms, opening windows, and using ceiling and floor fans as well as the exhaust hood above your stove. Typically I also light incense, as I find it blends well with fry smell and makes it more pleasant.

JOSEFINE MARTINA
CURAÇAO

Josefine Martina is the owner of Jojo-Ala, a popular snack shop (or snek, as it's known in Curaçao) in Pariba, an area just outside of the capital where many formerly enslaved people resettled after emancipation. The region is relatively rural, with single-lane roads, low hills, and grasslands peppered with low-lying dry brush—and, like much of Curaçao, it is akin to a desert. There, Josefine lives among her family, and has left the island only once, decades ago, to work in Sint Maarten for a short time. Their cluster of homes, while modern, are reminiscent of the compounds created by their indigenous and African ancestors.

As a resourceful and deeply independent person (she never married and has no children), Josefine has always wanted to work for herself, and opening Jojo-Ala was the key. Josefine had never thought of owning a restaurant and doesn't consider herself a particularly good cook. But her business came about because of her deep love for her people and a desire to do something steady and long-term that would be of and for Curaçao.

Jojo-Ala started as a bar that primarily served cocktails. One day, Josefine decided to start making chicken wings—not for sale, just to offer customers to keep them happy. Although fried chicken wings are perhaps not as popular in Curaçao as they are in other parts of the world, she has a secret spice blend (her grandmother's) and a special frying technique that produces phenomenally flavorful, crispy chicken. Her wings quickly became so popular that she switched gears and made them her thing.

The process is complex. Starting at 4:00 a.m., whole chicken wings, drumettes, and flats get tossed in Grandma's seasoning and are left to marinate for at least a day. Then Josefine pulls the previous day's batch out of the freezer and fills five deep pots halfway with vegetable oil. For the rest of the day, she's frying wings; batch by batch, starting in the first fryer, then moving to another hot fryer, and another if needed for optimal browning and crispiness. Folks drop by throughout the day, enjoying their wings, lingering late into the evening for drinks and conversation.

As with Josefine's wings, deep-frying with a skillful hand leads to a browned, crisped exterior that seals in flavor while keeping the insides juicy. And like other fried dishes on the island, her wings blend flavor with ancestry and resilience and are deeply tied to the island's complex past.

Josefine, ironically, doesn't even like chicken wings—she prefers more traditional Curaçaoan dishes like stewed saltfish. She says she'll retire someday and pack up the deep fryers that have been steadily sizzling for decades. But until then, Jojo-Ala will be open for a snek, a beer, and a long conversation with a lovely soul who embodies the complexities of her beloved island home.

RECORDS

JOJO-ALA CHICKEN WINGS

Using her grandmother's secret recipe, Josefine's flavorful wings are double-fried crispy. This recipe is an adaptation of hers, and also inspired by takeout lemon-pepper wings in my hometown of Atlanta. Deep-frying is among the ancestral techniques that are widely used in many African cuisines, and it was disseminated among communities of enslaved workers across the Americas and the Caribbean. While it's often considered a less healthy way of cooking, it has deep historical and cultural roots, and also reflects the ingenuity and resilience of people who developed methods for cooking over open fire using abundant oil and heavy pots.

SEASONING

2 Tbsp ground ginger

2 Tbsp sweet paprika

2 Tbsp onion powder

2 Tbsp garlic powder

2 Tbsp chicken bouillon powder

2 Tbsp dried lemon peel or lemongrass

2 Tbsp kosher salt

1 Tbsp smoked paprika

1 Tbsp Adobo Seasoning (page 39)

1 Tbsp dried oregano

1 Tbsp sugar

2 tsp ground annatto (achiote)

2 tsp cayenne pepper, plus more as needed

2 tsp freshly ground black pepper

CHICKEN WINGS

¾ cup [105 g] rice flour

4 lb [1.8 kg] chicken wings, tips trimmed (see Tips)

Vegetable oil, for frying

Lemon wedges and hot sauce, for serving

To make the seasoning: In a medium bowl, combine the ginger, sweet paprika, onion powder, garlic powder, chicken bouillon powder, lemon peel, salt, smoked paprika, adobo seasoning, oregano, sugar, annatto, cayenne, and black pepper and stir well with a fork to incorporate. If possible, transfer the mixture to a shaker, such as a repurposed spice bottle (see Tips).

To make the chicken: In a large bowl, combine the rice flour with 3 Tbsp of the seasoning mixture.

Dry the wings with paper towels. Transfer to a large bowl and sprinkle 2 Tbsp of the seasoning mixture on the wings. Let sit at room temperature while you prepare the oil.

In a deep fryer or deep wok, pour enough oil until it reaches the maximum allowed for the fryer, or at least 3 in [7.5 cm]. Heat the oil over medium-high until it is shimmering and reaches 375°F [190°C].

Line a large baking sheet with paper towels.

Just before frying, working in batches, dredge the wings in the seasoned rice flour. Fry the wings in batches, being careful not to crowd the fryer, until golden brown, 8 to 10 minutes. Transfer the wings to the paper towels.

Once all the wings have been fried, return them to the hot oil in batches and fry until deeply golden brown and crispy, being careful not to burn, 5 to 7 minutes more. Add more paper towels to the baking sheet as needed to drain the wings.

While the wings are still hot, transfer them to a clean, large bowl and generously sprinkle with more of the seasoning mixture—start with about ¼ cup [30 g], toss, then add another ¼ cup [30 g] to fully coat. Use less if you'd like a lighter flavor. Serve hot, with lemon wedges and hot sauce on the side.

TIPS   Josefine typically marinates her wings overnight using her grandmother's secret recipe, leaving them out to thaw for about 8 hours before frying. Add this extra step to boost the flavor if desired.

Whole chicken wings are preferred for this recipe, but you can also cut the wings into flats and drumettes if desired. This will shorten the cook time by a few minutes and stretch the recipe to serve more.

The recipe will likely yield more seasoning than you will use. Store leftovers in an airtight container in the pantry for future use.

FESTIVAL
JAMAICAN FRIED DOUGH

This classic Jamaican fried bread is sweet and filling, perfect for a quick snack or to pair alongside saucy dishes such as Stewed Oxtail (page 78). This recipe is inspired by Vivienne Monica Washington, *Islas* contributor Brigid Washington's mother-in-law, who lives in Kingston, Jamaica.

1 cup [140 g] all-purpose flour

2 Tbsp granulated sugar

2 Tbsp cornmeal

1½ tsp baking powder

¼ tsp kosher salt

⅛ tsp ground allspice

1 Tbsp unsalted butter, at room temperature

1 tsp vanilla extract

⅓ cup [80 ml] milk or water

2 cups [475 ml] vegetable oil, for frying

In a medium mixing bowl, combine the flour, sugar, cornmeal, baking powder, salt, and allspice and blend with a fork. Add the butter and use your hands to incorporate it until the mixture resembles small peas.

Add the vanilla and then slowly pour in the milk. Knead the mixture together with your hands to form a dough, using more milk or water as needed so that it is firm but not sticky. Cover the bowl with plastic wrap and allow the dough to rest for about 30 minutes.

Once rested, dust a workspace with flour and separate the dough into 7 or 8 equal-size pieces. Using your hands, roll each piece into an even 4 to 5 in [10 to 13 cm] log.

Line a baking sheet with paper towels.

In a deep skillet over medium, heat the oil until it shimmers and reaches 350°F [180°C] on a candy thermometer. Auntie trick: Test the temperature of the oil by adding a small piece of dough; it's ready once it sizzles and rises to the surface.

Gently add each festival and fry for 3 to 4 minutes on each side, or until evenly golden brown, 6 to 8 minutes total. Work in batches as needed so as not to crowd the pan. Once the festivals are cooked through, remove with a slotted spoon and place them on the paper towels to drain and cool slightly. Serve warm.

Island
Seychelles

Yield
25 fritters

Active Time
1 hour

Total Time
At least 6 hours

GATO PIMA
LENTIL CHILE FRITTERS

This is recipe developer Jenn de la Vega's favorite recipe in *Islas*. Gato pima come together easily and freeze particularly well. You can fry them straight from the freezer and eat them like you might falafel on salads, wrapped up in a burrito, or garnished with Spiced Yogurt Sauce (page 46).

1¾ cups [350 g] split red lentils (see Tip)

3 red bird's eye chiles, seeded if desired to mitigate spiciness, finely chopped

1 medium white onion, minced

1 bunch fresh cilantro, leaves and stems, finely chopped

1 tsp grated peeled fresh ginger

4 garlic cloves, minced

1 Tbsp cumin seeds

10 curry leaves, finely chopped

2½ tsp kosher salt

½ tsp freshly ground black pepper

¼ tsp ground cinnamon (optional)

5 Tbsp [50 g] all-purpose flour, plus more as needed

Vegetable oil, for frying

TIP Split yellow lentils can be substituted for the red lentils.

Rinse the lentils, then cover with water by a couple of inches and soak for 4 to 6 hours or overnight.

Drain the lentils in a fine-mesh sieve and rinse once more, then drain for 30 minutes. Add the lentils to a large food processor and grind into a coarse paste, adding 1 Tbsp of water at a time until the mixture is smooth but not watery.

Transfer the lentils to a large mixing bowl. Add the chiles, onion, cilantro, ginger, garlic, cumin seeds, curry leaves, salt, pepper, and cinnamon (if using). Gradually add 1 Tbsp of flour at a time until you have a thick paste that is still a bit moist, using about 5 Tbsp—though you may need slightly less or even more flour, so keep extra handy.

Line a baking sheet with parchment or wax paper.

Roll the mixture into rough 1 in [2.5 cm] balls, then transfer to the prepared baking sheet and refrigerate until ready to fry. You'll have about 25 balls.

In a large, deep frying pan, pour enough oil to reach 1½ in [4 cm]. Heat the oil over medium-high until it reaches 350°F [180°C]. Test the oil temperature by using a candy thermometer or adding a small piece of dough to the oil; it'll sizzle and rise to the surface if it's ready. Meanwhile, line a baking sheet with paper towels.

Fry the gato pima in batches, being careful not to overcrowd the pan, for 4 to 5 minutes on each side, turning as needed to ensure even browning and moving them around in the oil so they don't stick together. If the fritters start to brown too quickly, lower the heat.

Once the fritters turn a uniform golden brown, remove them from the oil with a slotted spoon and drain them on the paper towels. The fritters should be golden and crunchy on the outside and soft, fluffy, and moist on the inside. Serve hot if possible, though they are also delicious at room temperature.

PATES
FRIED MEAT TURNOVERS

These small, delightful fritters are a St. Croix staple. Pates can be made in any shape, but this recipe calls for crescents. While forming the pates, be sure to keep the dough moist by covering it with a slightly damp kitchen cloth.

4 cups [560 g] all-purpose flour

3 tsp kosher salt

2 tsp baking powder

2 tsp sugar

½ cup [90 g] shortening, chopped into pieces and chilled

1¾ cups [415 ml] cold water

3 Tbsp olive oil

1 yellow onion, chopped

1 green or yellow bell pepper, seeded and diced

1 celery stalk, diced

7 garlic cloves, minced

½ cup [24 g] chopped green onion, white and green parts

1 Tbsp fresh thyme leaves

1 tsp dried parsley

½ scotch bonnet pepper, seeded if desired to mitigate spiciness, minced

½ tsp freshly ground black pepper

Zest and juice of 1 lime

1 Tbsp tomato paste

1 lb [455 g] ground beef

3 cups [710 ml] vegetable oil, for frying

TIP To test if a pate is cool enough to eat, bite off a corner. If the steam emitted is too hot for your lips, give it another minute or you'll burn your tongue. Blow on it if you're impatient.

In a large mixing bowl, combine the flour, 2 tsp of the salt, baking powder, and sugar and mix well with a fork. Add the shortening and water and mix until evenly incorporated, with the texture of peas.

Transfer the mixture to a work surface and knead well for 1 minute. Cover with a clean kitchen towel and let rest at room temperature for 1 hour.

In a large sauté pan over medium-high, heat the olive oil. Add the onion, bell pepper, celery, garlic, green onion, thyme, parsley, scotch bonnet, remaining 1 tsp salt, pepper, lime zest, and lime juice. Cook until the vegetables are translucent and soft, 5 to 7 minutes. Add the tomato paste and cook, stirring, for another 3 to 5 minutes.

Lower the heat to medium, then add the beef and cook, breaking it up with a spoon, until the meat is browned, 10 to 12 minutes. Remove from the heat.

Dust a surface with flour, then roll out the dough ⅛ in [3 mm] thick. Using a 5 or 6 in [13 or 15 cm] diameter bowl or a dough cutter, cut circles out of the dough, setting them aside. Gather up the scraps, roll again, and cut until all the dough is used.

Ready a small bowl with ice water, then place about 2 Tbsp of meat filling in the center of each dough circle. Brush the edges of the dough with ice water and fold the dough in half over the filling, forming a half-moon. The pastry should be filled. Using a fork, press down the edges.

In a large pot over medium heat, heat the vegetable oil until the temperature reaches 325°F [165°C]. Meanwhile, line a plate with paper towels.

Working carefully, add the pates one at a time to the oil and fry for 3 or 4 minutes, turning a few times. The pates should rise to the surface and turn golden brown. Using a slotted spoon, remove the pates from the oil and let cool for a few minutes on the lined plate before eating.

Island
Samoa

Yield
12 panikeke

Active Time
20 minutes

Total Time
20 minutes

PANIKEKE LAPOTOPOTO
SAMOAN ROUND PANCAKES

While "pancake" is the easiest translation for this dish, these are not your traditional breakfast treats. More like Dutch poffertjes, these small, round fritters are lightly sweetened and delightfully dense. Very similar to Jamaican Festival (page 196), they're substantial and filling. Add a little mashed ripe banana and a dusting of ground cinnamon for a fruity variation.

2 cups [240 g] sifted all-purpose flour, plus more as needed

½ cup [100 g] superfine granulated sugar

2 tsp baking powder

¼ tsp kosher salt

1 egg, at room temperature

½ cup [120 ml] milk

Vegetable oil, for frying

Confectioners' sugar, for dusting (optional)

In a stand mixer fitted with the paddle attachment, combine the flour, sugar, baking powder, salt, egg, and milk and mix into a thick batter.

In a large pan, pour enough oil to reach 3 in [7.5 cm]. Heat the oil over medium until it reaches 350°F [180°C], using a candy thermometer to determine the exact temperature. The heat level is crucial, as too high a temperature will leave the panikeke raw inside, and too low will make them greasy.

Form balls of dough with two large tablespoons, using one to scoop the batter and the other to push it into the hot oil, forming them one by one and frying them in batches, four to five at a time, for 3 to 5 minutes, until golden brown. The balls should turn themselves in the oil; if not, give them a little nudge with a fork or chopstick to ensure even frying.

Enjoy hot or warm, dusted with confectioners' sugar if desired.

Island
Madagascar

Yield
28 fritters

Active Time
15 minutes

Total Time
35 minutes

MOFO ANANA
MALAGASY SPICED FRY BREAD

Similar to Gato Pima (page 197), these flavorful fried dumplings are a great snack but can also be eaten atop a salad or in a wrap. This recipe uses sambar powder, a curry blend that incorporates ground lentils; garam masala is a good substitute.

2 cups [280 g] all-purpose flour

1 Tbsp kosher salt, plus more as needed

½ tsp freshly ground black pepper

1 tsp sambar powder or garam masala

1 tsp baking soda

1 cup [30 g] finely chopped baby spinach or arugula

3 to 4 long green chiles, seeded if desired to mitigate spiciness, finely chopped

1 cup [140 g] finely chopped white onion

1 cup [160 g] finely chopped tomato

About 6 cups [1.4 L] vegetable oil, for frying

In a large mixing bowl, combine the flour, salt, pepper, sambar powder, and baking soda and mix well with a fork to fully incorporate. Add the spinach, chiles, onion, and tomato and fold to fully incorporate. Slowly add ¼ cup [60 ml] of water, mixing the batter with your hands or a rubber spatula, until it forms a thick paste.

Pour the oil into a deep skillet or Dutch oven until it reaches about 3 in [7.5 cm] deep, and heat over medium-high until it reaches 300°F [150°C]. Test the oil temperature by using a candy thermometer or dropping in a small piece of batter; it will sizzle and rise to the top when the oil is hot enough.

Meanwhile, line a baking sheet with paper towels.

Lower the heat to medium, then drop in 1 Tbsp of the batter at a time, in batches, being careful not to crowd the pot. Cook, turning frequently, until golden brown, 2 to 3 minutes each. Remove the fritters from the oil with a slotted spoon and transfer to the paper towels to drain. Serve hot.

Island
Haiti

Yield
10 fritters

Active Time
20 minutes

Total Time
30 minutes

AKRA
BLACK-EYED PEA FRITTERS

Also spelled *akara* or *accra*, this West African dish traveled to the Caribbean and Latin America during the transatlantic slave trade. Though it has a number of variations, most often its main ingredients are flour, cowpeas or black-eyed peas, and sometimes saltfish. This dish carries deep spiritual significance for many religious communities connected to the Yoruba people and is traditionally fried in red palm oil and prepared as an offering to certain orishas (Yoruba deities).

1 cup [165 g] black-eyed peas, soaked overnight and drained

½ cup [70 g] chopped red onion

1 scotch bonnet pepper, stemmed and chopped

½ cup [24 g] chopped green onions, white and green parts

1 egg, gently whisked

1 tsp kosher salt, plus more as needed

About 2½ cups [600 ml] vegetable oil, for frying

In a large food processor, combine the black-eyed peas, onion, scotch bonnet, and green onions and blend, adding 1 tsp of water at a time until completely smooth but not watery. Transfer to a medium mixing bowl, then add the egg and salt and mix well to incorporate.

Pour the oil into a large, deep skillet until it's at least ½ in [13 mm] deep. Heat over medium-high until hot but not smoking, about 375°F [190°C]. Meanwhile, line a baking sheet with paper towels.

Once the oil is hot, gently add spoonfuls of the batter and fry in batches until golden brown, 2 to 3 minutes each, turning once. Don't overcrowd the pan, as it will lead to soggy akra. Remove from the oil with a slotted spoon to the paper towels, drain, and serve hot.

TIP   A single wooden chopstick is a great tool for turning fritters in oil.

ISLAS

BADRU DEEN
TRINIDAD AND TOBAGO

By Sophia Ramirez

"Doubles, doubles!" Calls to action radiate from the roadside stands on practically every corner in Trinidad and Tobago. Under the canopies, sticky dough is fried into soft, pillowy flatbreads and topped with a saucy chickpea curry called chana. In two or three deft motions, chutneys and pepper sauces are spooned onto the chana and your doubles are up, served on white paper. They're eaten on the spot, using the remaining fried bread to scoop up the fallen chana. This is the island's number one street food.

Given their ubiquitous nature, you might assume this dish has a long history in Trinidad and Tobago. But in truth, they've been around for less than a century. According to Badru Deen, author of *Out of the Doubles Kitchen*, an Indian couple who arrived in Trinidad as indentured servants in the 1930s started selling a sort of doubles prototype out of a box on a bike. The snack sold for one cent. It was a brave attempt to escape the poverty that plagued post-indentured Indians in Trinidad and Tobago.

"It was, in a sense, a silent act of resistance," said Badru. "A protest against the colonial economic system of labor exploitation and subservience, in the miserable living conditions of abject poverty created by indentureship."

This Indian couple, Emamool and Rasulan Deen, were Badru's parents, and his memoir is a meticulous record of his family—the family who changed the culinary legacy of Trinidad and Tobago forever.

"The indomitable will of this husband-and-wife team to nurture their vision and withstand the early ridicule, shame, and stigma attached to street vending is a living testament of Emamool and Rasulan's unwavering courage to change the eating habits of a cruel society," said Badru. "Doubles in Trinidad are now a metaphor for human creativity in transcending one's social circumstances."

The family's ambition is magnified in Badru. You can now find doubles in some major US cities, and he wants to bring them into the mainstream.

But his version of events is not without opposition. After his father passed, Badru said others—including his uncle—started laying claim to the invention of doubles. "So I wrote a book about it just to prove that point and to give credit where credit was due," Badru says.

Badru's parents were illiterate, but they were responsible for his education. In desperate times, they stole Badru a two-volume dictionary so he could improve his English. After their doubles empire took off, they paid for his education overseas. Badru said he feels a responsibility to use this gift to preserve his parents' legacy.

Island
Puerto Rico

Yield
4 servings

Active Time
20 minutes

Total Time
30 minutes

MOFONGO CON GUISO

When I think of Puerto Rico, the island where I was born, I always think of mofongo. It's a traditional dish made by frying and smashing green plantains, often seasoned with garlic and chicharrón (fried pork skins)—and it's a favorite among my people. While it is certainly heavy and filling, it's also a marker of creativity and ingenuity and is a fusion of indigenous and African ingredients and techniques and Spanish flavors. It's prepared and served in dozens of different ways, such as in a rich, meaty tomato gravy; stuffed with meat or seafood; or formed into a ball and nestled in a clear broth. Many also make mofongo out of other starchy ingredients such as cassava and breadfruit. My grandmother Tata was an amazing cook, and she often made mofongo into a stuffing for our Thanksgiving turkeys. These two recipes are adapted from hers—a lighter preparation, brightened with lemongrass and shrimp, with a splash of fish sauce for added umami, and the other more traditional with a rich tomato guiso on the side.

GUISO

1 tsp olive oil

2 Tbsp Sofrito (page 38)

1 cup [240 ml] tomato sauce

MOFONGO

Vegetable oil, for frying

3 large garlic cloves

1 tsp kosher salt, plus more as needed

¼ cup [60 ml] olive oil

1 Tbsp fresh lime juice, plus more as needed

3 green plantains (see Tip)

1½ cups [48 g] chicharrón or pork cracklings, plus more for garnish (optional)

Lime wedges and fresh cilantro leaves, for garnish (optional)

To make the guiso: In a small saucepan over medium, heat the olive oil for 1 to 2 minutes, until shimmering. Add the sofrito, lower the heat to medium-low, and sauté until the liquid has evaporated, 3 to 5 minutes. Add the tomato sauce, partially cover the pan with a lid, and simmer over low for 7 to 10 minutes. The sauce will thicken and darken in color.

To make the mofongo: In a medium saucepan over medium-high heat, pour enough vegetable oil until it reaches 3 in [7.5 cm]. Line a bowl with paper towels.

While the oil heats, in a pilón or large mortar and pestle, crush the garlic and salt until a wet paste forms.

In a small saucepan over medium, heat the olive oil until just shimmering, about 5 minutes. Slowly pour this hot oil over the garlic, carefully stirring to incorporate. It'll sizzle, and the garlic may turn light green. Add the lime juice and stir to combine. Transfer this mixture—the mojo—to a small bowl.

Peel the plantains by cutting off both ends, then making three lengthwise slices through the skin. Carefully pull off the peel, starting at one of the corners, with the edge of your fingernail or the tip of your knife if tough. Cut the plantains into 1½ in [4 cm] rounds. (Be careful: Plantain skins can stain your hands and clothing black.)

continued

Heat the vegetable oil until it reaches a temperature between 350 and 375°F [180 and 190°C] and is shimmering—you can test by using a candy thermometer or adding a small piece of plantain; it will sizzle when the oil is hot enough. Add plantains in two or three batches, taking care not to crowd the pot. Fry until the plantains begin to brown, stirring lightly a few times, 6 to 9 minutes. Be careful not to let them get too dark, or they'll be hard and dry. Use a slotted spoon or mesh strainer to transfer the plantains to the paper towels.

If you have a large enough pilón, add the drained fried plantains and chicharrón (if using) until the pilón is three-quarters full. Mash the plantains (and the chicharrón, if using), alternating pounding and grinding. Once the mixture has condensed to about half its original size, add 1 heaping Tbsp of the reserved mojo, and continue grinding and mashing until fully combined. The mixture will look like stuffing.

If you don't have a pilón, combine the plantains, chicharrón (if using), and 1 heaping Tbsp mojo in a large wooden bowl. Using the bottom of a slender jar, mash the ingredients together to incorporate, rotating the bowl after each mash. Pound, grind, and mash until the mofongo is fully blended.

Form the mashed mixture into four individual mofongos, each roughly the size of a baseball, or press into the bottom of a small rice bowl, then turn each onto a plate or into a larger bowl. Serve immediately, garnished with extra chicharrón, lime wedges, and cilantro if desired. Spoon guiso over the mofongo.

TIP Choose plantains that are as green as possible. Yellow plantains will taste and behave dramatically differently. If you're adventurous, try a sweet and savory mofongo by combining the two.

Island
Puerto Rico

Yield
4 servings

Active Time
30 minutes

Total Time
45 minutes

MOFONGO WITH SHRIMP AND LEMONGRASS

LEMONGRASS STOCK

2 cups shrimp shells, from 1 lb [455 g] fresh or frozen shrimp

3 lemongrass stalks, rinsed well and cut into 4 pieces

1 large yellow onion, quartered

2 garlic cloves, peeled and smashed

3 ají dulce peppers or ½ red bell pepper, halved and seeded

8 fresh cilantro sprigs

3 fresh culantro sprigs

1 Tbsp fish sauce, plus more as needed

1 Tbsp kosher salt, plus more as needed

MOFONGO

2 cups [475 ml] corn or vegetable oil, for frying

4 green plantains, peeled and cut into 1 in [2.5 cm] rounds

1 Tbsp olive oil

4 large garlic cloves

½ tsp kosher salt

SHRIMP

1 lb [455 g] fresh or frozen shrimp, peeled and deveined, shells reserved

Fresh cilantro leaves, sliced avocado, lime wedges, and hot sauce, for garnish

TIPS The mofongo will fall apart a bit once you add the stock, so serve immediately.

I first made this stock as a way to use up reserved frozen shrimp shells, which impart a lot of flavor. You can use fresh or frozen shrimp, but it really is a great way to make use of discarded shells from the shrimp you're using in this recipe or that you've reserved from past dishes.

To make the stock: In a large stockpot, combine 8 cups [1.9 L] of water with the shrimp shells, lemongrass, onion, garlic, peppers, cilantro, culantro, fish sauce, and salt. Bring to a boil, then lower the heat and simmer for 20 to 30 minutes.

To make the mofongo: In a deep skillet over medium-high, heat the corn oil to 375°F [190°C]. To test the temperature, use a candy thermometer or drop in a small piece of plantain; it'll sizzle and rise to the surface if it's ready. Meanwhile, line a large plate with paper towels.

Gently add the plantains to the oil, working in batches as necessary, and fry for 5 minutes, flipping once, until golden brown. Remove the plantains from the oil with tongs and transfer to the lined plate.

Meanwhile, in a small skillet over medium, heat the olive oil, then add the garlic and turn off the heat, stirring the garlic for 1 minute until evenly cooked.

Working in batches, transfer the fried plantains to fill half your pilón or mortar and pestle, then add 1 Tbsp sautéed garlic, the olive oil, and salt. Mash the plantains with a continuous pressing motion, scraping the sides into the center so the plantains and seasoning are fully incorporated. Scoop out the mixture, which should have the texture of Play-Doh, and form into four tennis-size balls of 1 cup [240 g] of the mixture each. Place the balls in small individual soup bowls.

Strain the stock through a fine-mesh sieve into a medium pot, then bring to a boil. Taste and adjust the fish sauce and salt as needed.

To make the shrimp: Add the shrimp all at once to the stock, off the heat, and let sit until the shrimp are no longer translucent, 1 to 2 minutes. Divide the shrimp among the bowls with mofongo. Pour 1 cup [240 ml] or more of stock into each bowl. Serve immediately, garnished with cilantro, avocado slices, lime wedges, and hot sauce.

I
S
L
A
S

FISH AND FUNGI

Fungi (pronounced *foon-gee*), the national dish of St. Croix, has nothing to do with mushrooms. It's a variation on fufu, a pounded starch that's a staple of many regional African cuisines. Enslaved people brought this filling side dish to the Caribbean and Latin America, where it's often made with cornmeal instead of yams or cassava. Here, fried fish is paired with fungi, then doused in a flavorful sauce thickened with okra. It's comforting—and tells a rich story of adaptation.

2 Tbsp vegetable oil

1 large yellow onion, diced

1 green or red bell pepper, seeded and diced

1 habanero or scotch bonnet pepper, stemmed, seeded if desired to mitigate spiciness, and minced

1 celery stalk, diced

3 garlic cloves, minced

1 tsp fresh thyme leaves, or ½ tsp dried thyme

1¼ tsp kosher salt, plus more as needed

2 Tbsp white vinegar

1 cup [240 ml] canned crushed or puréed tomatoes

1 Tbsp tomato paste

¾ cup [115 g] thickly sliced okra (fresh or frozen)

1 cup [140 g] cornmeal

1 Tbsp unsalted butter

¼ cup [60 ml] vegetable oil, for frying

2 lb [910 g] fish fillets, such as grouper, tilapia, or red snapper

Lime wedges, for garnish (optional)

In a large sauté pan over medium, heat the oil. Add the onion, bell pepper, habanero, celery, garlic, thyme, and ¼ tsp of the salt. Cook for 10 minutes, stirring frequently, until the vegetables are tender and starting to brown. Add the vinegar, tomatoes, tomato paste, and ¼ cup [60 ml] of water. Lower the heat to low and cook for 10 minutes more, until the vegetables are softened and the sauce has thickened. Adjust the seasoning as needed and keep warm until ready to serve.

While the sauce is simmering, heat a small skillet over medium heat. Add the okra and enough water to cover it, cover with a lid, and simmer on low for 5 to 7 minutes, until the okra turns jade green. Drain and set aside.

In a medium pot over high heat, bring 2 cups [475 ml] of water and the remaining 1 tsp salt to a boil. Whisking constantly, gradually add the cornmeal in a thin stream. Lower the heat to low and simmer, stirring frequently, until the cornmeal is creamy but holds its shape on a spoon, about 10 to 15 minutes or longer as needed. If the cornmeal isn't quite tender, add more water a few Tbsp at a time until the fungi sets up. Add the butter and okra, then taste and add more salt as needed.

In a wide saucepan over medium-high, heat the oil until it shimmers. Working in batches as necessary, carefully place each fish fillet in the pan and fry, flipping once, until browned, about 2 to 3 minutes on each side. Remove the fillets with a slotted spoon.

To serve, put two scoops of the fungi and a fish fillet on each plate. Spoon the sauce over and around the fish. Squeeze lime wedges over the fish if desired.

FRIED YAMS

Yams are found across the tropics. Yellow, orange, purple, even white, the starchy-sweet tubers are often grated or pounded into a paste or masa, boiled and mashed, braised in stews, or, in this case, fried. Here, the process of deep-frying draws out then caramelizes the yams' natural sugar, resulting in a final product that's crisp on the outside and soft on the inside.

Kosher salt

2 lb [910 g] yams

5 to 6 cups [1.2 to 1.4 L] vegetable oil, for frying

Bring a large pot of water to a boil over high heat and season generously with salt.

Fill a large bowl with water and set a cooling rack over a baking sheet or a single layer of paper towels. Set aside. Working quickly to avoid oxidation, slice off the ends of the yams and peel the skin. Cut the yams into ¾ in [2 cm] rounds and transfer to the bowl of water. Cut each piece further into 1 in [2.5 cm] wide strips, returning the pieces to the water as they are cut.

Working in batches, drop the yams into the boiling water and blanch for 2 to 3 minutes. Remove from the hot water and transfer to the prepared rack to drain. Repeat the blanching and draining process for the remaining yam strips.

In a large skillet, pour enough oil to reach 1½ in [4 cm]. Heat the oil over medium-high until the heat reaches 350°F [180°C]. To test, use a candy thermometer or add a small piece of yam; it will sizzle when the oil is hot enough.

Working in two or three batches to avoid crowding, and replenishing the oil as needed, fry the yam strips, turning occasionally, until golden brown and crispy, 10 to 12 minutes total. Remove from the oil and drain on the rack set over the baking sheet or on paper towels. Season with salt and serve hot.

TIP To roast the yams instead of frying them, rinse and drain the yam strips after slicing and dry with paper towels. Transfer to a baking sheet and toss with ¼ cup [60 ml] of vegetable oil. Season with salt, then spread in an even layer. Roast at 425°F [220°C], turning occasionally, until tender and deep golden brown in spots, about 45 minutes.

I
S
L
A
S

TOSTONES
FRIED GREEN PLANTAINS

Green plantains are fried, smashed, then fried again for this beloved side dish that's eaten across Latin America and the Caribbean. It's perfect served alongside grilled meat, Pescado Frito (page 219), Griot (page 215), or Habichuelas Guisadas con Calabaza (page 145), or on their own topped with Mojo (page 46) or Guiso (page 207).

3 green plantains

Vegetable oil, for frying

2 tsp kosher salt, plus more as needed

Line a large plate or baking sheet with paper towels.

Peel the plantains by cutting off both ends, then make three lengthwise slices through the skin. Carefully pull off the peel, starting at one of the corners, with the edge of your fingernail or the tip of your knife if tough, then cut the plantains into 1½ in [4 cm] rounds (see Tips). (Be careful: Plantain skins will stain your hands and clothing black.)

In a deep skillet, pour enough oil to reach 1½ to 2 in [4 to 5 cm]. Heat the oil over medium-high until it reaches 375°F [190°C]. Test the heat by using a candy thermometer or putting a scrap of plantain in the oil; if it sizzles instantly and rises to the top, the oil is ready.

Using a pair of tongs, carefully add the plantain rounds until the pan is full, but not crowded. Fry the plantains in batches, flipping every couple of minutes, until they're golden brown and oil sizzles up through their centers, 3 to 5 minutes. Remove from the oil with tongs and drain on the paper towels. Adjust the heat as needed to maintain the oil's temperature.

Once all the plantain rounds are fried, press each into a flat disk using a tostonera press (see Tips). Refry the pressed plantains in batches, being careful not to crowd the pan. Fry for 2 to 3 minutes, flipping once or twice to ensure even browning. Don't let them get too dark, as they'll take on a bitter, burnt taste.

Carefully remove the tostones from the oil with tongs and return to the paper towels (replacing the paper towels as needed). Sprinkle liberally with salt and serve hot.

TIPS Cut the plantains only once you're ready to start cooking, as they will quickly turn brown.

Do not slice the plantains on the bias; this will make your tostones an uneven shape.

If you don't have a tostonera press, press the plantains on a small plate with the bottom of a wide coffee mug or cup. Be careful not to press too thin or they'll fall apart when refried.

GRIOT
FRIED BRAISED PORK

Pork shoulder is marinated, braised until just tender, then deep-fried and served with Pikliz (page 99), a crunchy, spicy cabbage relish. Like many dishes in this book, griot is usually reserved for celebrations. In keeping with celebratory dishes worldwide, it requires time and effort—and is so worth it.

EPIS

1 medium white onion, chopped

10 to 12 garlic cloves, chopped

2 green onions, white and green parts, chopped

10 fresh thyme sprigs, smaller stems pulled from the woody stems

2 cups [80 g] fresh parsley, stems and leaves coarsely chopped

1 scotch bonnet pepper, seeded if desired to mitigate spiciness, chopped

1 cup [240 ml] fresh orange juice

¼ cup [60 ml] fresh lime juice

1 Tbsp sugarcane vinegar or white wine vinegar

1 Tbsp kosher salt

¼ tsp freshly cracked black pepper

GRIOT

3 lb [1.4 kg] boneless pork shoulder, cut into 2 in [5 cm] cubes

4 cups [945 ml] vegetable oil, for frying

Steamed white rice, Pikliz (page 99), fried sweet plantains, and/or Tostones (page 213), for serving

To make the epis: In a food processor, combine the white onion, garlic, green onions, thyme, parsley, scotch bonnet, orange juice, lime juice, vinegar, salt, and pepper and grind into a loose paste.

To make the griot: In a large mixing bowl, combine the pork and the epis, and mix well to evenly coat the meat. Cover and marinate for 6 hours, or overnight if possible.

Preheat the oven to 450°F [230°C].

Transfer the pork to a Dutch oven or other large oven-safe pot, add 1 cup [240 ml] of water, and bring to a boil over high heat. Transfer the pot to the oven and roast, uncovered, for 35 to 40 minutes or until the pork is fork tender.

Line a baking sheet with paper towels. Using a slotted spoon, remove the pork pieces to the lined baking sheet to drain; reserve the braising liquid (see Tip). Using a separate paper towel, pat the surface of the pork to ensure there's no remaining moisture. Let dry for an additional 10 to 15 minutes.

In a separate pot over medium-high, heat the oil to 350°F [180°C]. Add the pork in batches and fry for 3 to 5 minutes, until deep golden brown.

Meanwhile, discard the used paper towels and line the baking sheet with fresh paper towels. Once crisp, transfer the pork to the paper towels to drain. Serve hot, with steamed white rice, pikliz, fried plantains, and/or tostones.

TIP The remaining braising liquid for the pork is incredibly flavorful and makes a great addition to other stewed pork dishes or chili. Strain and transfer to an airtight container, then refrigerate for up to a week or freeze for several months.

PAPAS RELLENAS
PICADILLO-STUFFED POTATO FRITTERS

Enjoyed across Latin America, papas rellenas are sinful. Potatoes are boiled and mashed, then stuffed with seasoned ground beef, formed into balls, and fried. They're laborious to make, so they're most commonly sold at cuchifrito stands in the Dominican Republic and Puerto Rico—as well as Caribbean diaspora enclaves such as Chicago, Miami, and New York's East Harlem—instead of made at home. But they are worth the effort, as they freeze well and can be pulled out any time for company. While these may seem like a snack, they are quite filling.

POTATOES

4 large russet potatoes, peeled and cubed

1 Tbsp kosher salt, plus more as needed

PICADILLO

1 Tbsp olive oil

½ cup [120 ml] Sofrito (page 38)

1 lb [455 g] ground beef

2 tsp ground cumin

1 tsp kosher salt

1 tsp freshly ground black pepper

1 Tbsp tomato paste

1 Tbsp white vinegar

PAPAS RELLENAS

2 cups [280 g] fine dry bread crumbs

1 cup [140 g] all-purpose flour

4 eggs

1 qt [945 ml] vegetable oil, for frying

To make the potatoes: In a large pot, combine the potatoes and salt and cover with water. Bring to a boil over high heat, then lower the heat to medium-low, cover, and simmer until tender, about 20 minutes. Drain and allow the potatoes to steam dry for 1 to 2 minutes. Place the potatoes in a large mixing bowl and mash thoroughly. Taste and add salt as needed, then set aside to cool to room temperature (see Tips).

To make the picadillo: In a large skillet over medium, heat the olive oil until shimmering. Add the sofrito and sauté for 5 to 7 minutes until it's fragrant and the liquid has fully evaporated. Increase the heat to medium-high and stir in the ground beef, breaking the meat apart with a wooden spoon. Cook until the beef is evenly browned, 5 to 7 minutes. Stir in the cumin, salt, pepper, tomato paste, and vinegar, and stir continuously until the tomato paste has dissolved and the flavors have melded. Transfer to a large mixing bowl and allow the beef mixture to cool to room temperature (see Tips).

Meanwhile, to make the papas rellenas: Line a baking sheet with parchment paper. Pour the bread crumbs and flour into two separate shallow dishes. Crack the eggs into a medium bowl and whisk well.

Scoop approximately ¾ cup of the mashed potato and split it into two equal portions. Take one portion and form it into a small bowl shape in your hand, then fill the cavity with approximately 2 Tbsp of the picadillo, being careful not to overfill (see Tips). Add the remaining portion of mashed potato, gently cup both hands around the relleno, and press together to seal the edges, rolling delicately to smooth into a round ball.

Gently roll each ball in flour, shaking off the excess. Dip a ball into the beaten egg and then gently roll in the bread crumbs. Toss the ball from hand to hand to remove any loose crumbs. Repeat with the remaining balls. Place the breaded potato balls onto the prepared baking sheet and refrigerate for 2 to 4 hours (or freeze for later use).

When ready to cook, in a deep-fryer or large sauce-pan, heat the vegetable oil until it sizzles and reaches 350°F [180°C] on a candy thermometer. Line a plate with paper towels for draining and set aside. Fry the potato balls in batches, using tongs to gently roll the balls around to ensure even browning. The balls should become crispy and golden brown, about 3 minutes per batch.

Remove the balls from the oil with a slotted spoon, drain on the prepared paper towels, and let cool a few minutes before serving hot.

TIPS To cool the potatoes and picadillo faster, spread each mix onto separate baking sheets and refrigerate for 10 to 15 minutes.

Store any leftover picadillo in the refrigerator for up to a week and enjoy as a snack or a quick meal with steamed white rice.

PESCADO FRITO
FRIED RED SNAPPER

Fishing is an extraordinarily complex issue in Puerto Rico. Much of the seafood eaten doesn't come from the island's own waters, in part because of arcane legislation that controls fishing rights. And yet, deep-fried whole fish is a staple on the island, particularly along the west and southwest coasts. There, you'll find red snapper that's lightly seasoned, fried, and served with Tostones (page 213), avocado salad, and steamed white rice. Frying turns the head and the tail into a crunchy fish chicharrón, and the skin and flesh cook evenly, keeping the flesh moist and the skin crisp. Bones are often a concern for those uncomfortable eating whole fish, but the simplest solution is to eat it with your hands. With practice, you'll find your fingers are remarkably adept at finding sneaky bones, and there's a special pleasure in picking out tender cheek flesh.

ADOBO

Juice of 1 lime (about 2 Tbsp)

1 Tbsp olive oil

2 medium garlic cloves, minced

1 tsp kosher salt

½ tsp ground cumin

½ tsp dried oregano

¼ tsp store-bought or homemade Sazón Seasoning (page 39)

FISH

One 1½ to 2 lb [680 to 910 g] whole red snapper, cleaned and scaled, head and tail on

Vegetable oil, for frying

Lime wedges, hot sauce, and chopped fresh cilantro leaves, for garnish

To make the adobo: In a large pilón or mortar and pestle, combine the lime juice, olive oil, garlic, salt, cumin, oregano, and sazón and grind together.

To make the fish: Score the fish skin, making three shallow crosswise cuts on each side, then place the fish in a deep container with a lid or in a large resealable bag. Pour the adobo over, rubbing it into the skin, head, and cavity. Let marinate for at least 30 minutes at room temperature, or 2 to 3 hours in the refrigerator. If marinating in the refrigerator, let the fish come to room temperature before frying.

In a deep, wide wok or pot large enough to submerge your fish, pour enough vegetable oil to reach a depth of at least 2 in [5 cm]. Heat the oil to 350°F [180°C].

Meanwhile, line a baking sheet with paper towels.

Pick up the fish by the tail, shake off excess marinade, and lower it headfirst into the oil. Use a pair of tongs to gently nudge the fish to prevent it from sticking to the pot. Have a splatter shield handy, as the oil will be very active at first.

Using a ladle, frequently baste any unsubmerged fish with hot oil, ensuring the fish cooks evenly. Fry until it turns golden brown, 5 to 10 minutes, watching carefully and removing immediately if it darkens quickly.

Using a set of heatproof tongs and a heatproof spatula, carefully lift the fish out of the oil and transfer it to the lined baking sheet. Let the fish rest for 2 to 3 minutes. Garnish with lime wedges, hot sauce, and cilantro.

ISLAS

ALCAPURRIAS DE JUEYES
CRAB-STUFFED FRITTERS

Fritters abound across the Caribbean. Some, like Jamaican Festival (page 196), are simply seasoned dough or masa. But many others are a dough or masa stuffed with flavorful meat or seafood. In Puerto Rico, alcapurrias are among the most coveted. Most often they're a snack, purchased at a roadside or beachside stand or kiosko, particularly in Loíza—a town on the northeastern coast that is the island's African heart. At home, they're often made over the holidays, as many hands make light work. The flavor is unmistakable: earthy green banana and taro cut by savory Sofrito (page 38), briny capers, and delicate crabmeat. The filling, which is called a *salmorejo* and used to make dishes such as Arroz con Jueyes (page 153), is usually made from local land crabs, but commercially available lump crab is a fitting substitute. This recipe is adapted from one by María Dolores "Lula" de Jesús, founder of El Burén de Lula in Loíza. Lula is considered by many to be a madrina, or godmother, of this and other dishes from the area with African origins.

ANNATTO OIL

¾ cup [180 ml] vegetable oil or lard

3 Tbsp annatto seeds (achiote) (see Tips)

MASA

Kosher salt

2 lb [910 g] white yautía (taro root)

2 green bananas (see Tips)

FILLING

½ cup [120 ml] Sofrito (page 38)

2 Tbsp drained capers, chopped

1 tsp store-bought or homemade Sazón Seasoning (page 39)

1 tsp kosher salt, plus more as needed

1 lb [455 g] lump crab meat (about 2 cups)

Vegetable oil, for frying

Hot sauce, for serving

To make the annatto oil: In a small saucepan over medium-high, heat the oil and annatto seeds. Once the oil starts to shimmer, remove from the heat, stir to combine, and let rest for 5 minutes. Using a fine-mesh sieve, strain the oil into a heat-safe container and set aside.

To make the masa: Fill a large bowl with cold water and a fistful of salt. Peel and chop the yautía and green bananas into 1 in [2.5 cm] pieces. Soak the pieces in the salted water until ready to use, to prevent browning.

Cut at least 32 squares of wax paper about 4 to 5 in [10 to 13 cm] square each. (Traditionally, banana leaves are used, but since they can be difficult to source, wax paper is an appropriate substitute.)

Drain the yautía and bananas, then dry with paper towels. Working in two batches, add half the drained yautía and bananas to a food processor with 1 Tbsp salt, and pulse until fully incorporated and the texture of chunky hummus. Repeat with the remaining yautía, bananas, and an additional 1 Tbsp salt.

Return all of the blended yautía and bananas to the food processor, turn it on, and gradually pour in ½ cup [120 ml] of the annatto oil, blending the mixture until smooth and dark yellow in color. Taste for salt, then transfer to a large bowl and refrigerate for 1 hour or more so it can set. You will have 9 to 10 cups of masa.

To make the filling: In a medium saucepan over medium, heat 3 Tbsp of the annatto oil. Add the sofrito, capers, sazón, and salt, and cook, stirring occasionally, until most of the liquid has evaporated, 5 minutes. Lower the heat to medium-low and add the crab meat, stirring well to incorporate. Cook for another 3 to 5 minutes, stirring occasionally, until the flavors blend and the crab has soaked up the seasoning. Adjust the salt as needed.

To assemble and fry: Create an assembly line on the counter or a long dining table, preferably atop a cloth or towels that you don't mind getting stained. From left to right, arrange the remaining 1 Tbsp annatto oil, wax paper squares, masa, crab filling, and a large plate or baking sheet. Have a finger bowl with water and a clean towel available in case your hands get messy.

Smear about ⅛ tsp of the annatto oil in a wide oval shape nearly to the edge of a wax paper square. Add about 2 Tbsp of the masa, then spread the masa in a wide oval over the annatto oil, leaving at least a ½ in [13 mm] border. Add 2 to 3 tsp of the crab mixture to the center of the masa, taking care not to overfill. Fold the paper in half, creating a half-moon shape with the masa, and seal the edge by pressing the masa lightly with your fingers, being careful not to let the filling spill out. Stack the folded, filled papers carefully on the plate, and refrigerate until ready to fry. (These fry up best when they've had time to rest in the refrigerator. If you'd like to prepare them ahead of time, you can refrigerate them for several hours, or store in the freezer for up to several months. They can be fried directly from the freezer.)

In a deep fryer or deep, heavy-bottomed pan over medium-high, pour enough oil to reach 2 in [5 cm] and heat until it reaches 350°F [180°C]. Working in batches, carefully transfer each alcapurria to the shimmering oil, first sliding it off the paper onto your hand, then carefully dropping into the oil. Gently nudge the alcapurrias with tongs to prevent them from sticking. (The filling may burst through the edges, causing oil to splatter, so keep a splatter guard handy, if you have one.) Turn each fritter a few times and cook until evenly dark golden brown, 5 to 7 minutes.

Remove the alcapurrias from the oil and drain on paper towels. Let rest for at least 5 minutes before eating, as they will be quite hot. Sprinkle each bite with your hot sauce of choice.

TIPS Green bananas are distinct from unripe bananas. They are much closer in flavor and texture to green plantains, but with a more delicate flavor.

If you can't find annatto seeds, replace the annatto oil with 3 Tbsp bacon fat, lard, or vegetable oil combined with 2 Tbsp of ground annatto.

Island
Philippines

Yield
4 servings

Active Time
45 minutes

Total Time
**At least 6 hours
30 minutes**

LECHON KAWALI
CRISPY FRIED PORK BELLY

Among the most popular fried Filipino meat snacks, lechon kawali is made by a technique that produces a browned, crispy exterior and an incredibly juicy, salty porky interior.

2 lb [910 g] skin-on pork belly

8 medium garlic cloves, smashed

2 dried bay leaves

1 Tbsp black peppercorns

½ cup [120 ml] soy sauce

Kosher salt

Vegetable or peanut oil, for frying

Sinamak (page 48) or CHamoru Fina'denne' (page 43), for serving

In a large pot, place the pork belly skin-side down and add enough water to completely cover. Add the garlic, bay leaves, peppercorns, and soy sauce. Bring to a boil over medium-high, then lower the heat and simmer, covered, until the pork is fork-tender but not falling apart, about 1 hour. Transfer the pork to a wire rack set in a rimmed baking sheet and season well with salt. Put the baking sheet in the refrigerator and chill, uncovered, until the flesh and skin are fully dry, at least 5 hours or overnight, if possible.

Remove the pork from the refrigerator, score the skin diagonally, then cut it into 2 in [5 cm] slices lengthwise (see Tip). Line a separate baking sheet with paper towels.

In a wok or Dutch oven over high, pour enough oil to reach 3 in [7.5 cm] and heat to 375°F [190°C]. Working in batches, fry the pork slices until uniformly browned and the skin has crisped and bubbled, 7 to 10 minutes. Transfer the pork to the paper towels and let rest for 2 to 3 minutes to allow it to drain and cool a little. Taste and sprinkle with additional salt if desired. Serve immediately with dipping sauces, such as sinamak or fina'denne'.

TIP For an alternate shape, leave the long slices intact, then use a sharp knife to make seven or eight evenly spaced horizontal slices from the meat side to the skin, stopping just shy of the layer of fat. Deep fry whole, then chop along the notches.

CHAPTER FIVE

GRILLING, ROASTING + SMOKING

Puerto Rico

While developing the recipes for this book, I fell in love with fire and smoke. I came to understand how to wield and preserve it, how to control it, and how best to use it to cook different kinds of food. And above all, I learned that all fires must be respected—and that respect cannot come from a place of fear. A fire is an entity, one that will sense your hesitation and whip around and burn you, as if to say "toughen up!" It's through my kinship with fires and in getting to know the native people and plants of Puerto Rico that I connect with my indigenous past, which has often felt enigmatic and out of reach. So I approach every fire with humility and gratitude in an effort to understand who the island is.

Puerto Rico's first inhabitants were the native Taínos, who also lived until the mid-sixteenth century in what's now known as Haiti and the Dominican Republic (together known as Hispaniola), Cuba, Jamaica, the Bahamas, and the northern Lesser Antilles. Their diet was largely caught and foraged: fresh fruits, seafood and river prawns, and starches like cassava and yams. We know they pounded ingredients in a large, waist-high wooden mortar and pestle called a pilón (today, small enough to fit on a countertop), used to make casabe—a cracker-like bread that you can still find, packaged, on the island today and in many Caribbean grocery stores.

The word *barbeque*, in fact, stems from the term *barbacoa* (also *barbaca* and *barabicu*, Spanish spellings derived from Taíno pronunciations). While in the United States barbecue is perhaps most often associated with pork ribs slathered in sticky-sweet red sauce, the word *barbacoa* doesn't refer to a dish. Rather, it's a structure, a latticed platform made of wood set over a fire pit, allowing smoke to billow up and both preserve and season the ingredients above (in essence, an ancient smoker). It's a backstory illustrative of the tangled roots and layered histories that underscore much of island cuisine.

But as in many other colonized places, Puerto Rican culture is one of mestizaje, or racial mixing. Invaded by the Spanish, the island and its native inhabitants were ravaged by colonization. The Taínos were enslaved and nearly decimated by exploitation, violence, and disease, their labor then replaced by enslaved African workers. Puerto Ricans are descended from this hybridity of cultures: indigenous, African, Spanish, and more. And even though the Taínos were so significantly diminished, hundreds of thousands of islanders still carry their DNA.

The smell of wood fire perfumes many landscapes in Puerto Rico. Roadside stands sell pinchos—skewered, grilled fatty pork or chicken thighs. Popular beaches such as Piñones are peppered with kioskos frying Alcapurrias de Jueyes (page 220) and grilling Churrasco (page 241), garlic-marinated skirt steak. Cooking meat over hot coals or wood fires is also the method used to prepare one of Puerto Rico's most iconic dishes, léchon—sumptuous marinated slow-roasted whole pig, the best of which can be found in mountainous Guavate.

The practice of grilling and smoking meat on the island owes as much to its colonial legacy as its indigenous origins. Pork, perhaps the island's most common staple animal protein, was introduced by the Spanish, among Columbus's cargo on his second voyage in 1493. The Spanish arrived in Puerto Rico accustomed to having (often salt-cured) meat daily, and worked quickly to cultivate pigs (and cows) on the island, later leading to a hybrid breed of runaway feral pigs who thrived on tropical fruit and reproduced freely. Over time, pork came to be the most readily available protein, and today it continues to be incorporated throughout Puerto Rican cuisine, seasoning Habichuelas Guisadas con Calabaza (page 145), Sancocho (page 176), Arroz con Tocino (page 292), and Pasteles de Masa (page 284).

Even though the origins of these dishes have complex roots, they are all stories of creativity and of thriving despite the odds. For hundreds of years Puerto Rico was a sugarcane colony, and its cuisine still reflects the starchy, calorie-rich ingredients such as rice and plantains brought to feed enslaved workers. The way these same ingredients are prepared today are a celebration, using many of the techniques in this book to infuse dishes with intense flavor. And the love of fire and smoke abounds, producing aromas that illicit a carnal response. After all, there are few things as intoxicating as the smell of barbecue. Whether it's charred chicken on skewers or caramelized sweet potatoes, the smoky aroma of grilled food lures people toward roadside stands and into neighbors' backyards across the island. Grilling is an invitation to gather, often outdoors, and to share a meal. It is arguably among the most sumptuous global traditions.

The perceptions of tropical islands are often predicated by colonizers and tourists. Rarely does the reality of life on the island match the postcard. Yes, Puerto Rico has beaches, rum, cars blasting reggaeton, and an abundance of rich fried food. Puerto Rico is also lush and very wet. El Yunque, Puerto Rico's iconic rainforest on the east of the island, is a magical place. Dense vegetation springing from every corner, delicate elechos (ferns), elegant imperial palms, fan-like yagrumo. It has one of the largest underground river systems on the planet, in addition to the above-ground interlocking rivers that bring water to all parts of the island. Island trees drip with tropical fruit—mango, guanabana (soursop), parcha (passion fruit), acerolas (sour cherries), and pink-fleshed guavas with their intoxicating aroma. Plantains, bananas, and breadfruit hang from herbaceous trees, while malanga and yautía—two varieties of indigenous taro—as well as cassava, lettuces, herbs, and gandules (pigeon peas) spring from the ground.

But like Guam and Hawai'i, Puerto Rico's agricultural capacity is dictated by a complex system of policies, in part influenced by the 1917 Jones Act, which privileges imported produce over that cultivated on the island. Locals struggle with a compromised electric grid and overall infrastructure, which disproportionately impacts marginalized communities and people living in the center of the island.

I haven't lived in Puerto Rico since I was a small child, and while I travel there often and feel an undying connection, I am like the other million Puerto Ricans living off island. In some ways the reality on the island feels too difficult to bear, but I know from my loved ones there, en la brega, they always seem to find a way. *La brega* is Puerto Rican slang for the singular struggle of living in an island nation—a rhythm that must be developed amid constant chaos—resourcefulness, and adaptation that will ensure your survival. Fire and smoke across cultures are often used as a way to give offerings, to honor ancestors. It feels fitting, then, that the island would be such a perfect representation/exemplification of the act of cooking by fire, both literally and figuratively.

GRILL

Wood-fire cooking is one of the earliest forms of food preparation on the planet. On every corner of the globe, people use open fires to cook in creative ways, sometimes using residual heat, slow-cooking whole animals, or grilling directly over an open fire to permeate ingredients with smoky flavor.

Smoke is magical and is best honed by cooking over an open hardwood or charcoal fire. A brush of oil and a hit of salt is often all you need to create dishes that sing with smoky essence. Another form of high-heat cooking, grilling also makes quick work of most ingredients, yielding results so delicious you want to eat them when they're still hot enough to burn your tongue. You'll find grilled dishes in other chapters, such as CHamoru Barbecue Chicken (page 60) or Pork Ribs (page 64), and marinating is often the first step in preparing ingredients for the grill. Play and experiment with the flavors and techniques in this chapter, perhaps replacing beef for chicken in sate (page 253) or shrimp for pork in Filipino Barbecue (page 249). And as is the custom across islands, prepare these dishes when you want to bring people together.

Working with open fires can be daunting at first, as it can take time to learn how fires behave and ensure that your food is cooked through without burning. Modern tools are available for those who want to be precise, such as smokers with sensors that will send a signal to your mobile device when ingredients reach a certain temperature. Personally, I prefer a simple grill heated with lump hardwood charcoal and additional foraged wood and kindling. I've spent most of my life living in places with outdoor spaces, which defines my approach. Below are some tips for getting started and for developing your own practice based on your home space and the tools you have on hand.

STARTING A FIRE

The simplest way to start a fire, even in challenging conditions, is with dry wood (such as packaged firewood available at grocery and hardware stores), kindling (small dry sticks, store-bought or foraged from your yard), and a starter such as fatwood. Build the firewood and kindling into a teepee, with plenty of kindling underneath as a foundation. Light either a piece of kindling or fatwood, holding it downward and lighting the bottom. Once it's

fully lit and the flame starts to climb up the stick, set it in a spot with several pieces of kindling, flame-side down. Watch the fire closely at the beginning, relighting the fatwood if it extinguishes too quickly, and adding more pieces of kindling, one by one, until the firewood catches. Resist the urge to add more firewood until you've got a solid fire going. Once you do, add your charcoal or more firewood as needed to keep the fire going long enough to prepare your dish.

GRILLS

A simple round charcoal grill with a lid is among the most cost-effective, reliable, and long-lasting tools for grilling at home. They're also adaptable and can be used for both quick and slow cooking. They can be a bit laborious, as you may need to remove the metal grate to replenish wood or coals if you're cooking large quantities. But they're a solid option on a budget and easy to move. If you are cooking a lot of food, a charcoal chimney starter—an aluminum cylinder with a grate on the bottom and a handle—is a great tool to have on hand, as you can start a batch of coals while your fire is still going, and simply pour them into the grill when ready to use.

For more precise grilling, and the ability to cook large quantities with ease, a gas grill is the way to go. You'll still get grill marks and smoky flavor in your food, though less concentrated smoke than with a wood fire.

And if you have the budget, there are plenty of models of dual gas-and-charcoal grills.

HOT AND COOL ZONES

Whether you're working with a charcoal or gas grill, it's crucial to establish hot and cool zones. On a gas grill these are often built in, either through an upper rack distanced from the heat or easily managed by adjusting the flame on one part of the grill. With a charcoal grill, however, you'll need to build your fire to one side, so that there's an area with little or no fire at all. This method is key to ensuring your ingredients get kissed by fire, developing as much char as you'd like, while still getting fully cooked through. Several recipes in this chapter call for using the cool zone during the grilling process—which helps you prevent ingredients from overcooking, particularly for meat, which also benefits from resting before serving.

FRUITS AND VEGETABLES

Asparagus	Mushrooms
Broccoli	Okra
Cabbage	Onions
Carrots	Peaches
Cauliflower	Peppers
Corn	Pineapple
Eggplant	Squash
Lemons	Sweet potato

SEAFOOD

Fish fillets	Scallops
Lobster	Shrimp
Oysters	Whole fish

POULTRY

Chicken pieces (dark and white meat)	Whole chicken
Duck pieces (dark and white meat)	Whole duck

PORK

Chops	Shoulder
Ribs	Tenderloin

MEAT

Beef chuck stew meat	Goat loin chops
Beef ribs	Lamb leg
Beef steaks (rib eye, strip, tenderloin, porterhouse, T-bone, skirt)	Lamb loin chops
	Lamb ribs

• Grill times vary wildly across ingredients, depending on the type of grill, heat source, outside temperature, and more. Taking a tip from chef Samin Nosrat, use all your senses—touch, smell, sound, taste, and sight—to determine when ingredients are done cooking. Engaging your senses in addition to following instructions and formulas will make you a better cook overall.

• Dark meat chicken and duck are ideal for grilling, as their fattiness keeps the meat moist under intense heat, caramelizing and charring nicely on a grill. Chicken breast is also sumptuous, though you should opt for breast that is not too thick, as it will take much longer to cook and has the potential to dry out.

• If you're grilling vegetables along with meat, consider starting with the vegetables. They take much less time to cook and minimal flipping, and you can put them on a hot fire for a short period of time, then let them rest while you dedicate more time and attention to your meat.

• When grilling firmer vegetables, such as carrots, sweet potatoes, and cauliflower, blanch them in boiling water for a couple of minutes beforehand to ensure they cook evenly.

• When grilling fish, opt for skin-on fillets or whole fish. Fatty fish such as salmon and mackerel, and firm-fleshed fish such as marlin and swordfish, work particularly well on the grill. No matter which fish you choose, generously rub it with oil before placing it on the grill so that it doesn't stick.

• It's important to let ingredients rest after grilling. Vegetables need only 3 to 5 minutes (although they're very tasty at room temperature if left to sit longer), and seafood needs only 5 minutes to rest. Thick cuts of beef, pork, and lamb, as well as whole chicken and duck, should rest for at least 15 minutes, whereas thinner cuts of meat, such as flank steak, need just 7 to 10 minutes.

ITEGE CARO
PUERTO RICO

On a sunny Monday afternoon, Itege Caro steps out onto the pale sands of Playa Stella in Rincón, Puerto Rico. The westernmost tip of the island, it's a far cry from the bustling, congested San Juan metro area. Many who visit the island don't make it this far west, as it takes several hours on the island's wild expressways, followed by incredibly narrow, steep mountain roads. There, high cliffs give way to stunning views of a seemingly endless ocean with dramatic waves that make it the so-called surf capital of the Caribbean.

Itege is my cousin, my prima hermana, or sister *and* cousin, as we were born just two months apart. As such we were treated like twins—posing in family photos wearing matching clothes my grandmother sewed for us. As children, we were incredibly close. She was largely raised by my grandmother, Tata, as her parents were both artists and constantly struggled with economic instability, substance abuse, and the emotional turmoil that follows. And so, we spent a lot of time together, particularly during my summers on the island with Tata, and the visits she made

to the mainland on holidays. In between, we wrote letters and spoke on the phone, often straining the long-distance phone bill. Along with Tata, Itege was my tether to the island.

I admired Itege, but we didn't always get along. I was quite different from her—a shy bookworm while she was beautiful, vibrant, and athletic. As we became teenagers, she seemed to glow, her skin emanating a lifetime in the sun, her thick hair hanging down to her waist. But as time passed our calls and letters became less frequent and we fell out of touch. She had children and became nomadic, moving between Colorado, Oregon, Puerto Rico, and perhaps other places. I similarly wandered, living in Holland, Atlanta, San Francisco, New York, and North Carolina.

I never expected for Puerto Rico to become such an important part of my life. I didn't return for over a decade, because once Tata and Itege weren't there I had no reason to go. But information about Itege would trickle in from time to time, and her experience on the island intrigued me. For years she lived on the beach and in the mountains, performed music, and became a farmer with deep knowledge of indigenous plants. Her four children, whom she homeschooled, grew up bathing in rivers, eating ripe fruit in the hills of Maricao.

My curiosity about the indigenous spirit of the island grew through Itege, through the few stories I heard from her when we would connect via text, or when my mom was able to get her on the phone. I wanted to know the island as she did. And on this sunny Monday in Rincón, I got a little closer.

She was joined on the beach by her three younger children—Asmara (twelve), Jahenok (nine), and Lalibela (five)—who stepped onto the beach as if they'd been born there. They came packing a box of ingredients: whole fresh coconuts, which they'd just felled from a palm; malanga, a local variety of taro that is much larger than smaller varieties such as yautía, typically with white or light pink speckled flesh; green plantains; carrots; onions; a jar of sofrito; coconut oil; some sazón; and basic tools—metal bowls and silverware, a machete for splitting cocos.

Itege and I grew up inspired by Tata's cooking. She was legendary, and her palate and flavor sensibility continue to inspire me. My home kitchen remains an ode to Tata, and I've filled it over the years with tools that reference my island home as much as my Southern upbringings—my pilón (wooden mortar and pestle) sits next to my seasoned

cast-iron skillet. But I love kitchen tools and over the years have amassed a collection of gadgets: pressure cooker, stand mixer, food processors of various sizes, a fancy blender *and* a hand mixer, and much more. In stark contrast, on the beach that day we had a lighter, a basic pot with a lid, a grater, and a knife. Itege repurposed a cinderblock for chopping while her youngest carefully grated plantain into a bowl.

In minutes she started a fire, digging a small ditch in the sand next to the stump of a palm tree. Along the shore, her kids gathered wood and brush, which Itege formed into a teepee and sparked with the lighter. There, she prepared a sancocho with the ingredients she brought, along with the water and grated meat from the coconuts, and some ocean water. Open fires are, of course, the cornerstone of grilling and smoking, but they're also used to make braises and stews, their ingredients infused with billowing smoke. As the dish simmered, I swam with her children, who transformed into marlins as soon as their toes hit the water.

I then sat in the sand next to the fire, catching up with Itege, who'd been having a tough year. She'd recently separated from the children's father after sixteen years together and was struggling to make ends meet as a single parent. She and the children lived in a camper on the beach for a few months while they found more

stable housing, a time she says was quite fun for them but incredibly difficult for her. For decades she'd dedicated herself to agriculture and herbology, work that was spiritually fulfilling but often difficult to make profitable. Most recently she's been making a living producing juices and tonics from native plants, fruit, and coconuts, which she sells at markets. Her struggles are not uncommon among islanders. It's challenging to work in agriculture in these vulnerable places, where weather systems can upend growing seasons and harvests, combined with rigid government policies.

The sancocho she prepared was as good as any I'd ever had, maybe better, as most traditional preparations are quite meaty while this was fresh and nourishing with a hint of smokiness. Like so many of the best dishes, the beauty lies in its simplicity. I marveled at how easily it came together, how flawless it was—and that, despite being prepared on a beach just a few feet from the edge of the ocean, no sand got in.

Family is a complicated thing. Mine is decidedly fractured, disconnected. Itege and I have been somewhat perceived as misfits, as we both chose creative lives guided by our hearts and ideas. Itege more so than I. Years passed where we didn't know exactly where she was, when she was off the grid without any technology. We worried, naturally, particularly once she had children. On this day I could see the toll a challenging life had taken in the deep furrow of her brow, hands worn and wrinkled by hard work. Her eyes, on the other hand, tell a different story. I've known those eyes my entire life and have never seen them so vibrant: gold-flecked pools of light, like a lioness.

Across islands I've met others with this gaze, brimming with ancestral wisdom, powerful and resilient as a result of surviving challenges. Their strength drips from their fingertips and into their cooking, which is so often kissed by the char and smoke of open flames.

RECITES

GRILLING, ROASTING + SMOKING

Island
Philippines

Yield
4 servings

Active Time
45 minutes

Total Time
At least 3 hours

CHICKEN INASAL
GRILLED ANNATTO CHICKEN

This citrusy, smoky chicken is as pretty as it is tasty. That's thanks to annatto oil, which gives the chicken a vibrant orange-red hue while keeping the meat moist and crisping the skin. If you don't have access to annatto seeds, simply use vegetable oil, as annatto doesn't impart any flavor. But for true inasal, annatto oil is a must.

ANNATTO OIL

1 cup [240 ml] vegetable oil or lard

3 Tbsp annatto seeds (achiote) (see Tips)

CHICKEN

3 lb [1.4 kg] chicken leg quarters

2 medium shallots, minced

3 garlic cloves, finely chopped

2 Tbsp grated peeled fresh ginger

½ cup [34 g] minced lemongrass

¼ cup [60 ml] calamansi juice, sour orange juice, or equal parts tangerine and fresh lime juice

1 Tbsp dark brown sugar

⅓ cup [80 ml] coconut vinegar or apple cider vinegar

1 Tbsp kosher salt

2 tsp freshly ground black pepper

To make the annatto oil: In a small saucepan over medium-high, heat the oil and annatto seeds. Once the oil comes to a simmer, remove the saucepan from the heat, stir to combine, and let rest for 5 minutes. Using a fine-mesh sieve, strain the oil into a heat-safe container and set aside.

To make the chicken: Dry the chicken pieces with paper towels. Gently, using your fingers, lift the skin from the meat, being careful not to tear or remove it. Score each piece of the chicken with three or four deep cuts, down to the bone.

In a large nonreactive mixing bowl, combine the shallots, garlic, ginger, lemongrass, calamansi juice, brown sugar, vinegar, salt, and pepper and stir well. Add the chicken to the bowl and toss with the marinade, pushing the paste deep underneath the skin. Marinate in the refrigerator for 2 to 4 hours, or overnight if possible.

When ready to cook, heat a grill to medium. Remove the chicken from the marinade, shaking off excess marinade. Brush the chicken with the annatto oil, then place on the grill skin-side down. Grill with the lid off for at least 5 minutes to avoid sticking. Flip, then cook for an additional 25 to 30 minutes, flipping often and brushing with annatto oil on each rotation. The chicken is done when the juices run clear when pierced with a knife and the skin is crisp and a deep golden color, or when the internal temperature reaches 185°F [85°C]. Let rest for 5 to 10 minutes before serving.

TIPS If you don't have access to a grill, this chicken can also be prepared in the oven. Preheat the oven to 400°F [200°C] and line a rimmed baking sheet with aluminum foil. Place the chicken in an even layer across the baking sheet, skin-side up, and brush with annatto oil. Bake for 35 to 40 minutes, brushing with annatto oil every 7 to 10 minutes. Cook until the internal temperature reaches 185°F [85°C] and the skin is crisp and a deep golden color.

Calamansi juice is available frozen or bottled, typically in Asian grocery stores. If you can't find it, substitute half tangerine juice and half fresh lime juice.

If you can't find annatto seeds, replace the annatto oil with 3 Tbsp bacon fat, lard, or vegetable oil combined with 2 Tbsp of ground annatto.

Island
Puerto Rico

Yield
4 servings

Active Time
15 minutes

Total Time
45 minutes

CHURRASCO
GRILLED MARINATED SKIRT STEAK

In Puerto Rico, churrasco is garlicky wood-grilled steak. It's distinct from its Argentinian and Brazilian origins (the word *churrasco* encompasses grilled meats in both Spanish and Portuguese) though prepared similarly. Like so many island dishes, churrasco starts by tenderizing a tougher cut of meat—in this case skirt steak—with a flavorful marinade. I add a bit of adobo to my churrasco seasoning and serve it with Wasakaka (page 47), an herbaceous lime juice–forward sauce from the Dominican Republic. Smoke is key to churrasco flavor, so it should be grilled over an open fire, though a gas grill or a cast-iron skillet will do. Special thanks to Raúl Correa, Xavier Pacheco, and René Marichal for sharing their wisdom on this dish and space at their beautiful restaurant, BACOA: Finca + Fogón. Serve with steamed white rice and Habichuelas Guisadas con Calabaza (page 145), garnished with fresh tomato and avocado slices.

1½ lb [680 g] skirt steak or tri-tip (see Tip)

3 large garlic cloves

1 Tbsp finely chopped fresh oregano

1 Tbsp white vinegar

2 tsp olive oil

1 Tbsp store-bought or homemade Adobo Seasoning (page 39, or preferably Loísa or Badía brand)

2 tsp kosher salt, plus more as needed

Wasakaka (page 47), for serving

Steamed white rice, for serving

Sliced tomato and avocado, for garnish

Dry the steak with paper towels and place in a large resealable bag.

In a pilón, a mortar and pestle, or a small food processor, combine the garlic, oregano, vinegar, olive oil, adobo, and salt and grind into a loose paste. Pour the marinade over the steak. Seal the bag and shake well to coat the meat, rubbing it in gently. Let rest on the counter for 10 to 20 minutes, or refrigerate overnight. Be sure to let the steak come to room temperature before grilling.

Heat a grill to 500°F [260°C].

Remove the steak from the bag and shake off excess marinade. Place on the grill and sear for 1 to 3 minutes. Using tongs, pull up a corner to ensure the steak has a good dark char, bordering on burnt in places, before flipping, then cook for 1 more minute for rare or 2 minutes for medium-rare. Be careful not to overcook, or the steak will be tough.

Remove the steak from the grill and let rest for 5 to 7 minutes. Taste and sprinkle with additional salt if desired. Slice into strips and top with wasakaka, or serve the sauce on the side along with steamed white rice. Garnish with sliced tomato and avocado.

TIP Skirt steak and tri-tip are very different cuts, but both work well for this recipe. Because tri-tip is typically a thicker, rounder cut, you'll need to flip it a few more times on the grill and cook a few minutes longer.

Island
Jamaica

Yield
4 to 6 servings

Active Time
15 minutes

Total Time
1 hour

JERK PORK TENDERLOIN

Jerk is a powerfully complex blend of spices and aromatics redolent with cinnamon, allspice, cumin, and chile. Historically, it's tied to Maroons fleeing enslavement in the Jamaican foothills, and it is among the most iconic flavors of the Caribbean. True jerk is grilled over an open fire and is as much a seasoning as it is an action—because you can "jerk" pork, goat, chicken, and even fruits and vegetables. Pork tenderloin is far from the traditional application, as the most common protein choices are dark, often gamey or gristly cuts of meat that stand up to complex flavors. But this leaner, lighter meat is an excellent vessel for jerk. It's especially good when marinated overnight and grilled, but is so simple to prepare it can easily be made for a weeknight celebration. A simple jam glaze at the end adds sweetness and tang, caramelizing under a quick broil. This pairs beautifully with Rice and Peas (page 160), fried sweet plantains, or a bright, fresh garden salad.

JERK

One 2 in [5 cm] piece fresh ginger, scrubbed and finely chopped

3 green onions, white and green parts, coarsely chopped

6 garlic cloves, finely chopped

1 Tbsp kosher salt

1 or 2 scotch bonnet or habanero peppers (optional)

2 Tbsp finely chopped fresh thyme leaves

2 Tbsp dark brown sugar

3½ tsp ground allspice

1 tsp ground nutmeg

½ tsp cayenne pepper

½ tsp ground cumin

½ tsp ground coriander

½ cup [120 ml] fresh lime juice

1 Tbsp vegetable oil

PORK

1½ lb [680 g] pork tenderloin (see Tip)

¼ cup [60 ml] guava jam or preserves or other tangy fruit jam, such as mango, peach, or apricot

1 Tbsp boiling water

½ tsp fresh lemon juice

To make the jerk: In a food processor or blender, combine the ginger, green onions, garlic, salt, and chiles (if using) and pulse until minced. Add the thyme, brown sugar, allspice, nutmeg, cayenne, cumin, coriander, lime juice, and oil, then blend on medium-high speed until the mixture becomes a fine paste.

To make the pork: Dry the pork tenderloin with paper towels. Using a sharp paring knife, cut a series of deep holes into the meat, about 1 to 2 in [2.5 to 5 cm] depending on the thickness of the tenderloin.

Transfer the pork to a resealable bag or container with a tight lid and pour the marinade over. Let sit at room temperature for at least 10 minutes, or refrigerate overnight if possible. Bring to room temperature before continuing.

Adjust the oven rack to the top third of the oven and preheat the oven to 400°F [200°C]. Line a rimmed baking sheet with foil, then place the tenderloin in the center of the sheet and transfer to the oven. Roast until the internal temperature is 145°F [62°C] in the thickest part, about 25 minutes, flipping every 10 minutes to evenly brown.

Meanwhile, in a small nonreactive bowl, mix together the guava jam, boiling water, and lemon juice.

Increase the oven heat to a high broil. Carefully pull the pan out of the oven and brush the tenderloin with the glaze. Return to the broiler for 5 to 7 minutes, until the pork is a toasty dark brown with some charred spots, brushing once more with any remaining glaze if desired.

Remove from the oven and set the tenderloin on a carving board to rest for about 5 minutes. Cut into slices and top with any juices.

TIP Many pork tenderloins are sold in packs of two. This marinade is enough for 1½ lb [680 g] of tenderloin, so you can prepare both tenderloins by leaving a little space between them in the oven, or you can freeze one for later. Raw marinated pork freezes very well for several months or up to a year, and the marinade will more fully penetrate the meat if you freeze it.

MAS HUNI
SMOKED TUNA WITH COCONUT

Tuna and coconut are commonly found in Maldivian cuisine, notably in this national dish. Quick to prepare and great for a snack or a simple lunch, this version of mas huni uses those same ingredients, but with valhomas (preserved, smoked tuna) instead of fresh. Valhomas can be difficult to source, but high-quality canned tuna in brine is a great substitute. The dish is a dynamic sensory experience—spicy, sour, sweet, and smoky. Serve it with chapati, naan, steamed white rice, or a simple salad.

½ scotch bonnet or habanero pepper, stemmed, seeded if desired to mitigate spiciness, and finely chopped (about 1 tsp)

½ small red onion, minced

½ cup [120 ml] fresh lemon juice

½ tsp kosher salt

Two 5 oz [140 g] cans valhomas or tuna in brine, drained (see Tip)

1 cup [80 g] unsweetened grated or shredded coconut

¼ tsp smoked paprika (optional)

In a large nonreactive mixing bowl, combine the scotch bonnet, onion, lemon juice, and salt. Using a muddler or the bottom of a large wooden spoon, macerate the mixture by pressing it against the bottom of the bowl. Stir the mixture well, then add the tuna and coconut and toss gently to incorporate.

Sprinkle with the smoked paprika (if using) and serve immediately, or let sit for 30 minutes at room temperature to deepen the flavors.

TIP   Smoked trout makes a delicious and readily available substitution for the tuna.

MASIKITA
PAPAYA-MARINATED BEEF SKEWERS

A popular street food in Antananarivo, Madagascar's capital, these flavorful skewers come together quickly. Papaya juice, a natural tenderizer, is blended with aromatic herbs and effervescent cola, rendering otherwise tough meat tender and caramelizing on the grill.

MARINADE

2 large garlic cloves, minced

One 5 in [13 cm] piece fresh ginger, peeled and grated

2 Tbsp soy sauce

½ cup [120 ml] papaya juice

⅓ cup [80 ml] cola

2 Tbsp lemon juice

1 Tbsp grated lemon zest

2 Tbsp tomato paste

3 Tbsp vegetable oil

1 Tbsp kosher salt

¼ tsp freshly ground black pepper

BEEF

2 lb [910 g] beef, such as flank steak or chuck roast, cut into 4 to 5 in [10 to 12.5 cm] strips

Twelve to fifteen 10 to 12 in [25 to 30.5 cm] bamboo skewers

To make the marinade: In a medium nonreactive mixing bowl, combine the garlic, ginger, soy sauce, papaya juice, cola, lemon juice, lemon zest, tomato paste, oil, salt, and pepper and stir well to incorporate, using a fork as needed to break up the tomato paste.

To make the beef: Place the beef in a large resealable bag or airtight container, then pour over the marinade. Marinate in the refrigerator overnight, or for at least 3 hours.

Put the bamboo skewers on a rimmed baking sheet and cover with water until submerged. Let the skewers soak until ready to cook.

Once the beef is marinated, reserve 1 cup of marinade, then thread beef onto the bamboo skewers.

Heat a grill to medium-high, then grill the skewers for 15 to 20 minutes, turning every 5 minutes with the cover on and brushing once or twice with the reserved marinade. Let the meat rest on the cool side of the grill for 7 minutes to cook off the marinade. Serve immediately.

SIDNEY-MAX ETIENNE
HAITI

Paula Hyppolite was determined that her son be born in Haiti. They were living in New York when she became pregnant, and she returned to Haiti in time for Sidney-Max Etienne to take his first breath there. His early years were spent on his family's land, connecting with nature and digging yams out of the soil. The family would roast the tubers over an open fire with the skin on, for a dish called patat boukannen.

They returned to the States when Sidney was just three, but interest in his homeland lingered. In particular, he grew interested in forests and permaculture. The fundamental ingredient for grilling and smoking—wood—is a complex issue in Haiti, where trees have been cut to produce charcoal and make space for farming at such a high rate that only about one percent of their primary forests remain. Sidney had been working as a graphic designer, but the looming environmental crises in Haiti, compounded by political and economic instability, earthquakes, and health crises, beckoned him home.

Sidney returned to Haiti at age thirty-two. He lived in a tent for the first two and a half years—enough time to plant enough trees so that he would feel justified using lumber to build his home. The first few years were focused on reforestation, but his mission grew over time. "During my first years here, I realized a few things,"

Sidney said. "One being that humans aren't separate from nature and we are indeed part of this planet's biodiversity. So it simply started as growing trees and flourished into growing communities."

With the help of his mother and his partner, Yi Liu, Sidney founded Grown in Haiti, a regenerative reforestation project committed to biodiversity and food sovereignty. He began by creating a nursery of diverse food-bearing trees, with the goal of helping local communities become more sustainable. They then started providing locals with saplings, access to the food grown on the property, tools, and workshops on improving soil quality and crop cultivation.

Today, Sidney looks out on sixty different plant varieties on the properties. "Water apple, Malay apple, baobab, lychee, bilimbi, star fruit, mata kucing, lontan, dragon fruit, mango, breadfruit, Caribbean almond, avocado, chupa-chupa, lime, lemon, Meyer lemon, grapefruit, sour orange, vanilla, cashew apple, moringa, Manila tamarind, guava, annatto, noni, ylang, jackfruit, durian, sea grapes, grapes, jaboticaba, maya breadnut, papaya, mamey apple, sapodilla, pond apple, custard apple, black pepper vine, passion fruit vine, squash vine, chocolate sapote, guama machete, sugar apple, calabash, cinnamon, bay leaf, allspice, ackee, various bananas, açaí palm, corozo palm, royal palm, Christmas palm, star apple, soursop, loquat, and snake fruit," he listed proudly.

In addition to growing and sharing edible plants, Sidney has started cataloging Haiti's endemic flora and fauna in the hopes of expanding preservation efforts across the island. "Whatever may or may not unfold, if I'm judging the future by what I'm seeing around me . . . it looks abundant and green."

Island
Philippines

Yield
6 servings

Active Time
30 minutes

Total Time
4 hours

FILIPINO BARBECUE PORK SKEWERS WITH PINEAPPLE MARINADE

This magical marinade pairs well with just about any kind of protein. While it is great for seafood, particularly shrimp, it's particularly good for tough, fatty pork shoulder. The natural enzymes in the pineapple tenderize the dense pork, allowing the marinade to infuse the meat with chiles, garlic, and soy. *Islas* recipe developer Jenn de la Vega recommends adding a bit of 7UP (not Sprite!) to add a bit of extra sweetness.

MARINADE

1½ cups [360 ml] pineapple juice

½ cup [120 ml] soy sauce

¼ cup [55 g] brown sugar

10 to 12 garlic cloves, minced

4 red bird's eye chiles

2 tsp kosher salt

2 tsp freshly cracked black pepper

PORK

2 lb [910 g] boneless fatty pork, such as belly or shoulder, cut into 1 in [2.5 cm] pieces

Twelve to fifteen 10 to 12 in [25 to 30.5 cm] bamboo skewers

Steamed white rice, for serving

Sinamak (page 48) or Toyomansi (page 45), for serving (optional)

To make the marinade: In a medium nonreactive mixing bowl, combine the pineapple juice, soy sauce, brown sugar, garlic, chiles, salt, and pepper and stir well to incorporate.

To make the pork: In a large resealable bag or airtight container, combine the pork and the marinade. Marinate in the refrigerator overnight, or for at least 3 hours.

Put the bamboo skewers on a rimmed baking sheet and cover with water until submerged. Let the skewers soak until ready to cook.

When ready to cook, thread the pork pieces onto the bamboo skewers. Reserve the remaining marinade.

Heat a grill to medium, then grill the skewers for 20 to 30 minutes, turning often to avoid burning, and brushing with the reserved marinade often. Rest on the cooler side of the grill or upper rack for 7 minutes to cook off the marinade.

Serve as an appetizer, or alongside steamed white rice and dipping sauces, if desired, such as sinamak or toyomansi.

Island
Seychelles

Yield
4 to 6 servings

Active Time
35 minutes

Total Time
1 hour

PWASON GRIYE
GRILLED RED SNAPPER

Because islands are surrounded by water, it's only natural that fresh fish is typically abundant. This is especially true in Seychelles. This dish celebrates some of the most iconic flavors found there: Fresh catch is rubbed down in Seychellois Massalé (page 40), a spicy, warming curry blend fragrant with cinnamon, clove, cardamom, and black pepper paired with a bright tomato chutney, sweet and sour with tamarind, which you can make while the fish marinates. This dish is ideally grilled over a wood fire, as the smokiness activates the spices and flavors in a unique way. The chutney will keep for at least 1 week in the refrigerator and freezes well for up to several months. The delicious fish, on the other hand, will be gone in minutes. Serve it with steamed white rice or Aros di Coco (page 293), Asar (page 104), or Salad Lalo Kreol (page 115).

FISH

2 large garlic cloves, minced

1 Tbsp minced peeled fresh ginger

2 Tbsp chopped fresh cilantro leaves

2¼ tsp Seychellois Massalé (page 40)

2 or 3 red bird's eye chiles, stemmed, seeded if desired to mitigate spiciness, and finely chopped

2 Tbsp vegetable oil

1 tsp kosher salt, plus more as needed

Freshly ground black pepper

One 2 to 3 lb [910 g to 1.4 kg] whole red snapper, cleaned and scaled, head and tail on (see Tip)

Steamed white rice, for serving

Lemon or lime wedges, for garnish

TAMARIND-TOMATO CHUTNEY

1 cup [160 g] chopped tomato

1 large shallot, chopped

1 jalapeño, seeded and chopped

½ tsp brown or turbinado sugar

2 Tbsp tamarind paste

2 large garlic cloves

4 whole cloves

1 cinnamon stick

½ tsp black mustard seeds

½ tsp cumin seeds

1 Tbsp fresh lime juice

1 tsp kosher salt, plus more as needed

¼ tsp freshly ground black pepper

To make the fish: In a large nonreactive mixing bowl, combine the garlic, ginger, cilantro, massalé, chiles, oil, salt, and a few grinds of pepper and blend well with a fork to form a paste.

Rinse the fish inside and out with cold water and dry with a paper towel. Slice three shallow cuts, about ½ in [13 mm] deep, into the thickest parts of each side of the fish. Season liberally with salt and pepper.

Add the fish to the bowl and rub the seasoning paste all over the fish, including into the slits and the cavity. Let sit at room temperature for at least 10 minutes, or refrigerate for up to 1 hour.

To make the tamarind-tomato chutney: In a blender or food processor, combine the tomato, shallot, jalapeño, brown sugar, tamarind paste, and garlic and grind into a smooth paste. Transfer the mixture to a deep skillet and add the cloves, cinnamon stick, and ½ cup [120 ml] of water. Cover and cook over medium-low for 7 to 10 minutes, until the chutney thickens and darkens.

Meanwhile, in a small skillet over medium, toast the mustard seeds until the seeds start to pop, 2 to 3 minutes. Add the cumin seeds and toast for 1 more minute, until the seeds darken and become fragrant.

continued

Add the toasted seeds to the simmering chutney, then stir in the lime juice, salt, and pepper. Cover and simmer on low for 10 minutes more, until the sauce thickens and darkens slightly, then remove from the heat and let rest, covered, while you cook the fish.

Heat a grill to 400°F [200°C].

Remove the fish from the marinade and shake off excess. Grill the fish for about 15 to 20 minutes, flipping carefully halfway through. Carefully remove from the grill using a large spatula (and tongs if necessary) and let rest for a few minutes before serving. Sprinkle the fish with additional salt if desired and serve with the prepared chutney alongside steamed white rice and lemon wedges.

TIP   This recipe also works well with whole grouper or sea bass. Alternatively, you can use fish fillets, grilling only on the skin side and reducing the cook time to 10 to 15 minutes.

Island
Indonesia

Yield
12 to 15 skewers

Active Time
40 minutes

Total Time
At least 3 hours

SATE AYAM
INDONESIAN GRILLED CHICKEN SKEWERS

One of the best-known Indonesian snacks, sate is spiced, skewered grilled meat. Beef, chicken, goat, and even shrimp are common, and are typically basted with kecap manis—the region's signature aromatic, thick sweet soy sauce—and grilled over a blazing hot fire. The key is to ensure the meat is cut just right: thin enough that it absorbs the marinade well, but not so thin that it won't stay on the skewers. This version calls for chicken thighs, and while the marinade and basting sauce require a little preparation up front, the dynamic flavor is well worth the effort. Serve on its own, as an appetizer with Coconut Peanut Sauce (page 43), or with steamed jasmine rice and a side salad for a flavorful, light dinner.

MARINADE

1 Tbsp grated peeled fresh ginger

1 Tbsp minced fresh lemongrass

2 large garlic cloves, minced

¼ tsp ground white pepper

2 tsp ground coriander

1 tsp ground cumin

½ tsp freshly grated nutmeg

1 tsp kosher salt, plus more if desired

1 tsp vegetable oil

½ cup [120 g] kecap manis

CHICKEN

1 lb [455 g] boneless, skinless chicken thighs, cut into 1 in [2.5 cm] cubes

Twelve to fifteen 10 to 12 in [25 to 30.5 cm] bamboo skewers

BASTING SAUCE

1 large shallot, thinly sliced

1 Tbsp minced fresh lemongrass

¼ cup [60 g] kecap manis

1 tsp fish sauce

2 Tbsp fresh lime juice

To make the marinade: In a small bowl, combine the ginger, lemongrass, garlic, white pepper, coriander, cumin, nutmeg, salt, oil, and kecap manis and blend well with a fork. Taste and adjust salt as desired.

To make the chicken: Transfer the chicken pieces to a resealable bag or airtight container, and pour over the marinade. Marinate in the refrigerator overnight, or for at least 2 hours.

Put the bamboo skewers in a rimmed baking sheet and cover with water until submerged. Let the skewers soak until ready to cook.

To make the basting sauce: In a small bowl, combine the shallot, lemongrass, kecap manis, fish sauce, and lime juice.

When ready to cook, heat a grill to medium-high. While the grill comes to temperature, thread three or four pieces of meat onto each skewer, lengthwise so that the chicken lays as flat as possible. Make sure the pieces are touching. Continue until you use all the chicken.

Brush each skewer with the basting sauce, then place them, basted-side down, on the grill, basting once again. Cook the skewers in batches if your grill is not large enough to hold them all, basting and turning for 4 to 7 minutes, until the chicken is charred and caramelized but not burnt. Serve immediately (or eat them right off the grill).

LEMONGRASS ADOBO GRILLED CHICKEN WITH PINEAPPLE

Inspired by the diverse communities of immigrants—Japanese, Chinese, Korean, Filipino, Portuguese, and Puerto Rican among others—who came to call Hawai'i home as agricultural workers, this recipe blends garlic, yuzu, ginger, adobo, and pineapple for a deeply tropical dish. Serve it as an entrée with coconut rice and sautéed bok choy, or on top of a green salad with lots of fresh cucumber.

2 Tbsp chopped fresh lemongrass

1 Tbsp chopped peeled fresh ginger

3 large garlic cloves

1 Tbsp Adobo Seasoning (page 39)

1 tsp kosher salt

1 Tbsp rice vinegar

2 Tbsp yuzu juice or sour orange juice (see Tips)

3 Tbsp chopped fresh cilantro leaves, plus more for garnish

1 tsp mirin

6 large boneless, skinless chicken thighs (about 1½ lb [680 g])

1 fresh pineapple, peeled and sliced into 1 in [2.5 cm] rounds

1 to 2 Tbsp grapeseed or vegetable oil

Lemon or lime wedges, for garnish

In a small food processor, combine the lemongrass, ginger, garlic, adobo, and salt and pulse until well chopped, stopping to scrape down the sides with a spatula as needed. Add the vinegar, yuzu juice, cilantro, and mirin and pulse to combine, scraping down the sides and lid of the food processor as needed, to form a loose paste.

Pat the chicken dry with paper towels, then place in a large resealable bag. Pour in the marinade and seal the bag, leaving a little air so the marinade can fully cover the chicken. Shake well and gently massage the marinade into the meat. Marinate in the refrigerator for 12 to 24 hours if possible, or for at least 30 minutes at room temperature.

When ready to cook, heat a grill to 400°F [200°C].

In a large nonreactive mixing bowl, toss the pineapple slices in the grapeseed oil until fully coated.

Remove the chicken from the bag, shaking off any excess marinade. Reserve the remaining marinade for basting.

Place the chicken and pineapple on the grill, turning every few minutes and basting the chicken between turns. If anything starts to burn, move it to the cool side of the grill (see page 233). Grill for 15 to 25 minutes, until the chicken is tender and breaks easily when pressed with tongs. The pineapple may cook more quickly than the chicken, so keep a close eye on it and flip often, brushing with additional oil if it starts to look dry.

Transfer the cooked chicken and pineapple to a rimmed baking sheet and tent loosely with foil. Let rest for 7 to 10 minutes before serving with lemon wedges.

TIP If you can't find yuzu or sour orange juice, substitute 1½ Tbsp fresh lime juice mixed with 1 tsp orange juice.

Island
Fiji

Yield
6 to 8 servings

Active Time
20 minutes

Total Time
**At least 1 hour
30 minutes**

FIJIAN LAMB BARBECUE

With a handful of simple ingredients, these flavorful lamb chops come together in minutes. This spice paste of garlic, ginger, chiles, and turmeric is adaptable and can be used to season chicken, beef, or pork as well. The lamb chops benefit from an overnight marinade, but if you're short on time, simply marinate them at room temperature for as long as you can.

2 lb [910 g] lamb chops, at least 1 in [2.5 cm] thick

3 large garlic cloves, minced

1 large jalapeño or serrano chile, seeded if desired to mitigate spiciness, minced

1 Tbsp grated peeled fresh ginger

2 tsp ground turmeric

2 Tbsp vegetable oil

1½ tsp kosher salt

Trim each lamb chop of excess fat and tendon.

In a large mixing bowl, combine the garlic, jalapeño, ginger, turmeric, oil, and salt and mix well with a fork to form a paste. Add the lamb and toss well to ensure the meat is evenly coated. Cover and marinate in the refrigerator for 12 to 24 hours if possible, otherwise at room temperature for at least 1 hour. (If refrigerating, take the chops out of the refrigerator at least 1 hour before cooking and bring to room temperature.)

Heat a grill to about 450°F [230°C]. Cook the chops, flipping every few minutes, until they are evenly browned with plenty of char, 7 to 10 minutes total. Transfer the chops to a rimmed baking sheet and tent loosely with foil. Let rest 5 minutes before serving, pouring any accumulated juices over the chops.

TIP Be careful not to overcook the chops, or the meat will be dry. The chops should reach an internal temperature of 160°F [68°C].

ISLAS

Island
Philippines

Yield
2 servings

Active Time
10 minutes

Total Time
30 minutes

ENSALADANG TALONG
GRILLED EGGPLANT AND VEGETABLE SALAD

Your next favorite cookout staple, this simple preparation of grilled vegetables is made more dynamic by adding pink bagoong alamang, a shrimp or krill paste that is sometimes labeled "salted shrimp fry." A little goes a long way! In contrast, ginisang bagoong is sautéed shrimp paste with a sweet, roasty flavor. Try a little bit with a slice of ripe mango to see how much you should add to your dish.

4 medium Japanese eggplants

2 medium plum tomatoes, halved lengthwise and sliced

1 medium yellow onion, halved

½ cup [120 ml] sugarcane vinegar or white vinegar

½ tsp sugar

¼ tsp kosher salt

¼ tsp freshly ground black pepper

Steamed white rice and sliced ripe mango, for serving (optional)

2 Tbsp bagoong alamang shrimp paste, for garnish (optional; see Tip)

Heat a gas or charcoal grill to medium-high.

Grill the eggplant, tomatoes, and onion—the eggplant will take 10 to 12 minutes per side to become fully cooked and soft, while the onion and tomato will take 3 minutes per side to become softened and lightly charred. Set each vegetable aside when it is ready.

Slice the eggplant lengthwise. Coarsely chop the tomatoes and onions, then scoop them onto the eggplant.

In a small nonreactive bowl, combine the vinegar, sugar, salt, and pepper, stirring to dissolve the salt and sugar completely. Pour over the tomato, eggplant, and onion. Serve with steamed white rice, mango, and shrimp paste on the side if desired.

TIP   To make this vegetarian, substitute equal parts white miso and minced capers, ground or blended to create a paste, for the shrimp paste.

Island
Martinique

Yield
4 servings

Active Time
30 minutes

Total Time
At least 2 hours 30 minutes

POULET BOUCANÉ
SUGARCANE SMOKED CHICKEN

Sold at roadside stands across Martinique, poulet bucané, or buccaneer chicken, is marinated overnight in a spicy, tangy sauce, then cooked over a smoky open fire. Traditionally it's set over sugarcane, making use of an ingredient that shaped Caribbean history in complex ways. For this recipe, chicken is spatchcocked and set over pieces of sugarcane inside a grill rack. This tool helps keep the sugarcane close to the chicken and enables you to flip the whole chicken safely to ensure it cooks evenly and gets maximum smoke.

CHICKEN

One 4 lb [1.8 kg] whole chicken, spatchcocked

6 large garlic cloves, minced

2 green onions, white and green parts, chopped

1 yellow onion, minced

2 or 3 red bird's eye chiles, stemmed, seeded if desired to mitigate spiciness, and chopped

1 tsp ground allspice

¼ cup [15 g] chopped fresh thyme sprigs

2 Tbsp kosher salt

¼ tsp freshly cracked black pepper

½ cup [120 ml] fresh lime juice

½ cup [120 ml] white rum

Three 7 in [17 cm] pieces fresh sugarcane (see Tips)

SAUCE CHIEN

2 Tbsp chopped fresh flat-leaf parsley

2 small garlic cloves, minced

1 small red bird's eye chile, seeded if desired to mitigate spiciness

1 green onion, white and green parts, minced

1 small shallot, minced

¼ cup [60 ml] fresh lime juice

¼ cup [60 ml] olive oil

¼ cup [60 ml] warm water

1 tsp kosher salt, plus more as needed

½ tsp freshly ground black pepper

To make the chicken: Rinse the chicken, remove bone shards if needed, pat the chicken dry with paper towels, and score the chicken breast, thighs, and legs through the skin. Transfer the chicken to an extra-large resealable bag or a container with a lid.

In a medium nonreactive mixing bowl, combine the garlic, green onions, yellow onion, chiles, allspice, thyme, salt, pepper, lime juice, and rum and blend with a fork. Alternatively, grind the marinade ingredients in a food processor.

Pour the marinade over the chicken, then toss well and massage to evenly coat. Marinate for at least 1 hour at room temperature or in the refrigerator overnight.

When ready to cook, heat a grill to 450°F [230°C].

Meanwhile, prepare the sugarcane by rinsing, then drying it well. Using a cleaver or other heavy knife (a machete or hatchet will do), cut the sugarcane pieces in half by holding the sugarcane upright on a cutting board, and carefully inserting the center of the knife through the center of the cane. Then, use your other hand to push the blade through, carefully banging your palm down on the top of the knife if needed.

continued

To make the sauce chien: In a 1 pt [475 ml] jar with a lid, combine the parsley, garlic, chile, green onion, shallot, lime juice, olive oil, water, salt, and pepper. Tighten the lid and shake vigorously to combine.

Once the grill reaches the desired temperature, place a 10 by 12 in [25 by 30.5 cm] grill basket over a large baking sheet. Lay the sugarcane pieces on the sheet, cut-side up. Carefully transfer the chicken from the marinade to the sugarcane, breast-side up. Close the lid of the basket and secure the latch, using an additional clamp if needed.

Place the basket on the grill and roast for 30 to 45 minutes, turning and basting every 5 to 7 minutes to cook evenly, ensuring you cook off the marinade (see Tips). Remove the basket from the grill and set over a clean rimmed baking sheet. Loosely tent with foil and let rest for 7 to 10 minutes, then remove the chicken from the basket. Transfer it to a cutting board and chop into eight pieces with a sharp cleaver, pouring over any reserved juices from the baking sheet. Serve with sauce chien on the side.

TIPS Sugarcane can be difficult to source. Lemongrass is a good substitute, or you can omit this ingredient altogether.

If the chicken starts to get too dark or burn in places, remove it from the grill basket, place it on a baking sheet, and finish in a 350°F [180°C] oven until the thickest part of the breast has reached 165°F [74°C], likely another 10 to 20 minutes.

Island
Puerto Rico

Yield
4 servings

Active Time
30 minutes

Total Time
**At least 1 hour
30 minutes**

CHULETAS AL CARBÓN
GRILLED PORK CHOPS

This may be the only pork chop recipe you'll ever need. Using a classic Puerto Rican adobo, a wet paste that is more flavorful and dynamic than the more commonly known ground spice blend, bone-in pork chops are marinated in garlic, vinegar, olive oil, and oregano with fresh-squeezed clementine juice for a bit of sweetness, then grilled over a wood or charcoal fire. If desired, boneless pork loin chops will also work with this recipe, though they'll cook faster and be less juicy. Double the recipe for your next cookout, and serve the pork whole or cut into slices on a large cutting board.

One 2½ to 3 lb [1.1 to 1.4 kg] bone-in pork loin chops, at least 1 in [2.5 cm] thick (see Tips)

3 large garlic cloves, minced

3 Tbsp store-bought or homemade Sazón Seasoning (page 39)

2 tsp kosher salt, plus more as needed

1 Tbsp white vinegar

2 tsp olive oil

1½ tsp dried oregano

½ cup [120 ml] fresh clementine juice

½ tsp freshly ground black pepper

Dry the pork chops with paper towels and place in a large resealable bag.

In a pilón, a mortar and pestle, or a small food processor, combine the garlic, sazón, salt, vinegar, olive oil, oregano, clementine juice, and pepper and grind into a paste. Pour the marinade over the chops. Seal the bag and shake well to coat the meat, rubbing it in gently. Let rest at room temperature for 30 minutes, or refrigerate for 12 to 24 hours.

When ready to cook, heat a grill to 400°F [200°C].

Remove the chops from the bag, shaking off excess marinade, and set on a rimmed baking sheet. Transfer the remaining marinade to a small bowl to use for basting (optional).

Place the chops on the hottest side of the grill and sear for 2 to 4 minutes on each side (see page 233). Move the chops to the cooler side of the grill and cook for 20 to 30 minutes, flipping often to avoid burning, and basting a few times if desired (see Tips).

Remove the chops from the grill once they are fully browned with plenty of char and their internal temperature reaches 140°F [60°C] at the thickest part. Transfer to a small rimmed dish, tent loosely with foil, and let rest for 7 to 10 minutes before serving. The chops can be served individually or sliced into thick strips and drizzled with the accumulated juices.

TIPS This recipe will also work for boneless pork loin chops; reduce the cooking time to 10 to 15 minutes.

If using the marinade to baste your chops, be sure to stop basting at least 5 minutes before you think they'll be done, to fully cook off the marinade.

CHAPTER SIX

STEAMING + IN-GROUND COOKING

Vanuatu

C louds of smoke and ash and sputtering molten lava erupt from the center of Mount Yasur on the southernmost tip of Vanuatu. Among the most active volcanoes on the planet, it's been bubbling continuously for more than 800 years. In Vanuatu lore, Yasur is believed to be the home of an enigmatic god-man named John Frum, living within the molten lava, waiting to be reborn. It's one of the few volcanoes on earth that you can approach on foot, making it an attraction for brave tourists. It's a beacon to the Ni-Vanuatu—the island's natives—of the origins of their volcanic archipelagic home, but also a potential signal of its demise.

Vanuatu is an old place, and home to the Ni-Vanuatu (or of-Vanuatu), a large ethnic group largely of Melanesian descent who are believed to have been on the island for about 3,000 years. Because of its size and relative isolation in the South Pacific, Vanuatu has retained much of its ancestral heritage and culture, which is apparent in the island's cuisine. Unlike neighboring Guam, whose cuisine has been heavily impacted by centuries of colonization and imposed ingredients (see page 54), the Ni-Vanuatu diet continues to be full of fresh, vibrant fruits and vegetables—jackfruit, pawpaw, papaya, cabbages, peppers, greens, breadfruit, cassava, taro, and yams. The most common style of cooking in Vanuatu is lovo, or in-ground cooking. Done in a variety of styles—traditionally in an in-ground clay oven, layered with hot stones, covered with banana leaves— the lovo mirrors the internal heat of the island's volcanoes.

Vanuatu is an archipelago comprising eighty-three islands set in a Y shape, only fourteen of which have surface areas of more than 62 sq mi [160 sq km]. Although relatively unknown outside the region, Vanuatu holds an important place in how the United States perceives the Pacific. During World War II, 100,000 American troops were stationed on one of these islands, Espiritu Santo, or Santo as it's known. (Once called New Hebrides, Vanuatu inspired a John Michener book that spawned the war-centered Rodgers and Hammerstein musical *South Pacific*.) Before leaving the island, the military tossed hundreds of pieces of war equipment into the ocean because the local government would not purchase them, causing a veritable ecological disaster. These artifacts can still be found underwater, as well as planes abandoned on land, their wings peeking out of dense jungle vines.

These Western associations aside, Vanuatu is truly a stunning place. Coconut plantations dot the islands, where copra—the pulp of coconuts— is harvested for oil and is the island's most important cash crop. Kava, sandalwood, white wood, and melektree are also important commodities, though they've been experiencing a decline in recent years due to decades of unregulated harvesting.

Colonization—first French, then British—and immigration from neighboring countries has brought together Polynesian, Melanese, Chinese, and Vietnamese people. Most Ni-Vanuatu speak English, French, and their adaptive native tongue Bislama—itself a creolized language with Spanish and other European influences. Colonization also left deep scars on the island. Beginning in 1847, tens of thousands of Ni-Vanuatu boys and men were forcibly removed or tricked into going to work as indentured servants on British sugar plantations in Fiji and Australia. Thousands died of exposure to illnesses and mistreatment, and many were simply never heard from again.

Being of an ancient civilization, the Ni-Vanuatu have preserved much of their indigenous culture and foodways. Social customs are egalitarian in nature, seeming almost utopian in an increasingly individualistic world. Their society is structured around an extended family unit, so if a child cannot be properly cared for, another family member will adopt them. All that you earn you must share, and if a family member falls on hard times, your responsibility is to support them. Meals are served family style, traditionally on the ground atop a cloth or sometimes banana leaves, everyone eating with their hands from the same dishes. Food is considered a fundamental right, and no one is allowed to go hungry, no matter the circumstance.

Vanuatu is an island paradise. And yet, in so many ways it is among the most vulnerable of them all. Unlike islands such as Seychelles, which has only recently had to deal with direct hits from violent storms, Vanuatu has always been battered by cyclones, and they're getting stronger. But like Seychelles, their coastline is being quickly eroded by rising sea levels. Local volcanoes could erupt at any time; in January 2022, the Hunga Tonga-Hunga Ha'apai underwater volcano near Tonga erupted, bringing tsunami waves to neighboring Vanuatu and offering a window into what may happen if its own underground volcano, Kuwae, should erupt one day. But these are the vulnerabilities they're used to, the ones that have bred a resilient, caring culture—and approaches to cooking that make extensive use of available resources.

Fundamentally, much of cooking is about turning the inedible edible, and doing so in a way that is nourishing and delicious. In Vanuatu, an island archipelago that is perhaps the least developed of any featured in *Islas*, you see how ingenuity and available resources combine to produce unique dishes that mirror other societies in similar climates and similar terrains across the planet.

The recipes in this chapter bring together dishes that use sustained heat and steam to cook rice, marinated meat and fish, and banana leaf–wrapped parcels.

Although in-ground earth ovens are commonly used to prepare these dishes, they are hard to come by in urban settings, so these recipes have been adapted for modern kitchens with an emphasis on preserving the spirit of these dishes and replicating their flavor profiles.

From Indonesia, Bebek Betutu (page 275) is whole duck marinated in garlic, chiles, and Balinese thousand-spice blend, then wrapped in banana leaves and steamed—perfuming and tenderizing the meat and creating a velvety sauce you can pour onto fragrant, turmeric-laced Indonesian Nasi Kuning (page 289). Puerto Rican Cazuela (page 294), among the few desserts in this book, is made by blending pumpkin and batata, or white sweet potato, with coconut milk, cloves, and star anise and then baking it inside banana leaves.

The complexity of island food is in the procurement of its ingredients and the enduring wisdom of its arbiters. Arguably, these recipes are among the most challenging in this book. They may be particularly unfamiliar to folks who haven't explored the tropics.

The recipes included are guides, many of which are sourced from islanders and family—including my grandmother's Pasteles de Masa (page 284)—adapted with common ingredients available in the United States. Before getting started, read the recipe carefully, get to know the ingredients, and then go for it.

STEAMING WITH BANANA LEAVES

There were too many variations across recipes in this chapter to provide meaningful instruction in other areas, so I've chosen to focus on steaming with banana leaves. Like coconuts and rice, banana leaves unite the tropics. Even though we think of them as trees, bananas and plantains are herbaceous plants, rhizomes that spring up from a network of interlocking roots. The fruit they produce is abundant and can be enjoyed in all stages of ripeness, and their leaves are an incredibly versatile tool. They provide a buffer to protect food from direct heat, a package within which food can be roasted or steamed, all the while perfuming food with an unmistakable earthy, slightly sweet, grassy aroma and flavor. Fresh, clean leaves

can be used to handle food, as serving dishes, and as the centerpieces for celebratory meals such as a Filipino kamayan buffet, where whole roast suckling pig, rice, vegetables, pickles, and sauces are set across a long leaf-covered surface and piled high. And because these plants dot the landscape, cooking with banana leaves ties body to earth in a special, visceral way.

People in the tropics have easy access to banana leaves, since there's likely a plant growing nearby. Even decorative banana plants, which grow well in hot, humid places across the planet, can be used for cooking and serving food. But even if you don't live in one of these environments, banana leaves are commonly found in the freezer section of Latin American or Asian specialty grocery stores. And because they're either readily available in the local environment or very affordable when store bought, they are an ingredient you can experiment with freely.

HOW TO WORK WITH BANANA LEAVES

Fresh banana leaves are far more flexible and watertight than frozen leaves. To start, rinse leaves in warm water and dry them with a clean towel. Right before using them, pass the leaves over a hot flame—either a gas range, grill, or open fire—in order to make them more pliable.

When working with frozen leaves, let them defrost on the counter overnight, in the refrigerator for a day, or out in the sun for a few hours. As with fresh leaves, rinse them, dry them, and pass them over a flame before using.

Banana leaves are an ideal casing for packets such as Seychellois Moukat (page 287), the key being to use exceptionally starchy ingredients such as cassava, yams, plantains, and cornmeal as a base for the tamal. As with Hawaiian Kālua Pua'a (page 278), banana leaves are also a functional, perfumed wrapper for meat. They hold up well to sustained high heat, so you can use them to steam raw meat, seafood, and vegetables.

Always firmly wrap banana leaf packets, ensuring there are no cracks in your leaves so that ingredients steam evenly and you don't lose precious juices. Tie the packets with kitchen twine like a present.

Allow the packets to rest at room temperature for at least 10 minutes prior to opening. When ready to serve, use kitchen sheers to cut the twine, then unwrap them carefully, allowing steam to escape from one end to avoid burning yourself.

TROUBLESHOOTING

• Frozen leaves are more likely to break than fresh leaves, even when they've been heated. Have extra leaves handy in case you need to layer them.

• If you are unable to source banana leaves, you can substitute ti or bamboo leaves. But if you're unable to find any leaves for the recipes in this chapter, parchment paper is a good substitute, particularly when wrapped with additional aluminum foil to lock in moisture and juices.

PRIMROSE SIRI
VANUATU

Santo, Vanuatu's largest island, is home to Primrose "Rose" Siri and her family, and where she runs her namesake restaurant, Rosie's, in Luganville. Her daughter is head server, and her nieces are cooks in this family establishment that offers catering for local businesses and medical facilities, as well as take-out and in-restaurant dining. A small restaurant with just ten tables, it's open Monday through Saturday and is busiest at lunchtime.

Primrose is forty-five years old, married—her husband is a local corrections officer—with three daughters ages twenty-six, twenty-two, and nineteen. While she lives on Santo today, she comes from Banks Islands, among the most remote cluster of islands in the chain along its northeastern edge. There, ancient traditions are very much preserved and practiced by locals, including her brother Sandy Sur, who orchestrates presentations of Vanuatu traditions for locals and tourists alike. This includes water music performances, where women stand waist-deep in water wearing dresses made of palm leaves and crowned with fuchsia flower garlands, while producing trance-inducing rhythms by slapping the water with their hands, singing soulful chants that bounce up from the percussive splashing.

Rose is always ready with a smile, a welcoming toothy grin with a bit of a wrinkle in her nose. She couldn't afford to go to university, so at age nineteen she got her first restaurant job as a server. The experience got her curious about cooking, and it wasn't long before she made her way into the kitchen. She loves to cook and believes that she infuses her own joy into the food she makes. Every dish she serves in her restaurant was prepared at home first, her family's happiness the highest form of praise for her food.

Like many restaurant owners in Vanuatu, Rose finds that people don't want to eat traditional, local dishes in restaurants. Her cuisine, as such, is a hybrid of European and Vanuatu dishes, such as lasagna with local small eggplants and chiles, as well as traditional ingredients like tomato paste and cheese. One of her signature dishes is nalot, a soft cassava or breadfruit dish similar in texture to a bread pudding, that's typically cooked on a hot stone over an open fire, then doused with rich coconut milk.

But perhaps her most popular dish is laplap—a traditional dish that exemplifies the kind of cooking that makes island food so special. Incredibly adaptable, almost like a casserole or a freeform tamale, it's made with finely grated starchy vegetables—whatever is on hand, such as yams, breadfruit, cassava, plantains—that are spread onto a series of overlapping banana leaves, often several feet long and wide. The starchy mash is topped with a variety of other fillings, also making use of whatever is available—such as vegetables, seafood, or chickens that were harvested or caught that day. This heavenly mixture is doused in rich coconut milk, topped with more banana leaves, then steamed over a lovo earth oven heated by hot stones. Rose's version uses yam, chicken breasts, onions, garlic, ginger, tomatoes, and herbs, and has been adapted from the traditional version into individual wrapped packets.

Rose's dedication to preserving her island's culture is admirable, and she has expanded her work beyond her family and customers and into a local NGO called SAMNA Food Revolution. Along with her cofounder and volunteers, they teach cooking classes to local community members. Their principal goal is to preserve ancestral dishes and cooking by demonstrating how these foods can be prepared quickly and with ease using modern tools, and creating new dishes that are inspired by tradition but more approachable. Rose frequently travels to other islands, where she relishes the opportunity to share her knowledge and love of food.

RECIPES

STEAMING + IN-GROUND COOKING

Island
Vanuatu

Yield
4 to 6 servings

Active Time
45 minutes

Total Time
1 hour 30 minutes

LAPLAP

The national dish of Vanuatu, laplap is typically a family affair. It is often several feet long, with alternating layers of a grated starch such as cassava or yam, seafood or chicken, herbs, spices, and fresh coconut milk. It then cooks slowly outdoors over an earth oven heated with hot rocks. It's one of Primrose Siri's signature dishes (see page 270), one she's adapted over the years into individual servings. This recipe is inspired from hers, using commonly available ingredients and cooked in the conventional oven for ease.

1 lb [455 g] boneless, skinless chicken breast, chopped into small pieces

1 small white onion, finely chopped

3 medium garlic cloves, minced

2 Tbsp minced peeled fresh ginger

¼ cup [20 g] chopped fresh cilantro leaves

2 tsp kosher salt

¼ tsp freshly ground black pepper

1 tsp ground turmeric

1½ cups [360 ml] canned full-fat coconut milk, well shaken and stirred

3 large banana leaves

2 lb [910 g] purple or white yams, peeled and finely grated

2 roma tomatoes, sliced

Preheat the oven to 425°F [220°C].

Combine the chicken, onion, garlic, ginger, cilantro, salt, pepper, turmeric, and coconut milk in a large mixing bowl and stir well to fully combine.

Cut the banana leaves in half crosswise. Cut eight 12 in [30.5 cm] lengths of kitchen twine. Set up your station in this order: twine, banana leaves, grated yam, chicken mixture, and tomatoes.

Set two pieces of twine crosswise, then top with a piece of banana leaf. Scoop ½ cup [70 g] of grated yam on top and spread lengthwise with a large spoon. Add ¼ cup [35 g] of chicken mixture, then layer on two tomato slices, being careful not to overfill.

Fold the banana leaves from the outside in, then tie up each parcel with twine like a gift. Place each on a large rimmed baking sheet, then transfer to the oven and bake for 45 minutes to 1 hour, pressing the top to test whether the packets are completely firm. If they're still a little squishy, let them cook for 10 to 15 minutes longer, checking along the way. Let the laplap rest for 10 minutes before serving. It should be enjoyed fresh and warm and should only be stored in the refrigerator for a day outside of the banana leaf as the texture can become mushy and the leaves can impart a bitter taste.

Island
Indonesia

Yield
2 servings

Active Time
1 hour

Total Time
1 hour 30 minutes

BEBEK BETUTU
ROAST DUCK IN BANANA LEAF

Bali is among the more than 17,000 islands comprising Indonesia, and its cuisine and culture are distinct. Indonesia is characterized by numerous Muslim communities that influence the cuisine, perhaps most notably in the absence of pork. But Balinese culture is heavily influenced by Hindu customs, which influence the art and music as much as the food. This ceremonial, ancestral Balinese slow-cooked duck dish is intended for celebrations. It starts with an incredibly fragrant paste of shallots, ginger, chiles, and spices, many of which originate from the region.

BALINESE SPICE PASTE

6 garlic cloves, halved

5 large shallots, halved

3 Tbsp fresh turmeric, peeled and finely chopped

6 candle nuts or macadamia nuts, chopped

5 Tbsp [63 g] finely grated peeled fresh ginger

5 red bird's eye chiles, stemmed, seeded if desired to mitigate spiciness, and thinly sliced

½ tsp ground white pepper

½ tsp freshly ground black pepper

1 tsp ground coriander

1 tsp ground cumin

¼ tsp ground cloves

¼ tsp ground nutmeg

1 tsp sesame seeds

1 tsp palm sugar or brown sugar

1 tsp kosher salt

DUCK

½ cup [120 ml] coconut oil

⅓ cup [80 ml] soy sauce

2 tsp dried shrimp paste

One 4½ lb [2 kg] duck, washed and patted dry (see Tip)

3 or 4 banana leaves, or greaseproof paper or aluminum foil

Preheat the oven to 350°F [180°C].

To make the Balinese spice paste: In a food processor, combine the garlic, shallots, turmeric, nuts, ginger, chiles, white pepper, black pepper, coriander, cumin, cloves, nutmeg, sesame seeds, sugar, and salt, and grind into a fine paste.

To make the duck: In a large mixing bowl, combine the coconut oil, soy sauce, and shrimp paste. Place the duck in the bowl and massage the duck with this marinade, then cover with plastic wrap and let sit while you prepare the remainder of the ingredients.

Using your gas stove or any other open flame, pass the banana leaves, one at a time, over the flame, moving constantly until they become soft and pliable, then wipe with a paper towel. Do not put the leaves directly into the flame or they will burn.

Cut a length of kitchen twine, as long as your wingspan, and place it on a work surface. Place two banana leaves lengthwise on top of the twine, slightly overlapping, then place the duck in the center.

continued

Add the Balinese spice paste to the remaining marinade, mix well, then use your hands to slather the surface and cavity of the duck with it. Cut another piece of kitchen twine and truss the duck with it, then wrap tightly in the banana leaves, adding additional leaves as needed to ensure an airtight packet. Pull the twine up on alternate sides, crisscross on the top like a gift, then carefully flip the parcel, bring the twine around, and tie a firm knot. Use more twine as needed to secure the parcel.

Place the parcel in a deep pan fitted with a roasting rack so that the duck is breast-side down on the rack. Pour in enough water to reach at least ½ in [13 mm], but not touching the duck. Cover the pan with foil.

Bake for 1½ hours, then transfer the parcel to a shallow baking dish. Unwrap the duck and transfer it to a cutting board. Let it rest for 10 minutes, then carefully separate the legs and thighs, and slice the breast. Pour the reserved juices from the cutting board and the baking dish into a small bowl and serve alongside the duck. Store leftover meat in the refrigerator for up to 5 days.

TIP   This recipe also works well with individual duck breasts. Roast for 15 to 20 minutes, less for more rare meat if desired, and let rest for 7 to 10 minutes.

MARIA BENEDETTI
PUERTO RICO

On a breezy but hot late-summer day, I drive up to Maria Benedetti's new home and farm. Tucked into the hills of Mayagüez, Puerto Rico, her mother's family's native home, it's the first farm she's ever owned despite having created three herbal learning centers based on traditional botanical medicine.

Maria is dressed in a vibrant, form-fitting rainbow tie-dyed top and teal pants, her curly red and silver hair voluminous and joyful.

"Que te preparo?" she asks. *What should I make for you?* I tell her it's up to her, whatever she'd like to show me, and she takes me out to the yard and instructs me to start harvesting what look like weeds from the garden. In fact, it's margarita silvestre (*Bidens sp.*), an indigenous plant that grows wild across the island, sometimes sprouting out of sidewalks and parking lots with floppy green leaves and small yellow-centered white blossoms. We pull it up, wash it, shake off the water, and add the leaves and flowers to a pot of simmering, salted water. She cooks the greens until they darken and become tender, then adds olive oil and freshly mashed garlic, and serves me a steaming bowl of nourishing broth and vegetables. She brings out roasted breadfruit and a pesto made of oregano brujo, a powerful native version of fresh oregano that's widely recognized for its medicinal properties. It's all delicious, and sourced from the garden that is just steps from her front door. This preparation is the key to Maria's work on traditional medicinal plants— the cornerstone of a storied career.

Maria grew up in Queens, New York, after her maternal family left Puerto Rico, in 1927, after their family home had been destroyed in a series of natural disasters. Growing up, her grandmother María Cristina Sotomayor Fernández de Benedetti came to their house on Wednesdays and cooked classic Puerto Rican dishes: rice with red beans or gandules with chicken, steaming

Pasteles (page 284), savory Papas Rellenas (page 216), and, on special occasions, sweet, creamy arroz con coco. Those meals, and a soundtrack of Tito Puente, Tito Rodríguez, Johnny Pacheco, and La Lupe, helped her to connect deeply with her Puerto Rican roots.

She went on to cultivate her own personal relationship with the island. With a passion for herbal medicine, she began to study Puerto Rican literature, history, culture, and folklore. This led her to interview women elders, who shared their wisdom of herbal remedies and traditional medicine, planting a seed she would later cultivate.

Her first trip to Puerto Rico was in 1987. She went with a camera, cassette recorder, and small bag of clothes, and interviewed farmers, herbalists, and elders about their knowledge of the healing properties of plants, collecting plant trimmings, photos, and notes in a giant New York City phone directory. This research would lead to her first book, *Earth and Spirit: Medicinal Plants and Healing Lore from Puerto Rico*. She ultimately settled in Mayagüez and began building a community of like-minded nature-lovers, dedicating herself to collecting the fleeting ancestral wisdom of her beloved island communities.

Maria's second book of oral history is focused on both healing and farming traditions of Puerto Rico amid ballooning environmental challenges. One of Maria's collaborators was Pablo Díaz Cuadrado, a farmer living near Lake Matrullas in Orocovis, a mountainous town in the central part of the island. He offered Maria the opportunity to farm on a woodland farm, cultivating coffee, diverse green and root vegetables and medicinal plants, while keeping bees. Together, they developed agritourism experiences focused on biodiversity and ecological regeneration. Maria kept studying medicinal plants and deepened her understanding with plant spirit medicine, taught by shaman Eliot Cowan.

Today, Maria is the director of Botanicultura, an ethnobotanical education project at her farm Villa Montuna, where she teaches botanical medicine, offers guided meditations, and collaborates with the trees, bushes, herbs, and grasses of her surroundings. Her home is a living library of malagueta (native bay rum with fruits known as allspice), breadfruit, mango, palmas, and a growing array of medicinals. But it's also an unparalleled library of books, flyers, pamphlets, interview transcripts, audio recordings, photographs, and seeds. There are few centers like hers, and she will continue to be a joyful steward of ancestral knowledge.

KĀLUA PUA'A
PORK ROASTED IN BANANA LEAVES

Nothing can replace the flavor of a whole pig wrapped in banana leaves and slowly roasted over hot coals buried in the ground. Nothing. This adaptation of that incredible dish is more an homage than a replacement—a way to bring island flavors into your kitchen in whatever way you can. It comes together incredibly easily and, unlike most pork roasts, does not require marinating. Salt and liquid smoke invoke the pit, while the banana leaf keeps the steam inside, infusing the pork with tremendous earthy flavor.

2 Tbsp coarse Hawaiian or pink Himalayan salt

2 Tbsp liquid smoke (see Tip)

5 to 6 lb [2.3 to 2.7 kg] boneless, skinless pork shoulder

3 large banana leaves

Preheat the oven to 375°F [190°C].

In a small ramekin or bowl, combine the salt and liquid smoke.

Using a sharp paring knife, cut ½ in [13 mm] deep slits on all sides of the pork shoulder. Rub the salt mixture all over the pork, making sure to get it inside the slits as well.

Cut four pieces of kitchen twine, each about the length of your wingspan. Set them atop a large cutting board crosswise, then overlap several layers of banana leaves, ensuring an airtight package. Place the pork in the center, then wrap tightly into a parcel. Pull up the edges of the strings and tie tightly, knotting each piece to secure the parcel.

Place the wrapped roast on a rack in a roasting pan, then add at least 1 cup [240 ml] of water to the bottom of the pan, until it almost touches the bottom of the roasting rack. Cover tightly with foil, then place in the center of the oven.

Roast for 6 hours, then remove from the oven and let rest, still covered, for 15 minutes so the pork can cool and the banana leaf–scented pork juices can meld.

Remove the foil, then transfer the parcel to a deep serving dish. Cut away the twine and top layer of leaves with a sharp knife or kitchen shears, then shred the meat with your fingers or two forks, mixing well with the juices. Serve warm.

TIP Liquid smoke might leave a strong smell residue on your hands. To avoid that, wear gloves when handling.

I
S
L
A
S

Island
Fiji

Yield
6 to 8 servings

Active Time
45 minutes

Total Time
2 hours

LOVO CHICKEN
IN-GROUND ROASTED CHICKEN

Similar to umu cooking used in American Samoa (see page 63), lovo is a style of in-ground pit cooking where various vegetables and proteins are combined, doused in coconut cream, then wrapped in a woven banana-leaf or palm-frond basket. The baskets are then set atop more banana leaves over an oven of hot stones, then covered with more banana leaves and left to steam. In addition to the meat and vegetables, this dish traditionally includes palusami—taro leaves stuffed with grated coconut and onion, which are incredibly flavorful despite their simple ingredients. This recipe is heavily adapted from the traditional method, using a grill and aluminum foil instead of rocks and banana leaves.

One 4 to 5 lb [1.8 to 2.3 kg] chicken, spatchcocked, breastbone removed

1 Tbsp sweet paprika

1 Tbsp ground turmeric

1 Tbsp brown sugar

1 Tbsp ground ginger

2 tsp ground cumin

2 tsp ground coriander

1 tsp garlic powder

1 tsp kosher salt

½ tsp cayenne pepper

¼ tsp freshly ground black pepper

2 Tbsp dark soy sauce

1 Tbsp vegetable or coconut oil

1 lb [455 g] taro root

1 lb [455 g] white sweet potatoes

1 small white onion, minced

1 cup [80 g] unsweetened coconut flakes

1½ cups [360 ml] unsweetened coconut cream

6 to 8 large taro or collard leaves, thick stems removed

7 or 8 large banana leaves

One 20 oz [570 g] can green jackfruit in brine, drained

Steamed white rice, for serving

Rinse the chicken, remove bone shards, and dry with paper towels.

In a large nonreactive mixing bowl, combine the paprika, turmeric, brown sugar, ginger, cumin, coriander, garlic powder, salt, cayenne, and black pepper and blend with a fork. Add the soy sauce and oil and whisk into a thick paste.

Place the chicken in the bowl and rub well with the spice paste, carefully pushing spice mix under the skin. Let marinate at room temperature while you prepare the remaining ingredients.

Fill a large bowl with cold water. Thoroughly scrub the taro root and sweet potatoes, scraping off any hairs that remain on the taro skin, then quarter and place them in the water. Let soak while you prepare the palusami.

In a medium mixing bowl, combine the onion, coconut flakes, and ½ cup [120 ml] of the coconut cream and mix well to combine. Spread one taro leaf on a large cutting board and scoop 2 Tbsp of the coconut mixture into the center. Fold the leaf in half widthwise, then fold the top of the leaf over and roll up into a tight package. Set aside and repeat with the remaining leaves and coconut mixture.

Heat a grill to 400°F [200°C].

To assemble the chicken, lay two 2½ ft [0.75 m] long sheets of aluminum foil on an extra-large rimmed baking sheet or cutting board. Overlap the sheets at least 2 in [5 cm] in the center, and overlap three to four banana leaves on the foil.

Lay the chicken, breast-side up, in the center of the banana leaves. Arrange the taro root, sweet potatoes, and jackfruit around the chicken, and top with the palusami packets. Pour the remaining 1 cup [240 ml] coconut cream over the vegetables.

Place two or three banana leaves across the top of the chicken and vegetables, enough to encase the whole package. Add one additional piece of foil, just big enough to cover the top of the chicken and vegetables, then pull up each side of the foil, crimping upward to hold any juices that may accumulate.

Carefully transfer the package to the heated grill. Cook uncovered for 1 hour, rotating every 15 minutes, until the internal temperature reaches 165°F [74°C]. Partially unwrap to check for doneness in one of two ways: Use a meat thermometer to check the temperature, or pierce the thickest part of the dark meat with a sharp paring knife—if the liquid runs clear, the meat is done.

Remove the package from the grill and let rest for 10 to 15 minutes. Carefully remove the foil, then transfer the leaf package to a large serving platter or lined tabletop. Pull back or cut away the banana leaves, then transfer the chicken to a cutting board and chop into eight pieces. Return the chicken to the platter, pouring the juices from the cutting board over.

Eat the chicken, vegetables, and palusami directly from the leaf package, dipping into the rich sauce at the bottom. Serve with steamed white rice, spooning reserved sauce on top.

TIP   If using a charcoal grill, you'll likely need to add more coals along the way. Have a charcoal BBQ chimney starter handy, and make fresh coals about 30 minutes into cooking. It's much more work, but it will add a smokiness that's closer to the flavor produced by in-ground roasting.

Island
Philippines

Yield
4 to 6 servings

Active Time
30 minutes

Total Time
45 minutes

PINAPUTOK NA ISDA
STUFFED FISH STEAMED IN BANANA LEAF

This showstopping whole fish dish is as beautiful as it is delicious. Typically served family style inside its banana-leaf wrapper, it's a common centerpiece for a kamayan meal, a communal Filipino feast.

One 3 lb [1.4 kg] whole snapper, cleaned and scaled, head and tail on

4 banana leaves (see Tip)

1 in [2.5 cm] piece peeled fresh ginger, ½ grated and ½ thinly sliced

6 garlic cloves, 3 minced and 3 smashed

Kosher salt

Freshly ground black pepper

⅔ cup [110 g] cherry tomatoes, 4 halved, remaining quartered

6 green onions, white and green parts, thinly sliced

1 long green chile, seeded and thinly sliced on the diagonal

1 small handful fresh cilantro sprigs

Steamed white rice and Toyomansi (optional; page 45), for serving

TIP   Parchment or foil can be substituted for banana leaves if necessary.

Rinse the fish inside and out with cold water and dry with paper towels. Make three shallow cuts, each about ½ in [13 mm] deep, into the thickest part of each side of the fish.

Using your gas stove or any other open flame, pass each banana leaf, one at a time, over the flame, moving constantly until they become soft and pliable. Do not put the leaves directly into the flame or they will burn.

Heat a grill to 400°F [200°C].

Place two banana leaves lengthwise, slightly overlapping, on a work surface and place the fish in the center.

In a small bowl, combine the grated ginger and minced garlic and mix to form a paste. Spread the mixture inside the cuts on the fish. Generously season both sides of the fish with salt and pepper.

Stuff the remaining sliced ginger and smashed garlic into the cavity of the fish and scatter the halved tomatoes and green onion around it, reserving a handful of green onion. Place another banana leaf on top and use kitchen twine to enclose the fish, making a tight parcel.

Place the parcel onto the grill and cook the fish for 20 minutes, or until the parcel inflates slightly and you can hear a popping sound. Check for doneness by carefully opening the parcel and using a paring knife to separate the flesh of the fish near one of the cuts. The fish is done when the flesh is white and opaque all the way to the bone. If it is still pink or translucent, rewrap and cook a few minutes longer.

Place the fish on a serving platter lined with the remaining banana leaf. Scatter the remaining green onions, the chile, cilantro, and quartered tomatoes over the fish. Serve with steamed white rice and toyomansi if desired.

I
S
L
A
S

PASTELES DE MASA

The process of making pasteles (see page 269), a Puerto Rican Christmas staple, is as important as eating them. There are many steps—cooking the meat; preparing the masa; cutting banana leaves, parchment paper, and twine to exactly the right lengths. But making them is a joy, a way to come together with family over the holidays, and every cook has a special touch. Perfect pasteles are the work of abuelitas and tias, grandmas and aunties, who seem to have a preternatural ability when it comes to this dish. This is my grandmother's recipe, and the smell of boiling pasteles is a time portal into her kitchen.

PORK

2 lb [910 g] boneless, skinless pork shoulder, cut into ½ in [13 mm] pieces

1 Tbsp olive oil

2 Tbsp finely grated peeled fresh ginger

1 cup [240 ml] Sofrito (page 38)

⅓ cup [80 ml] fresh orange juice

MASA

8 lb [3.6 kg] yautía or taro root, a mix of white and yellow

15 green bananas (see Tips)

2 cups [475 ml] milk

2½ Tbsp kosher salt

8 large banana leaves, or enough for twenty-four 12 in [30.5 cm] pieces

Kosher salt

½ cup [120 ml] Annatto Oil (page 291) (see Tips)

TOPPINGS

One 15.5 oz [440 g] can garbanzo beans, drained

One 10 oz [285 g] jar pimento-stuffed olives

1 Tbsp capers in brine, drained and chopped

1½ cups [210 g] black or golden raisins (optional)

Steamed white rice, for serving

Pique (page 49), for serving

To make the pork: Combine the pork, olive oil, ginger, sofrito, and orange juice. Let marinate while you prepare the masa, or overnight if possible.

To make the masa: Peel and chop the yautía and green bananas, and transfer to a large bowl with water so they don't brown. In a food processor, blend the drained yautía and green bananas with the milk and salt, working in batches depending on the size of your food processor. The masa will be thick and smooth, with no large pieces. Refrigerate until ready to use.

To cook the pork: Heat a large saucepan over medium heat. Add the marinated pork along with any remaining marinade, bring to a simmer, then lower the heat to low and cook, covered, for 30 to 45 minutes, until it's tender and falling apart. Try to resist the temptation to snack on it, or your pasteles will suffer the consequences.

Meanwhile, cut twenty-four 12 in [30.5 cm] lengths of kitchen twine. Cut twenty-four 12 in [30.5 cm] squares of parchment paper, then the same number and size squares of banana leaves.

Bring a large stockpot, about half full of water and 1 Tbsp of salt, to a boil. Once boiling, lower the heat to a low simmer until ready to cook the pasteles.

On a long table or countertop, set up your pasteles station in this order: twine, parchment, banana leaves, annatto oil, masa, pork, and toppings. Set two pieces of twine crosswise, then layer the parchment and then the banana leaves. Using a small spoon, spread a light layer of annatto oil on each leaf. Scoop 3 Tbsp of masa on top, spreading lengthwise in a rectangular shape with a large spoon. Add the pork, garbanzos, olives, capers, and raisins (if using) in a single layer—just a few pieces of each, being careful not to overfill.

Starting with the banana leaves, fold from the outside in, like a taco, to completely cover the pork filling with masa. Roll the leaf ends and tuck them underneath, then repeat the process with parchment paper, then tie up each parcel with twine lengthwise and crosswise, like a gift. Continue making packets until all the masa has been used. Leftover pork filling can be stored in the freezer for up to several months, or eaten with steamed white rice. Transfer the pasteles to the refrigerator if cooking immediately, or to the freezer if you plan to cook them later.

To cook the pasteles, add them in batches to the pot of boiling water, six to eight at a time depending on the size of your pot (see Tips), ensuring that all pasteles are covered with water. Cook for 1 hour, until pasteles are firm to the touch (you will have to cook for a bit longer if cooking from frozen; see Tips). When done, remove using tongs to a cutting board.

Let the pasteles rest for 10 minutes before serving. Cut twine, unwrap each pastel, and serve alongside steamed white rice with pique.

TIPS Green bananas are distinct from plantains, as they have a milder, sweeter flavor and are ideal for this dish.

If you put more than eight pasteles in the pot to boil, they will take 15 to 30 minutes longer to cook.

Pasteles can be boiled directly from the freezer, but will take closer to 2 hours.

If you can't find annatto seeds, replace the annatto oil with 3 Tbsp bacon fat, lard, or vegetable oil combined with 2 Tbsp of ground annatto.

KOBA
STEAMED BANANA-PEANUT PACKETS

Like many other Malagasy dishes, koba is simple, hearty, and satisfying. It's one of the few sweet dishes in this book, and a favorite among *Islas* recipe developers. Roasted peanuts and bananas are sweetened with honey and vanilla, blended with glutinous rice flour, then wrapped in banana leaves and steamed. Topped with a halved banana, they're very cute—as well as delicate yet rich—and make for a nice presentation.

1 cup [140 g] unsalted roasted peanuts

3 ripe bananas, chopped

1½ cups [210 g] glutinous rice flour

2 tsp honey

⅓ cup [65 g] brown sugar

1 vanilla bean

1 large banana leaf

In a food processor or mortar and pestle, finely grind the peanuts.

In a large mixing bowl, combine ¾ cup [105 g] of the peanuts with the bananas, rice flour, honey, and brown sugar and blend into a loose dough. Cut the vanilla bean lengthwise, scrape out the seeds, and mix them into the dough. The mass should be very sticky and pulpy.

In a small saucepan, bring 3 cups [710 ml] of water to a boil. Cut the banana leaf into four equal lengths, then place them in the boiling water for 5 minutes so that they become soft and pliable. Remove them from the water and dry with a clean towel.

Divide the dough into eight pieces. Spread one piece on each of the banana leaves in a rectangular shape. Sprinkle each rectangle of dough with the remaining ¼ cup [35 g] ground peanuts, then top each with a piece of the remaining dough. Fold the banana leaves over the dough like a package and tie with kitchen twine.

In a large pot fitted with a steamer basket or a bamboo steamer, bring 4 cups [945 ml] of water to a boil. Lower the heat to medium, place the koba in the steamer, cover the pot, and cook, covered, for 30 minutes.

Carefully remove the koba from the steamer with tongs and let cool for 5 to 10 minutes. Remove the banana leaf and serve whole or in slices.

Island
Seychelles

Yield
15 packets

Active Time
30 minutes

Total Time
3 hours

MOUKAT
BANANA AND CASSAVA PACKETS

These banana-cassava packets have a delicate flavor with a subtle sweetness.
They can be enjoyed as a dessert or served alongside savory dishes.

1 lb [455 g] cassava, grated, fresh or frozen and thawed

1 large banana leaf (see Tip)

1 lb [455 g] very ripe bananas, peeled

1½ cups [360 ml] canned full-fat coconut milk, well shaken and stirred

4 Tbsp [60 ml] sweetened condensed milk

1 tsp vanilla extract

¼ tsp ground nutmeg

1 tsp kosher salt

¼ cup [30 g] all-purpose flour, sifted

Coconut cream, for serving (optional)

TIP The moukat can also be assembled using parchment paper instead of banana leaves if desired.

Place the grated cassava on a clean kitchen towel, wrap it tightly, and place it in a large strainer set in the sink or over a bowl. Let drain for 30 minutes. Set a heavy object on top to extract as much moisture from the cassava as possible.

Once most of the moisture has been removed, place the cassava on a baking sheet and fluff it with your hands. Allow it to air-dry on the counter for a few hours. It's critical to ensure that the cassava dries out fully, or the moukat won't set up properly. You will end up with approximately 1 cup [240 ml] of cassava "flour."

Gently wash the banana leaf under cool running water, taking care not to tear or break it. Using a sharp knife or kitchen scissors, cut the banana leaf into approximate 10 in [25 cm] squares.

Preheat the oven to 350°F [180°C]. Using your gas stove or any other open flame, pass each banana leaf square, one at a time, over the flame, moving constantly until they become soft and pliable. Do not put the leaves directly into the flame or they will burn.

In a medium mixing bowl, mash the bananas completely with a fork. Add the coconut milk, sweetened condensed milk, vanilla, nutmeg, and salt and stir to blend. Fold in the flour, making a thick batter. Rest the mixture at room temperature for about 15 minutes.

Place about 3 Tbsp of the mixture in the middle of each banana leaf square and fold to create neat, small parcels and place them on a baking sheet. You can either tie the parcels with kitchen twine or leave them seam-side down. Take care not to press the filling or spread it out as you are making the parcels. They should also not be rolled too tightly, as the moukat will expand during cooking.

Bake for 30 minutes, until they feel firm when gently pressed. Remove from the oven and allow the parcels to cool completely before unwrapping. Slice and serve topped with fresh coconut cream if desired.

MANHA APIGIGI
COCONUT-CASSAVA PACKETS

Similar to Seychellois Moukat (page 287), delicately flavored and barely sweet, these cassava packets come together easily. Traditionally they are prepared over hot coals, but this recipe calls for a grill or bamboo steamer as an option. Serve alongside Pescado Frito (page 219) with Pique (page 49).

5 large banana leaves

5 cups [500 g] peeled, grated young coconut meat

3 cups [510 g] , peeled and finely grated cassava

¼ cup [30 g] tapioca starch

¼ cup [50 g] brown sugar

1 tsp kosher salt

1 cup [240 ml] canned full-fat coconut milk

Heat a grill to 400°F [200°C].

Prep the banana leaves per the instructions on page 269, then cut into 4 by 6 in [10 by 15 cm] sections.

In a large bowl, combine the coconut meat, cassava, tapioca starch, brown sugar, and salt and stir to combine. Slowly pour in the coconut milk, stirring until the mixture is a sticky but workable dough.

Form the dough into a 1 by 6 in [2.5 by 15 cm] log, ½ in [13 mm] thick. Wrap the log in banana leaves, then secure it with kitchen twine.

Grill the packets for 20 to 30 minutes, turning often, until the banana leaves begin to char and packets are firm to the touch. Serve hot or at room temperature. Store leftovers in the refrigerator for no more than 1 day, as the texture and flavor may become unpleasant.

TIP Manha apigigi can be steamed in a bamboo steamer for 25 minutes instead of grilling. See Yuca Con Mojo (page 119) for tips on sourcing cassava.

Island
Indonesia

Yield
4 to 6 servings

Active Time
25 minutes

Total Time
45 minutes

NASI KUNING
LEMONGRASS-TURMERIC RICE

This aromatic yellow coconut rice, seasoned with lemongrass and makrut lime leaves, is a staple in traditional Indonesian cuisine. It pairs well with any of the curries and braised dishes in this book, though it's particularly delicious alongside lighter seafood and poultry dishes such as Lemongrass Adobo Grilled Chicken with Pineapple (page 254) or Pwason Griye (page 251).

4 cups [800 g] jasmine rice, rinsed

2 large fresh lemongrass stalks, halved lengthwise

7 fresh bay leaves or daun salam (Indonesian bay leaves) (see Tip)

3 fresh makrut lime leaves

2 tsp kosher salt

1 Tbsp ground turmeric

1½ cups [360 ml] canned full-fat coconut milk, well shaken and stirred

In a large pot over high heat, combine the rice, lemongrass, bay leaves, makrut lime leaves, salt, turmeric, coconut milk, and 3 cups [710 ml] of water. Stir well to combine, submerging the lemongrass and leaves as much as possible.

Bring to a rolling boil, stirring continuously with a large wooden spoon to prevent the rice at the bottom of the pot from sticking. Allow to boil for 20 seconds, lower the heat to low, cover, and simmer for 15 minutes or until the liquid is mostly absorbed.

Remove the pot from the heat and let sit, covered, for an additional 10 minutes.

Gently fluff the rice with two forks, discard the lemongrass and leaves, and serve.

TIP   Daun salam, also known as Indian bay leaves, are central to Indonesian cuisine. They can be hard to source, and standard bay leaves can be used, though the flavor will not be the same.

BAIGAN VALO
FISH-STUFFED EGGPLANT

This incredibly rich side dish has a number of preparations across Pacific islands, particularly in Fiji. Traditionally cooked in a lovo, or in-ground earth oven, eggplant is stuffed with tinned fish and coconut cream, then steamed over hot rocks. This adaptation uses a stovetop and broiler for a wonderfully unique and flavorful dish. Serve with Fijian Lamb Barbecue (page 257) and Nasi Kuning (page 289) for an elegant, dynamic meal.

1 Tbsp vegetable oil, plus more for brushing

1 lb [455 g] Japanese eggplant (about 4 medium), halved lengthwise

½ cup [70 g] finely diced white onion

3 large garlic cloves, minced

One 8 oz [230 g] can milk fish in tomato sauce (see Tip)

1 cup [240 ml] unsweetened coconut cream

1 tsp soy sauce

Kosher salt

TIP   Tinned milkfish in tomato sauce can be found in Asian grocery stores, or online. Spanish mackerel in tomato sauce can be substituted.

Preheat the oven to 500°F [260°C].

Line a baking sheet with aluminum foil and brush lightly with oil. Place the eggplant on the baking sheet and brush it lightly with oil. Roast for 7 to 10 minutes, watching carefully so that it does not burn, until the flesh is tender when pierced with a fork. Remove the eggplant from the oven and let rest while you prepare the filling.

Heat the 1 Tbsp oil in a large skillet over medium heat. Once shimmering, add the onion and sauté until lightly browned, 7 to 10 minutes. Add the garlic and sauté for 30 seconds, until fragrant. Pour in the tinned fish and sauce and ¾ cup [180 ml] of the coconut cream, breaking the fish apart with a wooden spoon. Bring to a simmer, then lower the heat to medium-low and cook for 5 minutes.

While the filling simmers, use a small spoon to gently scoop the eggplant flesh from the center of each eggplant, being careful not to pierce the skin, and place it in a small bowl. Combine the eggplant with the filling, using a wooden spoon to break up any tough parts and stirring well to incorporate and create a thick, rich filling. Add the soy sauce, taste, and season with salt as desired.

Preheat the broiler to high. Evenly fill the eggplant shells with filling, then pour over the remaining ¼ cup coconut cream. Transfer to the oven and broil for 5 to 7 minutes, until the filling bubbles, watching carefully to ensure it doesn't burn.

Island
Guam

Yield
8 to 10 servings

Active Time
25 minutes

Total Time
45 minutes

RED RICE

A CHamoru cookout staple, this rich, porky rice is dyed vibrant red by annatto oil. It's incredibly flavorful and a beautiful addition to a meal. Serve alongside CHamoru Barbecue Chicken (page 60) or Ribs (page 64) or Filipino Chicken Inasal (page 238) or top with Puerto Rican Habichuelas Guisadas con Calabaza (page 145).

ANNATTO OIL

1 cup [240 ml] vegetable oil or lard

3 Tbsp annatto seeds (achiote; see Tip)

RED RICE

½ cup [70 g] diced yellow onion

¼ cup [12 g] chopped green onions, white and green parts

4 garlic cloves, minced

1½ tsp kosher salt, plus more as needed

½ cup [113 g] minced fried bacon, from about 3 strips thick-sliced bacon (optional)

3 cups [600 g] sushi rice or short-grain white rice, rinsed

2 cups [475 ml] chicken broth

To make the annatto oil: In a small saucepan over medium-high, heat the oil and annatto seeds. Once the oil starts to shimmer, remove from the heat, stir to combine, and let rest for 5 minutes. Using a fine-mesh sieve, strain the oil into a heat-safe container and set aside.

To make the red rice: In a deep, wide saucepan over medium-high, heat 3 Tbsp of the annatto oil until it is shimmering. Lower the heat to medium, then add the yellow onion and sauté until golden, 7 to 9 minutes. Add the green onions, garlic, salt, and bacon (if using) and sauté for 1 more minute, until fragrant.

Add the rice, broth, and 3 cups [710 ml] of water and mix well to combine. Increase the heat to medium-high and bring to a simmer, stir once more, and simmer uncovered until the liquid is mostly absorbed, about 5 minutes, shaking the pan intermittently. Lower the heat to low, cover, and cook for 10 minutes.

Remove the pan from the heat and let it rest for 10 minutes. Fluff the rice with two forks and let it rest for a few minutes more until ready to serve.

TIP If you can't find annatto seeds, replace the annatto oil with 3 Tbsp bacon fat, lard, or vegetable oil combined with 2 Tbsp of ground annatto.

Island
Puerto Rico

Yield
4 to 6 servings

Active Time
25 minutes

Total Time
1 hour

ARROZ CON TOCINO
RICE WITH SALT PORK

Steamed white rice is ubiquitous across the tropics. It's the most common accompaniment to island meals, from braises to fried fish. In Puerto Rico, arroz con tocino is a flavorful, rich variation, replacing the oil and salt that's usually added to white rice with salty pork. A lightweight aluminum pot or caldero is typically used for this dish, but a large, light, nonstick saucepan with a lid is a good replacement. In an exception to most rice preparations, do not wash the rice before cooking. I developed this recipe alongside my mother, who was adamant that rinsing the rice beforehand would make it mushy, and I trust her. This quick, easy side dish pairs well with saucy beans, greens, and stewed meats any day of the week.

5½ oz [155 g] salt pork or bacon

2 large garlic cloves, minced

2 cups [400 g] sushi rice or short-grain white rice

3 cups [710 ml] boiling water

Kosher salt

Salt pork can vary in saltiness and funk, so rinse it well and pat dry with a clean towel, then chop into ¼ in [6 mm] pieces.

Heat a large saucepan with a lid over medium. Add the salt pork and cook, stirring often, until browned and a substantial amount of fat has released, 7 to 10 minutes. Add the garlic and sauté for 30 seconds, until fragrant, then add the rice and stir until the rice is evenly coated with fat and starts to turn opaque.

Add the boiling water and bring to a boil, then lower the heat to medium-low. Simmer, uncovered, until the liquid has almost completely evaporated and the surface of the rice is dotted with little bubbly volcanoes, 7 to 10 minutes.

When there is no more liquid bubbling up from the holes, lower the heat to low, cover, and cook for 17 minutes without stirring. Remove from the heat and let it rest, covered, for at least 10 minutes. Taste to ensure the rice is fully cooked; if not, let sit for 5 to 10 minutes more. Fluff with a fork, season with salt as needed, and serve.

Island
Aruba

Yield
8 servings

Active Time
10 minutes

Total Time
30 minutes

AROS DI COCO
COCONUT RICE

Coconut rice is a staple across the Caribbean with countless variations. This version from Aruba incorporates shredded coconut as well as coconut milk for added texture and boosting the coconut flavor. Because coconut is ubiquitous across tropical islands, this rice pairs well with just about any dish in this book.

2 cups [400 g] jasmine rice

1 cup [240 ml] canned full-fat coconut milk, well shaken and stirred

½ cup [40 g] unsweetened shredded coconut

1 tsp kosher salt

Rinse and drain the rice in several changes of cold water, about three times, for at least 45 seconds per time, until the water runs clear.

In a medium saucepan with a lid, combine the rinsed rice, 1½ cups [360 ml] of water, coconut milk, shredded coconut, and salt and stir to incorporate. Bring to a boil over high heat.

Once boiling, stir, then lower the heat to low and cover the pot. Cook for 15 minutes, then remove from the heat and let sit, covered, for an additional 10 minutes. Fluff with a fork and serve.

CAZUELA
PUMPKIN, PLANTAIN, AND COCONUT PUDDING

Cazuela, a richly spiced crustless pie with a texture between thick custard and bread pudding, is a unique dessert with a complex history. The term means "cooking pot" in Spanish, but the key ingredients—batata (white sweet potato), pumpkin, and coconut milk—and the traditional cooking process speak to the island's African culinary history. It's flavored with ginger, cloves, cinnamon, and star anise—all brought to the Caribbean during the spice trade. This dessert has been prepared since at least the nineteenth century, and today it's largely reserved for holidays. While this treat may seem challenging at first glance, it is incredibly adaptable and can be prepared days in advance in a casserole dish, ramekins, or even foil cupcake tins.

1 or 2 large banana leaves, trimmed of stiff edges (optional)

3½ Tbsp salted butter, at room temperature

2 star anise pods

2 tsp kosher salt

1½ lb [680 g] white sweet potatoes (Korean or Dominican), peeled and chopped into 2 in [5 cm] chunks (about 4 heaping cups) (see Tips)

1½ lb [680 g] calabaza or pumpkin, seeded, peeled, and chopped into 2 in [5 cm] chunks (about 4 heaping cups)

1 large very ripe plantain, peeled and sliced into 2 in [5 cm] rounds (about 1 to 2 cups [140 to 280 g])

1 cup [240 ml] canned full-fat coconut milk, well shaken and stirred

3 eggs

2 Tbsp brandy

1 tsp vanilla extract

1 cup [200 g] dark brown sugar

½ cup [70 g] rice flour or all-purpose flour

1 tsp ground cinnamon

1 tsp ground ginger

½ tsp ground cloves

½ cup [70 g] golden raisins

Lightly sweetened whipped cream, toasted grated coconut, and dark chocolate shavings, for garnish (optional)

Using your gas stove or any other open flame, pass the banana leaves (if using), one at a time, over the flame, moving constantly until they become soft and pliable, then wipe with a paper towel. Do not put the leaves directly into the flame or they will burn. Tuck the leaves into a 2 qt [1.9 L] baking dish, overlapping as needed to cover the bottom and sides, and trimming any pieces that go over the edge of the dish with a sharp pair of scissors. Butter the banana leaves with 1½ tsp of the butter.

If not using banana leaves, grease ten 8 oz [240 ml] ramekins with 1½ tsp of the butter. If using ramekins, arrange them on a rimmed baking sheet.

In a large pot over high heat, bring 3 qt [2.8 L] of water to a boil. Add the star anise and 1 tsp of the salt, then add the sweet potatoes and boil for 10 minutes. Add the calabaza and plantain and boil for another 15 to 20 minutes, until everything is fork-tender. (Adding these ingredients in batches ensures they cook evenly, and that the calabaza, in particular, doesn't fall apart.) Transfer the vegetables to a large mesh strainer, discard the star anise, rinse with cold water, and let drain fully.

Meanwhile, preheat the oven to 400°F [200°C]. In a small bowl, combine the coconut milk, eggs, brandy, and vanilla. In a medium mixing bowl, combine the brown sugar, flour, cinnamon, ginger, cloves, and remaining 1 tsp salt.

Transfer the sweet potatoes, pumpkin, and plantain to the bowl of a stand mixer fitted with the whisk attachment, or a large mixing bowl if using a handheld electric mixer. Let cool for 5 to 10 minutes, then add the remaining 3 Tbsp butter and blend on medium speed until smooth, about 3 minutes. Add the coconut milk mixture and mix to fully incorporate. Add the flour mixture and mix until the mixture is silky smooth and resembles a loose pudding, about 2 minutes. Fold in the raisins.

Pour the mixture into the prepared baking dish or ramekins, and bake for 45 minutes to 1 hour (40 to 50 minutes if using ramekins). Test by poking the center with a toothpick or skewer; if it doesn't come out clean, bake for 5 to 10 minutes more. The cazuela should be firm, with a golden top.

Remove from the oven and place on a wire rack to cool, about 30 minutes. The cazuela should separate easily from the banana leaves or buttered ramekins, and can be eaten directly from the container or flipped onto a plate. If you unmold it, turn out the cazuela onto a large rectangular platter, then peel off and discard the banana leaves (if using). Garnish with whipped cream, toasted coconut, and/or dark chocolate shavings if desired.

TIPS   You can substitute canned for fresh ingredients by using one 15 oz [430 g] can each of pumpkin and sweet potato purée, omitting the plantain and star anise, and reducing the coconut milk to ¾ cup [180 ml] and the sugar to ½ cup [100 g]. It'll serve six instead of ten, and the flavor and texture will be slightly different but still very delicious. Use good-quality canned pumpkin and sweet potato purée for best results. Sweet potatoes in light syrup can also be used, but reduce the sugar even further in that case.

Cazuela can be enjoyed warm, at room temperature, or cold from the refrigerator, and can be prepared up to 2 days in advance. Cazuela batter can be prepared the day before and baked when ready.

Baked cazuela can stay out at room temperature, covered, for up to 2 days. To keep longer, cover with a lid or plastic wrap and store in the refrigerator for up to a week.

TROPICAL MENUS

Across these recipes, certain ingredients show up time and again. Ginger, chiles, garlic, citrus, and—of course—coconut and rice. And because the techniques in this book can also be found across the tropics, its sauces, pickles, and side dishes are remarkably interchangeable. Cooking my way across the islands has blurred the borders between spaces and ingredients. Allspice, particularly abundant in Jamaican cuisine, has become one of my favorite additions to grilled meat. Filipino Sinamak (page 48) now sits on the table alongside Pique (page 49) and my other favorite store-bought hot sauces. Here are recommendations for menus that pair dishes from across these far-flung places celebrating their powerful flavors and the people who wield them.

NO. 9

AKRA
BLACK-EYED PEA FRITTERS
Haiti 203

RICE AND PEAS
Jamaica 160

STEWED CURRY EGGPLANT
Trinidad 141

NO. 10

SINIGANG SA MANGGA
SOUR SEAFOOD STEW
Philippines 116

MOFO ANANA
MALAGASY SPICED FRY BREAD
Madagascar 202

BEBEK BETUTU
ROAST DUCK IN BANANA LEAF
Indonesia 275

NO. 11

CALLALOO
COCONUT-BRAISED GREENS
Jamaica 143

JERK PORK TENDERLOIN
Jamaica 242

FESTIVAL
JAMAICAN FRIED DOUGH
Jamaica 196

ARROZ CON TOCINO
RICE WITH SALT PORK
Puerto Rico 292

NO. 12

SOUP JOUMOU
Haiti 173

GATO PIMA
LENTIL CHILE FRITTERS
Seychelles 197

MINT-CILANTRO CHUTNEY
Mauritius 44

NO. 13

CHURRASCO
GRILLED MARINATED SKIRT
STEAK
Puerto Rico 241

WASAKAKA
Dominican Republic 47

COCO BREAD
Jamaica 109

NO. 14

KINILAW NA ISDA
FISH CEVICHE WITH
GINGER AND VINEGAR
Philippines 72

**ARROZ NEGRO
CON PULPO Y CALAMARES**
BLACK RICE WITH OCTOPUS
AND SQUID
Puerto Rico 163

NO. 15

SALAD PALMIS
PALM HEART SALAD
Seychelles 95

CARI DE POISSON ET POTIRON
PUMPKIN FISH CURRY
Seychelles 151

TOSTONES
FRIED GREEN PLANTAINS
Cuba 213

NO. 16

KOBA
STEAMED BANANA-PEANUT
PACKETS
Madagascar 286

LOVO CHICKEN
IN-GROUND ROASTED CHICKEN
Fiji 280

NO. 17

MANGO CHOW
Trinidad 108

PERNIL
MARINATED ROAST PORK
SHOULDER
Puerto Rico 73

AROS DI COCO
COCONUT RICE
Aruba 293

NO. 18

LEMON LASARY
LEMON CHILE PICKLE
Madagascar 96

LAMB COLOMBO
Martinique 182

NASI KUNING
LEMONGRASS-TURMERIC RICE
Indonesia 289

ACKNOWLEDGMENTS

Immense gratitude to the individuals and institutions that contributed to *Islas*. We do this work together.

Juanita Blaz

Perline Ernestine

Marie-May Jeremie

Itege Caro

Maria Benedetti

Primrose Siri

Josefine Martina

Badru Deen

Darryl Green

Tisa Faamuli

Rado Ambinintsoa

Sophia Ramirez

Stephanie Rodriguez

Jenn de la Vega

Brigid Washington

Cybelle Codish

Lauren Vied Allen

Gina Ishmael

Rija Ramamonjy

Cami D. Egurrola

Jessica B. Harris

Stephen Satterfield

Nik Sharma

Osayi Endolyn

Toni Tipton Martin

J. Kenji Lopez-Alt

Monica Ocasio Vega

Alejandra Ramos

Francis Lam

Alicia Kennedy

Savannah Shoemake

World Wildlife Federation, Madagascar

Danny Andrianasolo

Tovoniaina Andriatsiory

Mialisoa Raharimanana

Danny Ravelojaona

Ramartour Madagascar

University of North Carolina, Department of American Studies

The Stonesong Press

Alison Fargis

Adrienne Rosado

Chronicle Books

    Cristina Garces

    Tera Killip

    Steve Kim

    Jessica Ling

    Dena Rayess

    Keely Thomas-Menter

    Lizzie Vaughan

Peter Kim

Lolis Eric Elie

Dr. Jessica B. Harris

Kathy Gunst and John Rudolph

Joseph, Noelle, and Lucas Washington

Serena, Toriano, and Devin Fredericks

Kendall Surfus and Mike Martin

Kate Medley and Will Funk

Victoria Bouloubasis

Keia Mastrianni and Jamie Swofford

Cruz Miguel Ortíz

Natalia Vallejo

Maria Mercedes Grubb

Jamila Robinson

Chandra Ram

Martina Guzman

Nicole Taylor

Chef Robert Oliver

Güakiá Colectivo Agroecológico

Marissa Reyes-Díaz

Tarisse Iriarte

Frances Medina

Francisca Goris

Ninette Rodriguez

Steven West

Bruje Fuego

Duke Lemur Center

Charles Welch

Suzy Delvalle

Curaçao Tourist Board

Damaris Sambo

El Tigre Productions

Elan Bogarín

Jonathan Bogarín

Common Ground Kauai

    Oliver Niedermaier

    David Stevens

    Amanda Dugan

Mikol Hoffman

Gabriel Antune

BACOA Finca + Fogón

    Raúl Correa

    Xavier Pacheco

    René Marichal

Frutos del Guacabo

Lechonera El Rancho Original

Yvonne and Mark Webb

Elc Estrera

Xaris Martinez

Gerard Aflague

INDEX

NORTH
AMERICA

SOUTH
AMERICA

Puerto Rico

Curaçao

AFRICA

Madagascar